AF351852

VALENTINE'S DAY 1874

A Ruhr Valley Romance

Terence Valentine Alve

Valentine's Day 1874: A Ruhr Valley Romance

Terence Valentine Alve

© 2024 Terence Valentine Alve

Phone: +64 27 600 1926
Email: terry.alve@gmail.com

ISBN 979-8-2242008-5-6

First Edition Published January 2024

Second Edition Published July 2024 - Edited, Corrected and Reprinted
This revised edition includes details of the Alve Descendant Reunions 1995, 2015 and 2024 and Rosa Alve's grave restoration at Featherston, including the addition of a memorial to her baby sister Emma. Other formatting, textual and pictorial additions and corrections have been made.

Cover Image
St Augustinus Catholic Church, Gelsenkirchen, Germany which was being rebuilt at the time of Theresia and Carl Alve's marriage there on Valentine's Day 1874. The rebuild was completed in 1881 and the first service was held during February 1882.

Title Page Image
These two votive candles were lit by the author in St Augustinus Church, Gelsenkirchen during his visit there in August 2019 as he prayed, remembered and gave thanks for Theresia and Carl and his German forbears.

This book is dedicated to Alve & Möllers ancestors who lived in Germany pre 1876 and the many romances, predating Carl and Theresia Alve's, which issued in Alve and Möller genes arriving in Aotearoa New Zealand.

Table of Contents

Preface

Valentine's Day 1874 occurred during the sixty-one years this history records (1849-1910) about a Deutschland-Aotearoa New Zealand family. *Theresia Möllers* and *Carl Alve* married in the Ruhr Valley on this day, and just over two years later they disembarked from an emigrant ship at Port Nicholson, Wellington. This study celebrates their marriage and asks two primary questions. Why did they leave Germany when they did? And, what happened to them in New Zealand subsequently until 1910? In the process we will discover how their romance worked out!

Throughout I attempt to place our forebears in their familial, relational, sociological, historical and religious contexts through to *Carl's* death in 1910. For *Theresia and Carl* and their whānau (family), we have no well-worn, handed-down, oral or written whakapapa (genealogy) such as a better-educated or financially wealthy family might have left for their descendants. We are dealing here with German peasantry who somehow summoned the courage to do what many courageous, or desperate, Germans were doing at the time, viz. emigrate to the relatively new countries that were seeking and receiving migrant workers to advance their national infra-structure development, notably U.S.A., Canada, South Africa, Brazil, Australia and Aotearoa New Zealand. I will record what I know about the early life in Germany of *Carl and Theresia,* and their years in Aotearoa New Zealand until Carl's death. I will comment on the influences and people in their lives growing up in Prussia, during a time of significant social upheaval. Apart from a brief survey of Alve and Möllers ancestors, this work focuses on the years from Carl's birth in1849, through marriage until his death in 1910.

Carl's parents married on 1 February 1846 and *Theresia's* on 24 October 1848. They, with their daughter Anna Maria Catharina (Mary) aged one, emigrated from Germany leaving on 18 December 1875 via Bremerhaven. After four years working on building railways for the Aotearoa New Zealand Government *Carl, Theresia* and their multiplying family spent fifteen years farming near Eketāhuna in the Wairarapa until the winter of 1896 when they returned to the Featherston area as sharemilkers. They then bought and relocated to another farm in the Manawatū, across the Tararua Range where they regrouped as a family by the winter of 1902. There they carved out another farm from primeval bush that had been the domain of Rangitāne Māori people previously.

While some of the content of this writing was included in my earlier work, *Alve Road: How Do You Spell That?* published in 1994, this work benefits from subsequent research and paints a broader picture. For instance, I know much more about *Carl and Theresia's* siblings and parents, their ancestry and about people they associated with in Prussia, and during their sea voyage to

Aotearoa New Zealand and through their early years there. I have dug deeper to know more about the socio-politico times in which they lived during this period.

In preparation for the writing of this book, and the anticipated Alve Family reunion in Pahiatua February 2024, The *Alve Family Facebook Page* has served to connect several members of the extended family during 2023-24. Apart from this serving as a promotional tool to alert family to the Reunion and the publication of this book, it has also allowed for dialogue and pictorial content about the family to be more widely dispersed. I have appreciated getting to know, online, many younger members of the family that I never knew previously.

This book will prove worthwhile if just one Alve descendant adds to their knowledge of our Aotearoa New Zealand pioneer family's story. The chances are that person will share the facts with two or three more, and it will not be long before many more will know the information shared here. Perhaps one of these people will continue researching and, in time, add to this body of knowledge which will benefit future descendants: whānau of *Theresia and Carl Alve* who began a journey with their romance and their marriage on Valentine's Day 1874.

Terry Alve – Epiphany, 6 January 2024

Foreword

Figure 1 - Christine Rose (née Alve).

Hello to you all. Hallo an euch alle. Tena koutou katoa.

In late January 1999, on a rather chilly afternoon in Gelsenkirchen Germany, I stood with my partner Ken and daughter Victoria inside the new St Augustine's Catholic Church. We were on one of our annual round the world trips from our place of residence at the time in Papua New Guinea. As we gazed around the interior of this rather splendid building, I thought about the marriage of Carl and Theresia held at this site almost 125 years before. What thoughts of their future inspired them to make the courageous decision of moving to a land so far away? Now, another 25 years after that visit to Germany, we will gather to celebrate that union on the most romantic of days – 150 years later. I wonder what Theresia and Carl would think. I imagine they'd be delighted and proud that their brave decision, endeavour and hardship, has resulted in descendants who have made their way ably in the new world they relocated to.

During my forty plus years as a teacher, one of my favourite topics to explore with students was that of "Our Family Tree". It was an extraordinary theme which led to a flurry of letters, emails, phone calls and photographs pouring in to support the children's understanding of who they were, and where they came from.

Thanks to our own family historian Terry, our families have access to a rich resource of information about who we are and where we are from. Terry's dedication to his research, uncovering facts, solving mysteries, recording and relaying stories and finding photographs and charts, is invaluable. What a wonderful adventure this study of the Alve family has led him on. Think of the endless hours and years he has spent poring over documents and files, the many interviews he has conducted, the kilometres he has travelled both here in New Zealand and abroad and the people, both family and information sources, he has met during this lengthy period of dedication to extending our knowledge of the Alve family. We are indeed most fortunate, and our heartfelt thanks go to Terry for undertaking such an enormous task and the production of this wonderfully presented compilation of his findings. A true taonga!

God bless you all.
Gott segne Sie alle.
Ma te koutou e manaaki.

Christine Rose (née Alve), Taupo

Author Acknowledgements

My first acknowledgement must be to Alec Wallace (1899-1994) who enthused a young teenager in the 1960's by taking time to tell him about some early Alve family history. As a boy he knew Theresia and Carl Alve and their children, and he graphically told me of life on the Rangitāne farm as he perceptively highlighted personality characteristics of several of the early family members. He even told me what it was like at mealtimes. Alec was the younger sibling of Catherine Wallace who became Charlie Alve's wife Dolly, whom I knew as a boy. In a portent of things to come I wrote a three-page summary of Alec's observations, and these became the basis of my extensive research about the Alve family over these past sixty years. For the record I had the privilege of being the officiant at Alec's funeral in Christchurch when I was Vicar of Spreydon near where he lived in Gainsborough Street, Hoon Hay.

Fast forward to the early 1990s when, encouraged by my uncles Phillip and Ivan Alve, I began contemplating the writing of *Alve Road*. My uncles, and my brother Gordon, became my support base for this work. Gordon chaired a representative group of Alve descendants as they began planning and organizing the Easter 1995 family descendant reunion. This gave us a deadline for completing and printing *Alve Road* which was published at the end of 1994. During early 1994 I completed a tour around the country visiting several of the family and recording information that became the printed biographies of the first three generations of the family born in New Zealand – around one hundred and forty records. With Gordon's help I was able to include a very comprehensive and up-to-date genealogical list of all the family for inclusion in the book, using the newly developed computer software, *Family History System.* The eldest of the second generation of Alve descendants, Bill Busch, and his second son Ken made significant contributions to *Alve Road,* which I acknowledge here.

There have been a couple of representative family gatherings since 1995, notably the Easter 2015 Reunion gathering of fifty lower North Island Whānau who met at the Palmerston North Convention Centre. Again, my brother Gordon (R.I.P.) was instrumental in making this happen and he continued to assist me with the computer genealogy. Three second generation family died that year: Alve Purdom just before the Reunion and Joyce & Hilton Alve (both of whom attended) later in the year.

Since 2015 I have made *My Heritage* genealogical software my programme of choice. The database of Alve descendant information is extensive and helpful, allowing me to keep track of who's, who. As mentioned in the Preface, the *Facebook Alve Family* page has been a resource for keeping the family in touch with one another and helping to both solicit new information and promote the February 2024 Reunion. Thanks, Whānau, for contributing.

Mention of Peter Alve is also due - he died 9 October 2023. Peter's prodigious memory for names, dates and details of family members, and others, constantly amazed us. More than that, he regularly kept in touch with so many of us, often with a birthday or anniversary greeting. It was my privilege as an *Alve* researcher to benefit from Peter's ready reckoning. If I ever had a query about a family date or fact, Peter was often my first port of call. Thank you, Cousin Peter; may you rest in peace, and rise in glory. We remember also Peter's sister Julianne currently as she journeys into the future without her close one. Julianne pays particular attention to family graves, having lovingly and ably restored many headstones in recent times.

Christine Rose (née Alve), daughter of Hilton and Jean Alve, has kindly written a *Foreword* for this work for which I am most appreciative. Like me she is a third-generation descendant of Theresia and Carl and my second cousin.

Finally, I acknowledge my wife Margaret (née Milne) who not only suffered my many absences when I wrote her father's biography in 2022-23 but has subsequently lovingly supported me as I have prepared and written *Valentine's Day 1874* during 2023. Thank you – perhaps I will stop researching and writing soon Marg, or not!

Author Notes

In recent times the name for *New Zealand* has regularly had the Māori name for this land prefixed, thus *Aotearoa New Zealand*. Some are ready to drop the New Zealand bit and call *our land of the long white cloud* just *Aotearoa*. As I write amidst this transition, I use the name *Aotearoa New Zealand* throughout this work when referring to New Zealand. When quoting others' work, I will use their wording.

In Chapter Two I have *italicised* the names of those who are direct ancestors of *Carl Alve and Maria Theresia Möllers*. Also, the two Carl's – *Carl (Jnr)* and his father, *Carl (Snr)* – are thus identified to clearly distinguish them. The surnames *Alve and Alfe* respectively, have also been used to distinguish them, although it is noted that *Carl (Jnr)* was surnamed *Alfe* in his birth and marriage certificates.

Throughout this book, *Maria Theresia Alve (née Möllers)* is referred to as *Theresia* and not *Maria* as she was in *Alve Road*. *Carl* and the family knew her as *Theresia*, witness Bill Busch's reference to her in the Foreword to *Alve Road*. It was common practice to use second names e.g., *Mary* for Anna Maria Catharina Busch and *Dolph* for Rupert Adolph Alve. Also, while *Theresia and Carl (Jnr)* had a son *Carl Wilhelm* born in 1876, I will refer to him as *Charles (William)* or sometimes as *Charlie Alve*.

Proper names and quotations are mainly italicized without quotation marks.

I have liberally used diacritics, or accented characters, for German and Māori words and place names.

This second edition includes further minor editing and the addition of a report, in Appendix Eight, on the Alve Descendant Reunion 17-18 February 2024, including new awarenesses that were discovered and discussed there. It also includes information about Rosa Alve's grave restoration at Featherston Cemetery that includes recognition of her baby sister Emma.

DEUTSCHLAND GERMANY

Chapter One: Pre 1849 Germany

During the 1800s and before, the Alve family lived in Germany near where Neandertal [i] remains were discovered in 1856. This extinct species of archaic humans lived in Eurasia until about 40,000 years ago. The type specimen, Neanderthal 1, was found in 1856 in the Neander Valley. It is a small valley of the river Düssel in the German state of North Rhine-Westphalia, located about 12 km (7.5 mi) east of Düsseldorf, the capital city of North Rhine-Westphalia. The valley lies within the limits of the towns of Erkrath and Mettmann. It is within Bergisches Land known for its beautiful scenery, lakes, waterways, valleys and woodlands.

The Neandertal was originally a limestone canyon widely known for its rugged scenery, waterfalls and caves. However, industrial quarrying during the 19th and 20th centuries removed most of the limestone and dramatically changed the shape of the valley. It was during such a quarrying operation that the bones of the original Neanderthal man were found in a cave known as *Kleine Feldhofer Grotte*. Neither the cave nor the cliff in which the bones were located still exists. A significant Neanderthal museum [ii] has been established at this site.

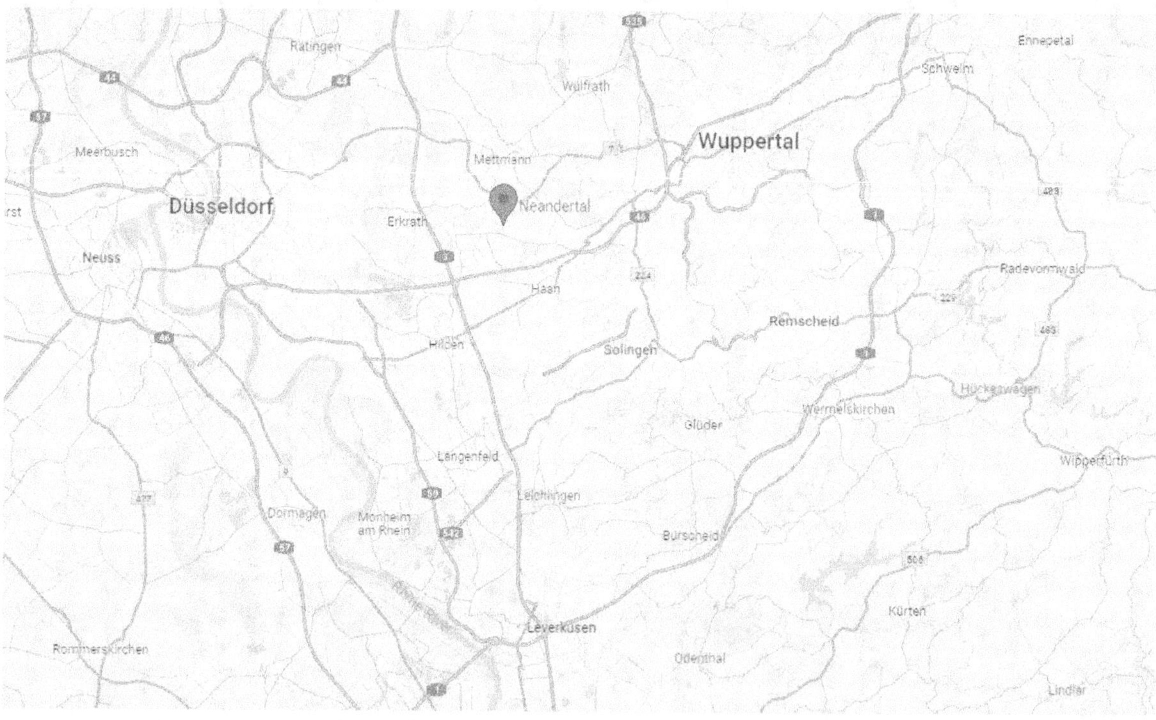

Figure 2 - Neadertal Valley and Museum in relation to Dusseldorf and Hückeswagen.

During the 19th century, the valley was called Neanderhöhle (Neander's Valley) and, after 1850, Neanderthal. It was named after Joachim Neander, a 17th-century Calvinist German pastor and hymnwriter. Neander is the Graeco-Roman translation of his family name Neumann; both names mean *new man*. Neumann lived nearby in Düsseldorf and loved the valley for giving him the inspiration for his compositions. The English hymn, *Praise to the Lord, the Almighty, the King of Creation* is one of his more popular works.

The 2010 Neanderthal genome project's draft report [iii] presented evidence for interbreeding between Neanderthals and modern humans. Most likely 100,000 years ago and again 65,000 years ago! Given Alve ancestors may have been present for a long time in this German region, it is conceivable that we may discover we have a smattering of Neandertal genes upon further investigation! After all, the direct line distance between Neander's valley and Hūckeswagen is just 25km or 50km by road.

Naturally there is a huge gap between this musing about prehistoric Germany and the beginnings of what we know about the Alve family that came to Aotearoa New Zealand in 1876. I attempt to bridge this gap in Appendix Four by offering a summary of German history: its key players and events.

We have oral history which relates to the sixteenth century and recorded ancestors who date from the middle of the seventeenth century.

Some Alve Oral Family History

Some New Zealand family members suggest that *Carl (Jnr) Alve* had Spanish ancestry. Certainly, the name *Alve* has a Spanish ring to it although, as we shall see, it was not always spelled this way. I believe *Carl's (Jnr)* wife, *Theresia*, reported this Spanish connection to her daughters, even suggesting that a Captain Alve (or like name) was perhaps a ship's captain in the Spanish Armada which after defeat in the English Channel foundered off Scotland and Ireland in 1588. Spanish casualties from England's defeat of the Armada were around 50%. If there was a Spanish Armada Captain Alve was he a casualty or a survivor? If there is Spanish ancestry, nothing is known about the reasons why a member, or members, of the family might have moved north from Spain to Germany, if they were not Germans fighting for Spain perhaps in defence of the Papacy.

Carl (Jnr) himself shared very little information about his ancestry and German background with his descendants. With the advent of DNA testing this assertion about a Spanish connection is challenged. Both I and my sister Margaret have had DNA tests and rather than a Spanish connection, we seem to have Scandinavian forbears in addition to Central European. Are these from the *Alves or Möllers*… perhaps they descend from other ancestral branches?

European history records that Spanish, as well as French and Scandinavian troops were in Germany during the *Thirty Years' War* (1618-1648). This protracted conflict followed the spread of Protestantism that originated in Germany with the Priest/Monk Martin Luther during the sixteenth century. This, combined with other political and sociological forces, created great unrest throughout Europe by the beginning of the 1600s. It is quite possible that a Spaniard could have found himself settling in Germany, whether intentionally or not, during this time. The possible Scandinavian connection may also relate to the *Thirty years War* mentioned above. To date I have been unable to link with any ancestor who has an obvious northern or Baltic connection.

As a result of the *Thirty Years' War* there was much social upheaval, as described by Diether Raff, [iv]

> *The population, decimated by war, eked out a living in shattered towns and cities. Industry, trade and agriculture were devastated. Economic recovery was impeded by enormous debts and by hordes of beggars and discharged soldiers who roamed about pillaging the land. The century (1650-1750) that followed the Thirty years War saw the German principalities, duchies and states weakened politically and impoverished.*

Just as the Thirty Years War ended, our first known ancestor appears: *Corß von Sassenbick* who was a shoemaker (Schuster)!

Earliest Known Ancestors

The earliest dated (Alve-Möllers) ancestors in my records are my seven times great grandparents: **Corß von Sassenbick** Born: May 1648. Occupation: Schuster in Klespe (a shoemaker in Klespe near Lindlar south from Hückeswagen) and, ***Entgen von Sassenbick (née von Scherkenbick)*** Born: Between May 1651 and Oct 1651. They Married: Oct 16 1678 - Wipperfürth, Cologne, North Rhine-Westphalia, Germany

Other early ancestors are:

- *Johann Peter Alffer* (1683-1756?) & *Anna Causmann* (?-c.1756)
- *Johannes Hermann Alffer* (1700-) and *Angela Alffer* (born Von Büchel) (1710-5 Dec. 1773) married 6 November 1734.
- *Angela's* parents were Father: *Christian Von Büchel*, Mother: *Margaretha Von Büchel*.
- *Angela's* husbands were *Johannes Hermann Alffer* and Thomas Schmitz.
- *Angela's* children were Johannes Georg Alffer, *Johannes Wilhelm Alffer*, Anna Richmund Altendorff (born Schmitz), Anna Elisabeth Stüttem (born Schmitz).

- *Angela's* siblings were Cunigunde Herzhoff (born Von Büchel), Johannes Adolf Zum Büchel. *Johannes Hermann's* parents were *Johannes Alffer* and *Anna Causemann* who were probably born around 1670-1680.

Between the early 1990s and 2023 when I write, knowledge of Alve ancestors has been extended back four generations, as above. In the early 1990s I was aware of the following ancestors:

- *Johannes Wilhelm Alfer* was born in 1740. His surname spelling reflects that used before 1820. Johannes's wife was *Anna Catharina Saszenbach.*
- *Johannes,* a farm labourer and *Anna* had several children including, *Wilhelm Melchior Alfer* - who was born in 1772 in the region of Wipperfürth east of the Rhine River, Düsseldorf and Cologne, and southeast of Hückeswagen. *Johannes* died in 1788 while living at Kluppelberg. Information about *Johannes and Anna* is contained in the marriage certificate of their son *Wilhelm* dated 1814.

Into the 1800s

In 1814 *Wilhelm Melchior Alfer* married *Anna Elizabeth Lamsfusz* in Hückeswagen which is adjacent the Wüpper River between Wüppertal and Wipperfürth. The Wüpper meanders through Bergische Land with its source near Marienhide in west Sauerland. It discharges into the Rhine near Leverkusen between Cologne and Düsseldorf. When I visited Hückeswagen in August 2019 I went for a walk with a local who was living next to where we stayed, Elena. As we were passing by the edge of town alongside the Wüpper river she mused that the river water changed colour from one day to the next as the weavers, in the 1800s, dyed their hand-woven fabric a different colour each day.

Wilhelm, our *Carl Alve's* grandfather**,** was employed as a cart driver and was living at Bundenberg when he married aged 42. It is not known if he was married previously. *Anna* was a widow, whose first husband, Peter Frielingsdorf died in 1811, the two having been married only a year before in 1810. Both Peter (1765/66) and *Anna* (1786) were baptised in the Hückeswagen Catholic Church along with their several brothers and sisters.

Anna was possibly the oldest of the family of *Johann Wilhelm Lamsfuß* and *Catharina Gertrud Kemmering*, that included: Joanny Wilhelmus Ferdinandus (1789), Anna Catharina Joanna Wilhelmina (1792), Petrus Wilhelmus (1795), Fridericus Wilhelmus (1798), Joan. Pet. Carolus (1801) and Petrus Joes. (1805). The name spellings are in the Latin of the church registers, rather than in the German of the people. *Johann* was a day labourer at the time of *Anna's* birth.

My wife Margaret and I travelled from Hückeswagen with Alve relatives from the United States (Linda Hulsen and Sue Heine) to the village of Lamsfuß during 2019. After visiting Kammerforsterhoehe, Wiehagen and Winterhagen to the west (places that all have an *Alve* connection), we drove south 15km to Lamsfusz before completing a circuit by returning to Hückeswagen via Wipperfürth. Perhaps a forbear or near relative of *Johann Wilhelm* Lamsfuß had a close association with the village of Lamsfuß (German spelling). I asked this question of a fellow German genealogist and my fifth cousin, Peter-Jorg Nöcken who was born in Hückeswagen in 1945. He does not know about this but referred me to a historian there. I am still awaiting a response. Peter, a retired judge, and I share *Johann Wilhelm Lamsfuß* as a common ancestor.

The marriage certificate of *Anna* and *Wilhelm Alfer* records that both their mothers were living at the time of the marriage and gave their assent. An interesting feature of their marriage certificate is the reference to the *Law Book of Napoleon*, another sign of the earlier French occupation. The following translation of the German is taken from this document, [v]

> *After I had perfectly convinced myself that the marriage sought for is not opposed by any legal obstruction, to the two engaged persons the sixth chapter of the law book of Napoleon was read out which deals with marriage, and the question was put to them whether it was their determination to mutually connect themselves in marriage. Both the engaged persons answered this question, 'Yes'. I have therefore, in the name of the law, declared Wilhelm Melchior Alfer and Anna Elizabeth Lamsfuß as a married couple and made the present document about this action.*

The above certificate and marriage were completed by Johann Georg Oules (possibly a Frenchman), the Burgermeister of Hückeswagen. *Anna's* brother Ferdinandus Lamsfusz (see above) was a witness to the marriage, signing the certificate and indicating that he was employed as a cloth weaver at the time. The registers also indicate that Ferdinand married Maria Brandenberg in 1812. Space and time do not permit me to record here this family line.

The first half of the nineteenth century in Germany saw a rapid population explosion. This resulted from conditions like those experienced in England fifty years before, with the coming of the industrial revolution. A consequence was unemployment in the villages and a movement of people to the cities where industry was increasingly being established. *Wilhelm* and *Anna Alfer* had at least four children during this period: Maria Catharina Carolina (1815), Furtina (1818), *Carl Wilhelm (Snr)* (1821) and Christina (1825). Each of their birth certificates records *Wilhelm's* occupation as a *day labourer*, probably indicating that the family lived close to the breadline with no secure, long-term employment. By the time of *Carl's (Snr)* birth in 1821 the "r" had been dropped from the surname.

Wilhelm died in 1830, leaving *Anna* a widow again with a young family to raise. We do not know their fortunes except that their daughter Maria married Joseph Feldmann in 1845 and before he married, *Carl (Snr)* found employment as a cloth weaver, possibly through the influence of his uncle Ferdinand. Difficult social and economic times were looming which would have undoubtedly affected the family adversely.

The Alfer - Alfe - Alves of Hückeswagen

We have noted above that the name change Alfer to Alfe occurred about the time of *Carl's (Snr)* birth registration in 1821. The change from Alfe to Alve came over several years before *Carl (Jnr)* came to New Zealand. His birth was registered Alfe although his father, or his representative, signed Alve. The births of his two sisters (Rosette and Anna Maria) were also registered as Alfe but his brothers were all registered Alve.

Figure 3 - Hückeswagen Coat of Arms.

The village of Hückeswagen is situated on the river Wüpper. Two dams, Bevertal and Wuppertal, are near the city. Hückeswagen's location is in a narrow valley. The nearby castle mountain (hill) is notable. It is located approximately 40km away from Cologne. Nearby towns are Radevormwald, Wipperfürth, Wermelskirchen and Remscheid.

The coat of arms of Hückeswagen [vi] was granted on August 9, 1892. The arms show in the upper part the lion from the arms of the Counts of Berg, who bought the area in 1260 from the Counts of Hückeswagen. The lower part is a symbol for the textile industry, which has been important to the town since the late Middle Ages. The combination of lion and spindle appears first in a seal from 1555.

On 18 October 1875 Hückeswagen, now a city, was connected to the railroad network. During the period of industrialization, Hückeswagen had a significant textile industry. Cloth available in

Hückeswagen today testifies to the great prosperity of the industrial families. The importance of the town as the center of the local area has been reduced in the last few decades as the neighbouring town Wipperfürth received some municipal and public facilities to establish itself as an important center.

Hückeswagen is in the Wüpper Valley in the beautiful Bergischeland. Addressing the Alve Family Reunion at Highden near Awahuri during the Manawatū Easter Reunion 1995, guest speaker Rolf Panny waxed lyrical about this area when he said,

> *Bergischeland - paradise - it's like a fairy tale and so I want you to know if you go there, and some of you will, then take along Grimms' fairy tales and compare the fairy tales to the lives and practices of the people over there that have stayed the same for the last 800 - 1,000 years, and that I think is the point we make: Carl and Maria... because people in those days couldn't imagine what this was - New Zealand - Neueseeland - so far away...*

By around 1820, hundreds of water-powered mills were producing textiles, lumber, shingles and iron in automated processes here. In even more workshops in the hills, highly skilled workers manufactured knives, tools, weapons and harnesses, using water, coal and charcoal power. As the machines became bigger and moved from waterpower to steam power, locally mined coal and charcoal became expensive and there was not enough of it. The Bergischeland industries ordered more and more coal from the new coal mining area along the Ruhr. Impressive and expensive railways were constructed through the hilly Wüpper region, to bring coal, and later steel, in from the Ruhr Valley, before being used to export it.

Beckum - the Spahrs, Wittings and Möllers

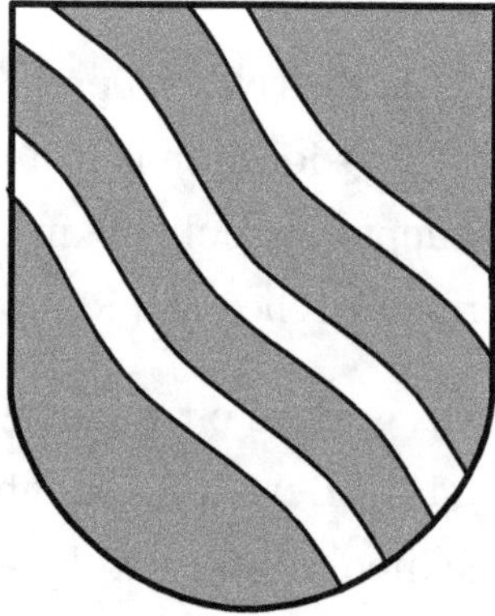

Figure 4 - Beckum Coat of Arms.

Several Neolithic stone cists are the earliest traces of humans in Beckum around the three brooks – Kollenbach, Lippbach and Siechenbach. Because of these three brooks, the town was eventually named Bekehem, later Beckum, meaning home upon the brooks. The three brooks are so symbolic of the area that they appear on the town's coat of arms as three silver wavy lines on a red background. The brooks converge near the town centre and form the river Werse, which flows past Ahlen and Münster to the River Ems. Beckum is situated in the southeast corner of agriculturally orientated Münsterland. Due to Münsterland's varied landscape of fields, pastures, hedgerows and small forests, it is often compared to a park. A range of low hills, the Beckum Hills, surrounds Beckum in the south and east. In the nineteenth century, chalk and cement industries developed in the area, and in 1827 the first cement plant opened in Beckum. Eventually the town became one of the most important and largest cement production areas in the world.

My records of *Theresia Möllers'* family are nowhere near as robust as they are for the Alves. *Theresia's* marriage certificate records her parents as *Bernhard Wilhelm Möllers* (b.1829) and *Katharina Spahr* (b.1825). *Bernhard* was a weaver. Their parents respectively were *Joann George* and *Gertrud (née Kloppenborg) Möllers* from Bevergern which is 100km northwest of Beckum; and *Heinrich Spahr and Adelheid (née Witting)* from Beckum.

So, the Beckum connection is essentially through *Theresia's* mother *Katharina* who lived there from birth. When and why, *Bernhard Möllers* came to Beckum to marry is unknown: perhaps his search for work led him there as a young man, just as *Carl Alve's* search for work led him to Gelsenkirchen and meeting *Theresia Möllers*. *Bernard* was a weaver and may have also, perhaps after marriage, moved to Gelsenkirchen for work. Was he conscripted into the Prussian Army during the 1870-71 Franco-Prussian War? Possibly he may have lost his life early through war, accident, pestilence or otherwise. This may be why his daughters grew up in an orphanage in Gelsenkirchen. Perhaps someday a future researcher will sight death records for him and his wife *Katharina Spahr* and discover why *Theresia* and her older sister were confined to an orphanage during their teenage, if not childhood, years.

Chapter Two: The Later Alve and the Möllers Families

The Revolutionary Spring (1848)

With the increasing industrialisation of Prussia, the smaller factories in Bergischeland could not compete with the growing number of large factories in the Ruhr Valley towns near the coal. Railways had arrived in the 1830's, followed soon after by steam engines, power-looms, ovens and hydraulic presses. Employment was increasingly to be found in the cities and coal mines, away from the villages. The plight of the weavers is recounted in the poetic song below which spread through the textile districts, like Hückeswagen, in 1844 and was incorporated into Gerhard Hauptmann's dramatic writing of the 1890's *Die Weber* (The Weavers). It recounts in haunting terms the terrible effects the events of the 1840's had on the victims of the industrial revolution in Germany.

Die Weber	The Weavers
Hier wird der Mensch langsam gequalt,	This is where people are slowly racked,
Hier ist die Folterkammer,	this is the torture chamber,
Hier werden Seufzer viel gezhalt	this is where countless groans,
Als Zeugen von dem Jammer.	evidence the depth of our pain.
Ihr seid die Quelle aller Not,	You are the source of the misery,
Die hier den Armen drucket,	that here afflicts the wretched,
Ihr seid's die ihm das trockene Brot	It is you who steal dry bread
Noch von dem Munde rucket.	out of the mouths of the poor.
Ihr fangt stets an zu jeder Zeit,	You who are always prompt,
Den Lohn herabzubringen,	to reduce our wage still further,
Und andre Schurken sind bereit,	while other scoundrels wait,
Dem Beispiel nachzuringen.	to follow your dread example.

The social discontent expressed in this poem issued in the uprisings of the *Revolutionary Spring of 1848* which saw much of Europe, including Germany, in turmoil. All of Europe was aflame with conflict and discontent. Parallel political tumults spread like brush fire across the entire continent, leading to significant changes. The men and women of Europe in 1848 saw the urgent challenges of their world as shaped profoundly by the past and saw themselves as inheritors of a revolutionary tradition.

It was a moment when political movements and ideas—from socialism and democratic radicalism to liberalism, nationalism, corporatism, and conservatism—were tested and transformed. The insurgents asked questions that sound modern to our ears: What happens when demands for political or economic liberty conflict with demands for social rights? How do we reconcile representative and direct forms of democracy? How is capitalism connected to social inequality? The revolutions of 1848 were short-lived, but their impact on public life and political thought throughout Europe and beyond has been profound.

> *Looking back at the revolutions from the end of the first quarter of the twenty-first century, it is impossible not to be struck by the resonances,*

Christopher Clark writes. [vii] He suggests that,

> *if a revolution is coming for us, it may look something like 1848.*

The uprisings came close to Hückeswagen and Gelsenkirchen as this report [viii] suggests.

> *On 9 May 1849, uprisings occurred in the Rhenish towns of Elberfeld, Düsseldorf, Iserlohn and Solingen. The uprising in Düsseldorf was suppressed the following day on 10 May 1849. In the town of Elberfeld, the uprising showed strength and persistence, as 15,000 workers took to the streets and erected barricades; they confronted the Prussian troops sent to suppress the unrest and to collect a quota of Landwehr conscripts. In the end, the troops collected only about 40 conscripts from Elberfeld. A Committee of Public Safety was formed in the town, to organize the citizens in revolt... On 17-18 May 1849, a group of workers and democrats from Trier and neighboring townships stormed the arsenal at Prüm to obtain arms for the insurgents. Workers from Solingen stormed the arsenal at Gräfrath and obtained arms and cartridges for the insurgents. Frederich Engels (the rich close friend of Karl Marx) was active in the uprising in Elberfeld from 11 May 1849 until the end of the revolt. On 10 May 1849, he was in Solingen and making his way toward Elberfeld. He obtained two cases of cartridges from the arsenal at Gräfrath and carried them to Elberfeld...*

I noted earlier the unrest and social upheaval occasioned by the collapse of the cottage weaving industries in Bergischeland and Westphalia and other places. This armed revolution, as short lived as it was, was another more sinister outcome of this pain. Pain that certainly was felt by both the Möllers and Alve families, both of whom had counted weaving as a primary source of income during the first half of the nineteenth century.

Carl Alve was born January 1849 amid this Revolutionary Spring. It had been forty plus years since Napoleon's forces raped and pillaged Bergischeland during the first decade of the 1800s. The enemy this time was not the French, nor any other foreign army; it was internal strife as the peasants sought to have a greater share of the wealth of Prussia.

For the families of Carl and Theresia Alve, despite the Revolutionary Spring, life was a perpetual struggle to obtain the rewards of their labour, determination and resilience. As we shall see, his quest would take them on a long journey that included work in coalmines along the Ruhr Valley, boarding an emigrant sailing ship for a ninety-nine-day journey to Aotearoa New Zealand, being a railway family working in the Remutaka Range, a forestry and small farm family in the forty mile bush living near Eketāhuna for sixteen years and, as dairy farmers who developed, with their children, a larger land holding at Rangitāne in the Manawatū during the last ten years of their marriage.

The chapters that follow explore the life and times and romance of this venturesome couple who were born in humble circumstances to become the progenitors of an Aotearoa New Zealand family who at this time have, one hundred and fifty years after their marriage, left us a legacy which values family togetherness, hard work and social responsibility.

The Later Alves

Carl Wilhelm (Snr) Alfe was 24 when he married Sybilla Catharina Bosbach aged 21, a servant girl of Huckeswagen, on 1st February 1846. Sybilla was born in 1825 at Cuerten (Kurten), the daughter of Wilhelm Bosbach and Maria Catherina Orth. Her father, like Carl's, had died prior to their marriage. It is recorded that Carl's and Sybilla's mothers both consented to the marriage.

Carl (Snr) and Sybilla had at least seven children whose births were registered at Huckeswagen between 1846 and 1862. Three of their children died young: Hubert (1854-1857), Hugo (1856-1857) and Ernst Albert (1862-1864). Their early deaths probably reflect the harsh conditions of the time and the poverty of the family. Just as diphtheria was a child-killer in New Zealand later, it may also have been in Germany and a factor in some of these child-deaths. Interestingly, Carl and Theresia were also to lose three of their children at a young age: Emma and Rosa, possibly named after Carl's older sister, as infants in 1896 and Anna, possibly named after Carl's younger sister, in 1906 to goiter at the age of twenty-six.

Sybilla's Death Record

Name	Anna Sibilla Bosbach
Birth	Circa 1826 Kürten
Residence	Gelsenkirchen, North Rhine-Westphalia, Germany
Death	23 May 1875 Gelsenkirchen, North Rhine-Westphalia, Germany
Age	49

We have no death record for Carl Alfe (Snr)

The Children of Sibilla and Carl

Rosetta Alve	1846 –

Carl Wilhelm Alve	1849 – 1910
Ewald Alve	1851 – 1917
Hugo Alve	1856 – 1857
Hubert Alve	1854 – 1857 Hubert's death certificate is available via an endnote [ix]
Anna Maria Alve	1858 – 1911
Ernest Albert Alve	1862 – 1864

Those who became adults were:

Rosette Alve

Rosette (Rosa or Rosalia) was born on 19 August 1846. She married Matthias Hausmann. They had at least two sons born in Gelsenkirchen: Hubert (1873-1912) and Heinrich Matthias (1880-1881). Hubert's death in 1912 was registered in Bonn.

Carl Wilhelm Alve

Carl Wilhelm (Jnr) whose family is a primary subject of this history, was born on 29th January 1849. Note his cemetery headstone inscription in Palmerston North, Aotearoa New Zealand wrongly has his birth year as 1850.

Ewald Alve

Carl's brother Ewald (b.1851) has long intrigued me. He first came to my notice in the 1990's when I received a copy of Carl and Theresia Alve's marriage certificate, I think via Hilton or Jean or their daughter Christine Rose (née Alve). I included it in *Alve Road*. The certificate has Ewald's signature as one of the two witnesses to the marriage. My interest was further piqued when I noticed more recently that he was witness also to the marriage of his younger sister Anna Maria in November 1875, twenty-one months later.

In 2022 *My Heritage* published extensive German death records from 1874-1938. Transcribed, Ewald's death record reads:

Name	Ewald Alve
Gender	Male
Birth	Circa 1852 Hückswagen, Kreis Lennep
Death	13th June 1917
Place	Suttrop, North Rhine-Westphalia, Germany
Age	65
Wife	Katharina (born Scharfenberg)

For the record, Suttrop is about 115km east of Gelsenkirchen via the A44.

The same German death record release also gives us insight into Ewald's family situation. His wife Katharina died 1926 in Gelsenkirchen and, if I am not mistaken, a witness to this is Ernst Alve, possibly their son. Her death record suggests she was born about 1843 in Heek, near the border with Holland, which is about 80km north of Gelsenkirchen.

Name	Katharina Alve (born Scharfenberg)
Birth	Circa 1843 Heek, North Rhine-Westphalia, Germany
Residence	Gelsenkirchen, North Rhine-Westphalia, Germany
Death	19 May 1926 Gelsenkirchen, North Rhine-Westphalia, Germany
Age	83

As I mention in Appendix 1 when writing about Emma Ida Alve, Ewald and Katharina also had a daughter Emma Alve who died young. She lived (1885-10 September 1887). Did correspondence between the brothers or their spouses prompt the naming of Emma Ida?

Anna Maria Alve

Name	Anna Maria Limbach/Hulsen (born Alve)
Birth	14 Aug. 1858 Hückeswagen, Lennep, Rhein, Prussia, Germany
Marriage to:	Carl Limbach 27 Nov. 1875
	Gelsenkirchen, North Rhine-Westphalia, Germany
Marriage to:	Henry Herman Hulsen 12 Feb. 1877
	Dusseldorf, Nordrhein-Westfalen, Germany
Immigration	1882 to USA
Death	17 July 1911
	Marseilles, La Salle, Illinois, United States

Children of Anna Maria to Carl Limbach (-1876) and to Henry Hulsen (1847-1900) were:

Charles Frederick Hulsen	1875 - 1957 (born Limbach, adopted by Henry Hulsen)
Maria Rosalia Hulsen	1878 - 1882 (died in Gelsenkirchen)
Anna Hulsen	1881 - 1882 (died aboard ship to USA)
Anna Maria Hulsen	1885 - 1965
Elizabeth Hulsen	1890 - 1895
Henry Herbert Hulsen	1892 - 1960
Herman Hulsen	1896 - 1944
Mary Anna Hulsen	1883 - 1958 (married: Quaintance)
Rose Elizabeth Hulsen	1888 - 1964 (married: Dropek)
Bennard Hulsen	1894 - 1970

Emma Myrtle Hulsen   1899 - 1974 (married: Johnson)

The Later Möllers

Bernhard and Katharina Möllers were married in Sankt Stephan Catholisch Church, Beckum on 24 October 1848 during the revolutionary spring described above. Their children were as follows:

Gerhard Möllers

Recently German death records became available in *My Heritage* (genealogy programme), and these provide information about Theresia's brother Gerhard's partner, some children and his death in Gelsenkirchen during 1926.

Birth:	Circa 1850 - Beckum, North Rhine-Westphalia, Germany
Residence:	Gelsenkirchen, North Rhine-Westphalia, Germany
Death:	16 February 1926 - Gelsenkirchen, North Rhine-Westphalia
Age:	76.
Civil Registration Office:	Gelsenkirchen

(Volume: P9-07_00675; Entry #: 348.)

Gerhard married and fathered at least three children with Theresia Moenninghof (b.1837) whom he married in the Katholisch Church, Ibbenbüeren, Westfalen, Prussia on 4 November 1868. Ibbenbueren is very near to Bevergern where Gerhard's father Bernhard lived as a child. Their children's christening dates are Gerhard Heinrich (8 November 1869), Heinrich August (15 December 1871) and Maria Elisabeth (7 February 1874 - 11 July 1888, Ibbenbüeren). I note that Theresia was about twelve years older than Gerhard. I also note that these three children were all born before Theresia and Carl Alve married in Feb. 1874.

Maria (Mary) Catherine Herbers (née Möllers)

Theresia had an older sister - Mary Catherine (1853-1895) – whom I believe lived in the Gelsenkirchen orphanage with her. Mary later emigrated to Aurora, Illinois, USA. Her first marriage was to a man whose name was thought to be "Miller". She had a second marriage to a Dutchman – John Herbers (1846-1908). They had at least six children: Deanna (possibly from her first marriage), Catherine, John, William, Tony (Antone) and, the youngest - Emma (married - Heiman) who was two when her mother died.

Emma lived in Aurora, Illinois and her children were Harold and Dorothy. Emma was reported as saying her Mother Mary had two brothers named Gerard and Albert. Descendants of Mary Herbers in the USA are recorded below. Some of these American cousins have corresponded with Alve descendants in Aotearoa New Zealand throughout this century. Gwen Davie (née Purdom) corresponded with Florence Herbers (wife of Tony) in the 1920's and 1930's. Ivan Alve corresponded with Emma Heiman (née Herbers) and more recently with Vera Burgess (née Herbers). Ivan's daughter Theresa Flintoff (née Alve) has had contact with Darlene Smith (née Aldrich), granddaughter of Tony & Florence Herbers, and daughter of Ethel Aldrich (née Herbers). Other Alve family members may have also corresponded.

Maria Theresia Alve (née Möllers)

Theresia (1856-1942) married Carl Alve in 1874. They are the primary subjects of this writing.

Two younger Möllers children

There were at least two other younger children: Johann Adolph Möllers (b.1859) and Anna Margaretha Spahr (b.1861). Does Anna bearing the name Spahr, not Möllers, suggest there was a marriage split before she was born? I have no further information about these two. Interestingly, Theresia Alve's youngest child Rupert Adolph (b.1902) was possibly named after this uncle. And possibly Anna Alve (1880-1906) after this aunty, as well as her paternal aunty Anna Maria Limbach/Hulsen (née Alve).

Chapter Three: Bismarck, Krupp and The Franco-Prussian War 1870-71

These two influential and prominent German men were very much at the centre of the life and circumstances of the Prussian, and emerging German, state during the period 1846-76.

- Bismarck's leadership in the Franco-Prussian War (1870-71) and the subsequent Kulturkampf persecution of Catholics had far-reaching effects for many, including the Alves.
- Krupp used Ruhr Valley coal and human resources to make steel products, especially for armaments and railway construction in Prussian and much further afield.

In this chapter I take a closer look at these two notables to appreciate how their influences converged to drive a peasant German couple to risk the privations and dangers of leaving their homeland, for the promised prospect of a better life far away in Aotearoa New Zealand. I will also offer some perspectives on the Franco-Prussian war which was the pivotal event during Theresia's and Carl's lives in Germany before they emigrated. Both Bismarck and Krupp were key players in this conflict between the military forces of France and the emerging German state.

Otto von Bismarck – Politician

Figure 5 - Otto von Bismarck.

From his origins in the upper class of Junker landowners, Bismarck rose rapidly in Prussian politics from the year before Carl Alve was born – 1848 – the year of the Revolutionary Spring. From 1862 to 1890 he was the president and foreign minister of Prussia. Before that, he was the

Prussian ambassador to Russia and France and served in both houses of the Prussian parliament. He masterminded the unification of Germany in 1871 and served as the first chancellor of the German Empire until 1890, in which capacity he dominated European affairs. He had served as chancellor of the North German Confederation from 1867 to 1871, alongside his responsibilities in the Kingdom of Prussia. He worked with King Wilhelm I of Prussia to unify the various German states.

Noted European historian Norman Davies wrote [x] at the end of the twentieth century,

> *Otto von Bismarck (1815-98) bestrode the Germany of the late nineteenth century much as the German Empire, which he designed, bestrode the rest of Europe. He, more than anyone else, was the architect of the European order which emerged from the turmoil after 1848, the year when he entered politics, and whose revolutions he detested. He was a man of immense contradictions both of personality and policy. The 'Iron Chancellor', of fearsome countenance in Reichstag or diplomatic encounter, he was in private a hysteric, an insomniac, and, as recently revealed, a morphine addict. He was a landed Junker, wedded to his estates at Schonhausen and Varzin, who presided over Europe's mightiest programme of industrialization. He was an antiquated Prussian conservative and monarchist who despised his sovereign, who adopted the nationalism of the liberal opposition, and who gave Germany both universal suffrage and social insurance. He was a victorious militarist who was infinitely suspicious of the fruits of victory. He was the hero of so-called German unification who chose to keep greater Germany divided. The key to his success lay in a marvelous combination of strength and restraint. He built up positions of great power, only to disarm his opponents with carefully graded concessions that made them feel relieved and secure. 'You can do everything with bayonets', he once said, 'except sit on them.'*

> *Yet Bismarck's reputation is a mixed one. No one can deny his mastery of the political art; but many question his morality and his intentions. For German patriots and conservative apologists, he was the person who gave his country, and his continent, an era of unparalleled stability: one has only to see what conflicts arose after his downfall when William II 'dropped the plot'. For liberal critics, however, he was and remains, in the words of Isaiah Berlin, 'a great and an evil man'. They see him as an aggressor, who used war as a conscious instrument of policy (and what is worst, succeeded); as a cheat who used democratic forms in order to preserve the undemocratic Prussian Establishment; as a bully, who bludgeoned his opponents with the blunt instruments of state power – the Catholics with the Kulturkampf, the Poles with the Colonization Commission, the social democrats with proscription. He would not have denied it. He believed, no doubt, that minor surgery and small doses of nasty medicine were well*

> *justified if major diseases were to be kept at bay. To quote a rare admirer of a leftist persuasion, 'The history of modern Europe can be written in terms of three Titans: Napoleon, Bismarck, and Lenin. Of these three…Bismarck probably did the least harm.'*

The King granted Bismarck the titles of Count of Bismarck-Schönhausen in 1865 and Prince of Bismarck in 1871. Bismarck provoked three short, decisive wars against Denmark (1865), Austria (1866), and France (1870-71). Following the defeat of Austria, he replaced the German Confederation with the North German Confederation, aligning the smaller North German states with Prussia, but excluding Austria. Receiving the support of the independent South German states in Prussia's defeat of France, he formed the German Empire – which also excluded Austria – and united Germany. With Prussian dominance accomplished by 1871, Bismarck used balance of power diplomacy to maintain Germany's position in a peaceful Europe. However, the annexation of Alsace–Lorraine caused French revanchism and Germanophobia. Bismarck's Realpolitik and powerful rule at home led to him being called the Iron Chancellor. Juggling a very complex interlocking series of conferences, negotiations and alliances, he used his diplomatic skills to maintain Germany's position. Bismarck disliked colonialism because he thought it would consume German resources rather than reaping the benefit of it but reluctantly built an overseas empire when it was demanded by both elite and mass opinion.

As part of his domestic political maneuvering, Bismarck created the first welfare state in the modern world, with the goal of undermining his socialist opponents. In the early 1870s, he allied himself with the low-tariff, anti-Catholic Liberals and fought the Catholic Church in what was called the Kulturkampf (culture struggle). This failed, as the Catholics responded by forming the powerful German Centre Party and using universal male suffrage to gain a bloc of seats. Bismarck responded by ending the Kulturkampf, breaking with the Liberals, and forming a political alliance with the Centre Party to fight the Socialists. He was loyal to his ruler, German Emperor Wilhelm I, who argued with Bismarck but supported him against the advice of Wilhelm's wife and son. While the Imperial Reichstag was elected by universal male suffrage, it did not have control of government policy. Bismarck distrusted democracy and ruled through a strong, well-trained bureaucracy with power in the hands of a traditional Junker elite. In 1888, which came to be known as the Year of the Three Emperors, the German throne passed from Wilhelm I to Frederick III to Wilhelm II. The new emperor dismissed Bismarck from office, and Bismarck retired to write his memoirs.

Bismarck is best remembered for his role in German unification. As head of Prussia and later Germany, Bismarck possessed not only a long-term national and international vision but also the short-term ability to juggle complex developments. As a result, he became a hero to German nationalists, who built many monuments honouring him. Historians praise him as a visionary who was instrumental in uniting Germany and kept the peace in Europe through adroit diplomacy. He has been criticized for his domestic policies such as Catholic persecution and the centralization of executive power, which some describe as Caesarism. Furthermore, he has been criticized by opponents of German nationalism, as nationalism became engrained in German culture, galvanizing the country to aggressively pursue nationalistic policies in both twentieth century World Wars.

Alfred Krupp – Industrialist

Figure 6 - Alfred Krupp.

Alfred Krupp, byname *The Cannon King*, German: *Der Kanonenkönig*, (born April 26, 1812, Essen, died July 14, 1887, Essen, Germany), was a German industrialist noted for his development and worldwide sale of cast-steel cannon and other armaments. Under his direction the Krupp Works began the manufacture of ordnance (c.1847).

His father, Friedrich Krupp, who had founded the dynasty's firm in 1811, died in 1826, leaving to his son the secret of making high-quality cast steel, together with a small workshop in which production had come almost to a standstill. Taking full charge of the firm at the age of 14, Alfred soon extended production to include the manufacture of steel rolls. He designed and developed new machines, invented the spoon roll for making spoons and forks, and manufactured rolling mills for use in government mints. He won new customers, extended his firm's purchases of raw materials, and secured funds to finance the expansion of his works. At the first world exhibition, the Great Exhibition, in London in 1851, he exhibited the largest steel ingot ever cast up to that time (4,300 pounds).

It was with the advent of railways that the rise of the firm really began. At first, railway axles and springs of cast steel were the only products made in this field, but in 1852 Alfred Krupp manufactured the first seamless steel railway tire. Later he adopted three superimposed railway tires, the "three rings", as the trademark of the firm. He was also the first to introduce the Bessemer and open-hearth steelmaking processes to Europe (1862 and 1869).

To prove the quality of his steel, Alfred Krupp turned to making cannons. Initially he could not sell his guns in Prussia, and the first orders came from Egypt (1856), Belgium (1861), and Russia (1863). As a result, however, of the performance of Krupp guns in the Franco-German War of 1870–71, the firm came to be called, *the Arsenal of the Reich.* Alfred Krupp was in many ways the founder of modern warfare. At the time of his death, he had armed forty-six nations.

Recognizing early the human problems of industrialization, Alfred Krupp created a comprehensive welfare scheme for his workers. As early as 1836 he instituted a sickness and burial fund, and in 1855 he established a pension fund for retired and incapacitated workers. In 1861 he began to build housing settlements, hospitals, schools, and churches for his employees. His workers became fanatically loyal to him. He had started his steel plant with seven workers; at his death the enterprise was employing 21,000 persons.

Krupp's marriage was not a happy one. His wife Bertha was unwilling to remain in polluted Essen in Villa Hügel, the mansion which Krupp designed. She spent most of their married years in resorts and spas, with their only child, a son named Friedrich.

While I do not suggest that Carl Alve was employed by Krupp, the coal he helped mine around Gelsenkirchen would certainly have been used by the Krupp conglomerate. The Krupp base at Essen is a stone's throw from Gelsenkirchen where the Alves and Möllers lived. This was very apparent when Margaret and I arrived at our hotel on the edge of the Stadtgarten, Gelsenkirchen on a very hot Friday 23 August 2019. From our tenth story room we had a grandstand view of an airship flying about 5-6 kilometres away towards the southwest in the direction of Essen. Krupp's influence included industrial pollution, high migration into the Ruhr region, employment, social interaction and other socio-political ramifications.

The Franco Prussian War 1870-71

I take time here to reflect on some of the history of this short war because I believe that as a twenty-one-year-old, Carl Alve was profoundly affected by it, at least psychologically. We have no record that he served on the front lines in northern France, but he was of an age that meant conscription into the Prussian army. The army that morphed into the German army which subsequently fought two world wars in the twentieth century. It was steel from the Ruhr Valley, forged into railway engines, carriages and tracks that ensured the speedy mobilization of the army that headed for France in 1870. And they took with them munitions also forged from Ruhr steel.

The Prussians were there before the French could blink an eye! Such was the organization and military dominance of the Prussians at that time. We also know, as is the way of war, that many atrocities happened during the war with raping, pillaging and summary executions commonplace.

Let's go back and remind ourselves about the backdrop to the Franco-Prussian conflagration.

When in 1869 the Spanish throne was offered to the Prussian king's cousin, Prince Leopold of Hohenzollern-Sigmaringen, Napoleon III, French Emperor, perceived this as an effort to encircle France. He twice sent his ambassador, Vincent Benedetti, to the Prussian King Wilhelm 1 at Bad Ems (a spa town near Koblenz on the Rhine), once to demand that acceptance of the offer be withdrawn (which it was on 12th July) and a second time to demand that under no circumstances should a member of the Hohenzollern family accept the Spanish throne in the future. The king politely refused the second request. Bismarck received a telegram from Bad Ems (the Ems telegram) giving a detailed account of the interview between William I and the French ambassador, which he proceeded to edit and abridge for the press in such a way that the French appeared to seek a humiliation of the Prussian monarch, and the monarch's rejection of Napoleon's demands seemed insultingly brusque to the French.

The French responded by declaring war on Prussia on 19 July 1870. When the French were decisively defeated at Sedan in September, it appeared as though Bismarck would be able to score a third rapid victory in seven years. But guerrilla warfare broke out, and Paris held out despite the capture of the emperor. Bismarck, however, stirred anti-French passions to such a fever pitch that in January 1871 the four southern states joined the North German Confederation to create the German Empire. The lesser German solution, with seven million German-speaking Austrians excluded, was the result of Bismarck's three wars. He was showered with honours and hailed as a national hero.

> *The Franco-Prussian War or Franco-German War, often referred to in France as the War of 1870, was a conflict between the Second French Empire and the North German Confederation led by the Kingdom of Prussia. Lasting six months (from 19 July 1870 to 28 January 1871), the conflict was caused primarily by France's determination to reassert its dominant position in continental Europe, which appeared in question following the decisive Prussian victory over Austria in 1866. According to some historians, Prussian chancellor Otto von Bismarck deliberately provoked the French into declaring war on Prussia to induce four independent southern German states—Baden,*

Württemberg, Bavaria and Hesse-Darmstadt—to join the North German Confederation; other historians contend that Bismarck exploited the circumstances as they unfolded. All agree that Bismarck recognized the potential for new German alliances, given the situation as a whole.

The Germans deployed a total of 33,101 officers and 1,113,254 men into France, of whom they lost 1,046 officers and 16,539 enlisted men killed in action. Another 671 officers and 10,050 men died of their wounds. Total battle deaths of 28,306. Disease killed 207 officers and 11,940 men, with typhoid accounting for 6,965. 4,009 were missing and presumed dead; 290 died in accidents and 29 committed suicides. Among the missing and captured were 103 officers and 10,026 men. The wounded amounted to 3,725 officers and 86,007 men. [xi]

We have no record written, or verbal that I am aware of, that Carl Alve was caught up in the Franco-Prussian War, nor the earlier Austrian war. Perhaps coal mining was considered an essential industry, and he was spared military service. Perhaps he did not pass muster as fit enough to serve. Or his involvement with the Prussian military during this war, and the subsequent occupation of the French territory of Alsace-Lorraine, may have taken him close to, or into the front line, fighting against the French. If it did, then he would have been squarely confronted with the horrors of nineteenth-century warfare. Did this inform his decision to emigrate? Mindful that old soldiers are notably reticent in talking about their experience of active warfare, we do not know what Carl's association was with these Prussian wars.

As we shall record later, Carl's fellow emigrant aboard the Gutenburg – Heins Briesemann – was involved in this war and, according to his descendants, was profoundly affected by this involvement. His subsequent emigration was perhaps a consequence of the ill effects of his Franco-Prussian war service 1870-71 – perhaps a case of PTSD. Offside with his family in Germany, he joined the Alves on the emigrant ship Gutenburg at the end of December 1875 and spent the rest of his life in Stratford in Taranaki, Aotearoa New Zealand.

The Logistics of the 1870-71 Franco-Prussian War

It has intrigued me how the scales of power were reversed as France struggled in this short war. This small, insightful commentary is a view of how Prussia won this war with their superior warfare logistics. [xii]

Prussia had already demonstrated four years ago, in the war against Austria-Hungary, how immensely important fast troop deployment via railway was. The Prussian, "Blitzkrieg" then resulting in Austria's defeat in a mere six weeks "had shocked

Europe." But still, the French failed to realise how much of a game changer railway transport really was.

If you remember, it was France which declared war on Prussia in 1870. And the French brass had a somewhat decent plan for an offensive into Germany along the Rhine. However, before they even started to assemble the widely spread armies néeded for that offensive, the Prussians were already aligned along the border and immediately pushed into France. In only three weeks, 1500 German trains had transported 640,000 soldiers, 170,000 horses and nearly 1600 artillery to the front. In contrast, France had a better railway net, but they never had planned and trained with that for military purposes. So, French trains had to stop or even turn around, because not all the designated troops for these trains had arrived.

This caught the French command completely by surprise. They had planned to attack, and before their armies were there, they now had to defend themselves.

*Also, the weapons depots of the French were centralised. Assembling the French troops meant the units marched (**marched!** while Prussians were **riding trains**) to certain logistic hubs, to where most weapons and ammo were to be delivered first, then the units would equip themselves with the arms, and then proceed to the area that they would have been employed. In contrast, Prussian units had their arms depots decentralised near their own barracks and would basically travel to their designated areas already fully equipped.*

There were some additional factors in play. One, numbers. Bismarck's clever propaganda made the independent southern German nations like Bavaria join the Prussian troops - while the French had fully expected that those nations would stay neutral. So, France faced a much stronger army than they had believed they would.

Then, weapons quality. The French did have more modern, advanced rifles - and the Prussians knew that. However, the Prussians had more modern, advanced artillery - and the French did not know about this.

So, when the somewhat sub-optimally organised French armies retreated, the advancing Prussians managed to encircle the largest French army around the fortified French city of Metz, isolating this army and effectively taking them out of the fights. Then they proceeded and did this again against another French army at Sedan.

Only, the Sedan troops were under command of emperor Napoleon III himself. When the Germans captured Napoleon at Sedan, France wasn't defeated - they had huge reserves that they still could have drawn upon. But the central command was gone, and the government was in utter chaos. So, the Prussians could advance towards Paris itself.

But, and I cannot stress this often enough, the main deciding factor was logistics.

It will be a task for a future researcher to inspect any surviving records of personnel involved in this war to determine if Carl Alve served or, if he somehow avoided involvement. I understand that there are detailed records available, but I have been unable to access them.

Figure 7 – Superior rail transportation of armaments, horses and soldiers into battle areas was key to Prussia prevailing in the Franco-Prussian War 1870-71.

Figure 8 - Defeating their powerful French neighbour to the west was the crowning glory for the (German) Confederation and signaled the birth of the German Empire. Read more at: https://www.magzter.com/stories/culture/History-of-War/1870-FRANCOPRUSSIAN-WAR

Figure 9 - The Prussian Army (1870-71) was composed not of regulars but conscripts and reservists. Service was compulsory for all men of military age; thus, Prussia and its North and South German allies could mobilize and field some 1.2 million soldiers in time of war, which it did within 18 days of mobilization. The sheer number of soldiers available made possible the mass-encirclement and destruction of entire enemy formations. Every able-bodied man had to serve in the army for three years, then he was released to the reserves for four years and after that he was on call to the national guard for five more years. Compared to the French, the Prussian soldiers were better educated with compulsory primary education that was not the law in France till after the war. An estimated 33,100 officers and 1,113,000 men took part in the war.
https://francoprussianwar.com/prussianmarch.htm

Chapter Four: Gelsenkirchen and Valentine's Day 1874

Gelsenkirchen Town

Gelsenkirchen was first documented in 1150, but it remained a tiny village until the 19th century, when the Industrial Revolution led to the growth of the entire area. In 1840, when the mining of coal began, 6,000 inhabitants lived in Gelsenkirchen; in 1900 the population had increased to 138,000. In the early 20th century, Gelsenkirchen was the most important coal mining town in Europe. It was called the "city of a thousand fires" for the flames of mine gases flaring at night... On the Emscher River (a tributary of the Rhine), it lies at the centre of the Ruhr, the largest urban area of Germany, of which it is the fifth largest city after Dortmund, Essen, Duisburg and Bochum... After Gelsenkirchen had become an important heavy-industrial hub, it was raised to city status in 1875: the year the Alves emigrated from there to Aotearoa New Zealand. [xiii]

Figure 10 - Gelsenkirchen Coat of Arms.

Up until the middle of the 19th century, the area in and around Gelsenkirchen was only thinly settled and almost exclusively agrarian. In 1815, after temporarily belonging to the Grand Duchy of Berg, the area comprising the city of Gelsenkirchen (City Crest pictured) passed to the Kingdom of Prussia, which assigned it to the province of Westphalia.

After the discovery of coal – lovingly known as 'Black Gold' (*schwarze Gold*) – in the Ruhr area in 1840, and the subsequent industrialisation, the Cologne–Minden Railway and the Gelsenkirchen Main Railway Station were opened. In 1868, Gelsenkirchen became the seat of an Amt within the Bochum district which encompassed the communities of Gelsenkirchen, Braubauerschaft, Gelsenkirchen-Bismarck, Schalke, Heßler, Bulmke and Hüllen. The cities of the *Ruhrgebiet* are from west to east: Duisburg, Oberhausen, Bottrop, Mülheim an der Ruhr, Essen, Gelsenkirchen, Bochum, Herne, Hagen, Dortmund, Lünen, Bergkamen, Hamm, Castrop-Rauxel and the districts of Wesel, Recklinghausen, Unna and Ennepe-Ruhr-Kreis. This area includes the Ruhr River, on its southern side, which has its source near the town of Winterberg in the mountainous Sauerland region in the east, at an elevation of approximately 670 metres (2,200 ft). It flows into the lower Rhine at an elevation of only 17 metres (56 ft) in the municipal area of Duisburg.

By 1850, there were almost 300 coal mines in operation in the Ruhr area, in and around the central cities. The coal was exported or processed in coking ovens into coke, used in blast furnaces, producing iron and steel. Consequently, the population climbed rapidly. Towns with only 2,000 to 5,000 people in the early 19th century grew in the following 100 years to over 100,000. Such was the growth trajectory of Gelsenkirchen. Skilled mineworkers were recruited from other regions to the Ruhr's mines and steel mills and unskilled people started to move in. From 1860 onwards there was large-scale migration from places like Silesia, Pomerania, East Prussia and Posen to the Ruhr. Skilled workers in the mines were often housed in *miners' colonies*, built by the mining firms. By 1870, over 3 million people lived in the *Ruhrgebiet* and the new coal-mining district had become the largest industrial region of Europe.

Gelsenkirchen and the Alves

Various members of the Alve family made their way to Gelsenkirchen in the late 1860s and early 1870s. At one level the reasons for moving to the *Ruhrgebiet* were the same: that's where the work was in the coal mines. Both families, the Alves and the Möllers, had been weavers, and both were influenced by the events of the 1840s and 1850s – the struggles to adjust to the demise of the cottage weaving industry. They had been impacted by the wars of the 1860s against Denmark and Austria and especially the 1870-71 Franco-Prussian war and really, they had no choice but to go where the money was.

What we do not know are the details of how this massive social upheaval impacted the Alve family. As we shall discuss, Carl's mother likely lived beyond Carl's wedding, but it is possible his father died before he and the members of his family moved north to the *Ruhrgebiet*. Sometime before his marriage to Maria Theresia Möllers in Gelsenkirchen in 1874, Carl (Jnr) Alve moved north. It may well be that around 1870 Carl (Jnr) and his brother Ewald were employed there as coal miners in Gelsenkirchen.

Or it may be that Carl was conscripted into the Prussian army before leaving the Hückeswagen area, or afterwards. The law required all men on reaching the age of 20 to undertake military service for three years and thereafter be a reservist. While there are many reports of 20-year-olds not doing military service for a range of issues, Carl reached 21 years of age in January 1870. A few months later the Franco-Prussian war of 1870-71 was fought and this required extra recruitment which makes it conceivable that Carl both trained for and possibly fought in this war.

If this speculation is right, there is no mention of it in family records or in anecdotal memories that I am aware of. Carl may not have become a coal miner (Bergmann) until sometime in 1871-72 after his military service in this case.

The distance from Gelsenkirchen to Hückeswagen via the A1 and A43 is 65km and takes about an hour nowadays by car. My wife Margaret and I travelled this route when we were driven via FlixBus by a Russian man as we travelled between these two towns in 2019. A lot of the journey was through forested hills and I recall seeing signs indicating that deer are a road hazard!

Gelsenkirchen and the Möllers

At some point the Möllers girls Catharina and Theresia found their way to Gelsenkirchen from Beckum, about ninety kilometres southwest. Did they come in order to be placed in the care of St Augustine's Catholic orphanage, or had their parent/s moved to live in the Ruhr Valley? It is my understanding that the Bishop of Paderborn Konrad Martin was in charge of both localities and perhaps the Gelsenkirchen Catholic orphanage was best equipped to care for two sisters in their situation at the time. Did the girls move to Gelsenkirchen ahead of, or after, members of the Alve family started arriving in Gelsenkirchen?

It is most likely that Theresia and her older sister Catharina were residents in the orphanage and school in Gelsenkirchen run by the Poor Handmaids of Jesus Christ (*Ancillae Domini Jesu Christi or ADJC*), founded in 1851 by Saint Maria Katharina Kasper in Dernbach (Westerwald) in the diocese of Limburg, further south. [xiv] St Maria Kasper was canonised by Pope Francis in 2018.

Figure 11 - Saint Maria Katharina Kasper founded the Poor Handmaids of Jesus Christ (Ancillae Domini Jesu Christi or ADJC) order in 1851. Theresia and Catherine Möllers lived in their Gelsenkirchen orphanage to 1874.

The turmoil of war in 1870/1871 on the one hand and the smallpox epidemic in the winter of 1871/1872 are possible reasons why the girls needed institutional care. [xv] In 1873, sixteen Catholic nuns were active in Gelsenkirchen, four of them school sisters and twelve nurses. To date we have no information about the fate of their parents who may have been incapacitated, or dead, when the girls were minors. As a result of Bismarck's *Kulturkampf* the school *ADJC sisters* had to end their service in 1874, and the convent and school were sold. Theresia married just before this happened.

Carl Alve and Theresia Möllers Meet

What were Carl and Theresia doing during the three years 1871-1873?

As discussed, during this time Carl possibly discharged his military obligations as a twenty-one year plus Prussian. We do not know when he moved from Hückeswagen to Gelsenkirchen, but it is likely that he was coal mining in the *Ruhrgebiet* along with the many others who had come from all over Germany and beyond to make this region the most industrialised in the world. He was likely living in mine provided accommodation. As he worked hard underground, we can be certain he was alert to any suggestion to improve his lot.

Steel magnate Alfred Krupp's wife Bertha talked of *polluted Essen* as she justified living away, in a spa town with her son. Essen was only twenty kilometres from Gelsenkirchen and wherever Carl was living, it is likely to have had a highly polluted atmosphere. Undoubtedly with so many young, newcomers flocking into the area, there was a buoyant social life and some of this will have revolved around the local Catholic church to which Carl and Theresia belonged.

All manner of questions arise about their relationship. We have the report that it may have been Theresia's brother Gerhard who introduced them. Gerhard had married in 1868 and had children at the time. He may well have been Theresia's (and her sister's) guardian. She was seventeen when they married, how old was she when they met: fifteen or sixteen? Did they meet in 1871 or 1872 or 1873? We know they married on Valentine's Day February 1874 when the priest was Father Schulte.

Father Ludwig Schulte, Gelsenkirchen Parish Priest (1833-1884)

Pfarrer (Father) Ludwig Schulte [xvi] was the Parish Priest of Sankt Augustinus Catholic Church, Gelsenkirchen from 1872-1884. He was born on the 18 March 1833, the son of a carpenter in Wenholthausen. He studied in Arnsberg, Bonn, Munster and Paderborn and got ordained to the priesthood there in 1858, through Bishop Konrad Martin.

He started his first and only chaplaincy at the parish church of St Johannes Baptist in Dortmund. Then he was ordered to be the priest at St Augustinus, Gelsenkirchen after the beginning of the Cultural War. Because of the growing number of obligees joining the new church, it was too small after its completion, so the industry pastor collected enough money on his collection journey to build a new church.

Its walls had already risen above the first St Augustinus Church in 1874. In the same year Theresia and Carl married and the confessing Bishop Martin was put into prison in Paderborn during the *Kulturkampf.*
Through plans from architect August Lange the new impressive church was finished in 1881, nowadays the provost church, one of the biggest churches in the *Ruhrgebiet*. The first service in the newly built church took place in February 1882.

Pastor Schulte died on 27th November 1884 in Gelsenkirchen. The grateful community built a monument in the shape of a still visible column and on top the figure of a good herder, standing at his grave on the new cemetery at the *Kirchstrasse.* [xvii]

Pfarrer Schulte was very much the family priest ministering, not only to Carl and Theresia but also to their siblings, notably Anna Maria Alve – her marriages, child baptisms and deaths…. One of the church register entries upon the death of her child Anna notes that she was, *poor.* Subsequently there is a USA report that hers was the poorest family in Depue! This impoverished background belies the fact that her descendants have made very good in the United States in many disciplines including medicine, engineering, education, music, politics, religion, etc.

Figure 12 - Coalminer memorial outside St Augustine's Catholic Church, Gelsenkirchen.

Carl and Theresia Marry

Maria Theresia Möllers was aged seventeen when she married Carl Wilhelm Alve. She lived in an orphanage with her sister Catharina who was a little older. As far as we know, her parents were not around for the wedding; she was an orphan. Theresia néeded court permission to marry as a seventeen-year-old, presumably in the absence of permission from her parents. Carl's mother Sybilla was most likely at their wedding. She died the following year on 23 May 1875, in Gelsenkirchen.

There has been an oral tradition in the family, sourced to Theresia herself, that their wedding service on Valentine's Day 1874 was held with several couples marrying together – as many as

Figure 13 - Maria Theresia Möllers and Carl Wilhelm Alve – Married 14th February 1874, St Augustine's, Gelsenkirchen.

sixteen I suggested in *Alve Road*. When I put this to a researcher at the Essen Catholic archives she commented in an email,

> *At Valentin's day 1874 a lot of couples got married at the St. Augustinus church in Gelsenkirchen. But I have to be honest to say, that St. Augustinus was a really big parish, and it can be a coincidence. I have never heard about 'mass marriage' at Valentine's Day, although it sounds very cute,* she wrote.

Attached to the same email were two pages containing marriage information about ten couples who were married by Pfarrer (Father) Schulte, the St Augustine's parish priest, on Saturday 14 February 1874, including the Alfes (sic). While there is no endorsement in the record that confirms the oral tradition, it is possible that a 'mass' marriage, with as many as ten couples involved, was conducted by the Priest. Perhaps a St Valentine's Day special service!

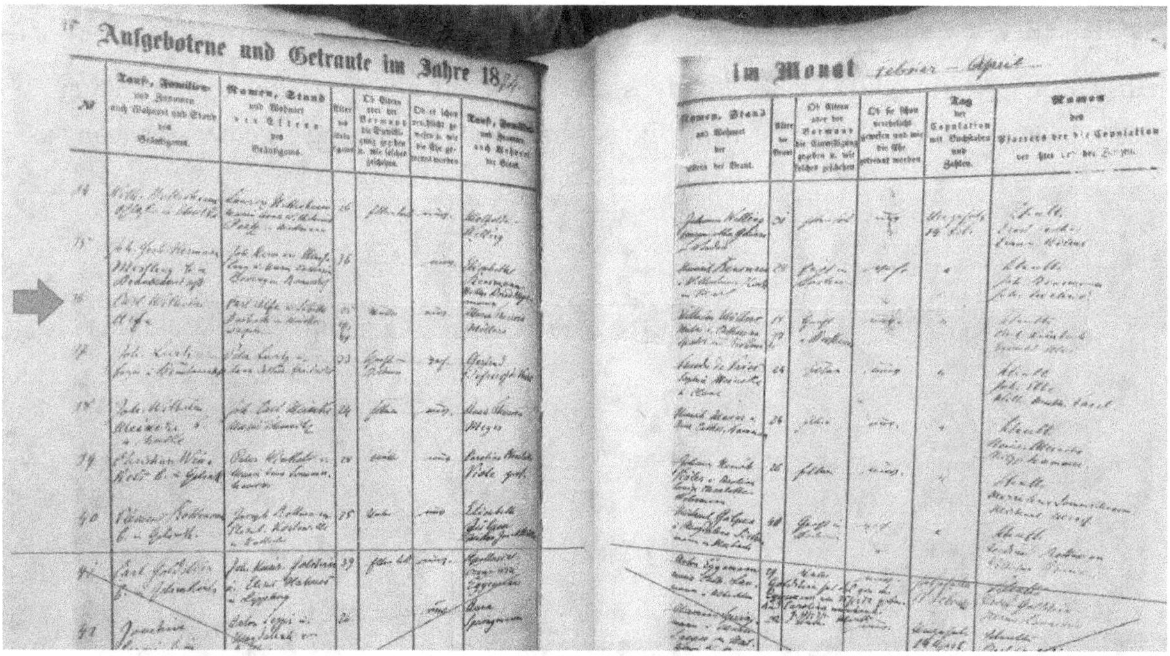
Aufgebotene und Getraute im Jahre 18
im Monat

Figure 14 - Carl Alve & Theresia Möllers married 14 February 1874 with nine other couples!

The same researcher made the point that,

> *... the church St Augustinus and everything in it was (in) 1944 absolutely destroyed by bombs and fire... (therefore) we do not have the original church books. But we have copies from the 1930s, which were made by the Nazis for the proofs of being Aryan.*

The Theresia=Carl marriage certificate copy below was passed on by Christine Rose (daughter of Hilton Alve). The details are self-explanatory and identify parties to the marriage, their parents and names of witnesses, including Carl's brother, Ewald.

The other interesting fact revealed in the email from Essen was the name of the orphanage where Theresia and her sister lived prior to her marriage,

> *"It was run by nuns from the 'Poor Handmaids of Jesus Christ' in German, 'Arme Dienstmädge Jesu Christi'."*

A query has been forwarded to their secretaries asking for more information which, to date, has not been answered.

In the original church book entry (below), the witnesses to the wedding were Ewald Alve (Alve not Alfe) and Carl Leinsbach, or similar.

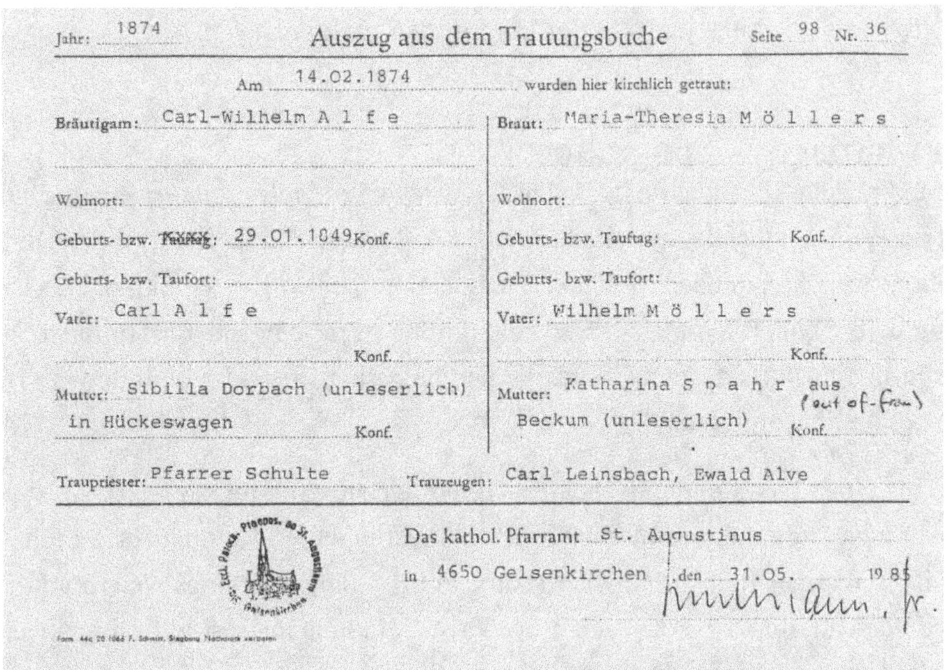

Figure 15 - A copy of Carl and Theresia's Marriage Certificate.

We have earlier noted Ewald was Carl's younger brother who also was a formal witness to the first wedding of his younger sister Anna Maria. Who was Carl Leinsbach? Anna Maria's first marriage was to Carl Limbach on 26 November 1875. Is it possible that these *Carls* might be the same person? It would be unsurprising if Anna's husband-to-be was at Theresia's and Carl's wedding, twenty-one months before Anna married him. Or perhaps it was the Valentine's Day 1874 wedding that brought Carl Limbach and Anna Maria Alve together? Or am I being too speculative and romantic in making the suggestion?

Theresia and Carl soon became expectant parents. Anna Maria Catharina was born in Gelsenkirchen on 1 December 1874. It is likely that Father Schulte was called upon to baptise Mary soon after her birth, as was the family custom of the Catholics. Just as there were many weddings in the Ruhr Valley in those days, as young people found their way to work in the coal mines and associated industries, so we can surmise that baptisms were regular also.

I will explore reasons why Theresia and Carl were prompted to consider emigration in chapter six. Perhaps it was Mary's arrival that confronted them with a desire to provide her, and other children they might bear, with better opportunities to improve their lot in life than they believed a future in Germany might offer them. This, combined with the reality that many young people, and not so young, were heading for the ports of Hamburg and Bremerhaven in search of brighter and more exciting futures abroad. Similar motivations are apparent today as people migrate from one country to another in search of a better life for their children.

Between Marriage & Emigration

It has intrigued me that Carl was described as a farm worker (*ackerslautern*) on the ship's manifest of passengers when he travelled to Aotearoa New Zealand. Was this an aspirational statement about what he intended to do in Aotearoa New Zealand, as he did, or was it something he was doing before he left Germany? Had coal mining been replaced with farm work as his occupation during his latter days in Germany? Did he perhaps farm for a while with Hermann Schormann before they emigrated?

It interested me when I took a long walk west from the centre of Hückeswagen in August 2019 that I discover a working dairy farm, pictured, at a locality called Kammerförsterhöhe. This is where Carl lived with his family and where some of his younger siblings were born. Had he as a youth indeed been a farm worker as well as a weaver? Had his interest in farming been piqued and had he deep down yearned to be a dairy farmer? I'll never know, but it intrigues me that he may have worked out, by coming to Aotearoa New Zealand, a deep-seated yearning. Perhaps addressing it just before he left Gelsenkirchen by doing a bit of dairying so that he could described himself as *ackerslautern* for Sir Julius Vogel, who was looking for farm workers and fit and healthy men to build roads and railways in Aotearoa New Zealand before they received land grants to become farmers.

Carl and Theresia's son Henry Alve with Theresa (née Wagner) his wife, my grandparents, established a Friesian stud at Rangitāne during the 1930s and named it *Westfalia* – the German region around Gelsenkirchen and Hückeswagen. Interesting!

Anna Maria Hulsen (née Alve)

Carl's younger sister Anna Maria Hulsen (née Alve) was to marry twenty-one months after him, less than a month before Theresia and Carl left Germany with little Mary, never to see one another again.

Figure 16 - A working dairy farm on the western edge of Hückeswagen at Kammerförsterhöhe in 2019.

Anna Maria Alve married Carl Limbach in St Augustine's, Gelsenkirchen on 26 November 1875. Anna was just sixteen. On 10 November 1875, just before their wedding, Anna gave birth to a son who was named Friedrich Carl Limbach. His godparents were Carl Alve and Rosa Alve – our Carl's elder sister. In September 1878 Rosalia Hausmann – the same Rosa – was also godparent for Maria Rosalia Hulsen who subsequently died in July 1882 before her mother left Germany with Friedrich and Anna to join her second husband Hermann Hulsen in Illinois, USA.

Figure 17 - Anna Maria Hulsen nee Alve.

So, Carl was probably around on 10 November. Were he, Theresia and Mary able to stay on for Anna and Carl Limbach's wedding a couple of weeks later, or did their pending emigration preclude that? It is possible that the wedding was the very last time that the Alve family adult siblings – Rosa, Carl, Ewald and Anna – were together. Their mother Sybilla had died earlier in 1875. We know Ewald continued living in Gelsenkirchen for some time afterwards.

After Carl Limbach's very premature death, Anna remarried when she and Hermann Hulsen became husband and wife on 12 February 1878. Hermann adopted Anna's baby Friedrich Carl Limbach and gave him his surname. Hermann left for the U.S.A. mid 1881 before arriving in Depue, Illinois where he found work as a coal miner. They had two daughters in Germany: Maria Rosalia who died before Anna left to join her husband Hermann in the USA in 1882; and Anna, who died of scarlet fever while on the boat crossing to USA in 1882. She was buried at sea. So, Anna arrived with her firstborn Friedrich Carl to meet Hermann in Illinois. They subsequently had several children together in the U.S.A. before Anna died in 1911, just one year after her brother Carl Alve died in New Zealand.

Anna Maria's great grand daughter, Linda Hulsen Daniel gives us this insight into her search for the family of Anna Alve – a search that was long and complicated. Her perseverance was rewarded as she relates here in her reflection about the challenges of being a family historian and genealogist looking for a German ancestor.

> *The Hulsen family has been searching for information about Henry (Hulsen) for over 100 years! We knew that he was born in 1847 but had no definite birthdate or birthplace. We could place him in Gelsenkirchen, Germany in 1878 at the time of the birth of his daughter. The family believed that he had married Anna Maria Alfa or Alpha in Dusseldorf about 1877 or 1878. My sister, Sue Hulsen Heine lives in Germany. She was able to obtain some civil records of the birth and death of Maria Rosa and the birth of Anna all of which occurred in Gelsenkirchen. Sue also found a civil record of the birth of Anna Maria Alve – after we figured out the correct spelling of her surname. Note that the name would have been pronounced 'Alfa' in German and in fact has had several different spellings.*

> *The civil records we obtained did not mention that Anna had an older brother – Carl Wilhelm Alve Jnr. who had immigrated to New Zealand. We discovered this about 5 years ago (2014) when I noticed Terry Alve's research on Ancestry. Terry has done an amazing amount of work on the Alve family history and has written a book about it (Alve Road)! We know that both Carl Alve and Anna Maria Alva were in Gelsenkirchen in the autumn of 1875, but there is no record of communication between them after that for the rest of their lives.*

> *Sue Heine was never able to find records in Dusseldorf. She was told that the records had been destroyed in the war. We wondered whether 'Dusseldorf' was the correct place*

to search. It might have been that family members in the U.S. were told that events happened 'near Dusseldorf' rather than in Gelsenkirchen because Dusseldorf was a name, they would have recognized in the early 1900s in Illinois and Gelsenkirchen was obscure. Therefore, we decided to look further in Gelsenkirchen.

Sue called St. Augustine Roman Catholic Church in Gelsenkirchen several times. This past summer, she was told that all church and civil records had been collected in Essen Germany. Sue called Essen. We sent a list of 6 records we wanted – knowing that often church baptism records yield more information than civil birth records. The staff members at Essen were terrific! They not only located all 6 records, but sent translations as well...

The Archivist who helped us in Essen reported that in fact church and civil records had been transported to Koln during WW II and had been destroyed. However, during the Third Reich, it was very important to the Nazis to discover people's heritage. This was called 'Ariernachweis' or Aryan proof. Nazis went to the churches and demanded the record books. When churches refused to hand them over, the Nazis sent in people to copy the records. The records we have today are the copied records that survived.

Henry Hulsen left Anna Maria in Gelsenkirchen with Carl, Maria Rosa, and Anna. Henry arrived in New York 24 Oct 1881 on the ship "Nederland" and continued to De Pue Illinois to find work as a coal miner. Ben Hulsen (son of Henry) wrote a story about this life which should still exist in the families of his children.

While Henry was gone, Maria Rosa died in Gelsenkirchen. Anna Maria then left with Carl and baby Anna on the ship 'Belgenland' for New York. (Baby) Anna died of Scarlet Fever during the passage and was buried at sea.

Ben Hulsen reports that their family was the poorest one in De Pue. Henry and Anna had 9 more children there... The family owes thanks to Grace Hulsen Higgins who started all this historical research, to Sue Derrick Rockwell for many contributions, and especially to Terry Alve.

Linda Hulsen Daniel - Nov. 2019

As far as I know, the first contact between Carl Alve's descendants and Anna Maria Hulsen (née Alve)'s descendants was in 2015, as Linda Daniel and Sue Heine exchanged correspondence with me and subsequently, we met together (with my wife Margaret) in Hückeswagen, Germany in late August 2019. We travelled together south in Sue's car along the Rhine River through Köln where we visited the great Catholic cathedral, Koblenz where we had lunch, Rudesheim for afternoon tea and to Frauenstein near Wiesbaden where Margaret and I stayed three nights. We had dinner and attended a *Rheingau* musical concert together with Linda and Sue at the Kloster Eberbach Abbey the night before we left Frankfurt, Germany for Manchester in England.

Subsequently, I have remained in contact with Linda, whose husband Steve Daniel died in April 2021, and Sue. Linda remains living in Denver, Colorado and Sue Heine, her sister, lives between her apartment in Florida and her German home in Bechtheim, a little north of Wiesbaden.

Figure 18 – L-R: Sisters Sue Heine and Linda Daniel great granddaughters of Anna Maria Hulsen (née Alve) with Terry Alve in 2019 at Kloster Eberbach, a former Cistercian monastery near Eltville in Rheingau, Germany.

Chapter Five: Emigration to Aotearoa New Zealand

Figure 19 - Rolf Panny, German historian, addressed the 1995 Alve Descendant Reunion.

Rolf Panny, German Historian at Massey University, Palmerston North in his address to the Alve Descendant Reunion during Easter 1995 [xviii] highlighted one of the costs German emigrant families faced in the 1800s when he said,

> *And remember that those who left were considered by most of their neighbours as failures, escaping, not bearing the hardship of life that was theirs.*

Later in his address, Panny invited those present to,

> *Imagine an underfed farm worker goes out into the neighbouring woods and he poaches a hare or a deer. Have you ever heard that the penalty for that was capital (punishment). That was during the time when the landlords and the owners of the land had the law on their side, and they were absolutely cruel. So, Carl and Maria did the right thing because they came to a land of favour.*

Why did they leave Germany? Rolf Panny in the same address said this,

> *Carl and Maria are saying to you through me, 'We are glad that you are all here together. We would not have dreamt that this would be the result of a sudden and probably unwise decision at the time.'... Today we would say that it was the most wonderful thing they have done because none of your faces would be here. And of course, they come from a country that is the home to the Brothers Grimm and their story is almost like a fairy tale, it really is. If somebody had written this as a fairy tale it would*

have ended also on the line that Carl and Maria lived happily ever after, had they not died. And I think that's an important consideration, that their life in the early days was not always happy. In fact, it was very, very hard and Mrs Clausen (the Manawatū mayor who was present) whose husband was Danish would also tell us that many of the emigrants from Germany and Scandinavia were told at the start that forty acres were waiting for them in New Zealand. Now tell me, if someone said to you today, "You can have forty acres in Canada, or, you can have $500,000 to start a new life in America" you'd have to think twice.

In his book, *A History of Germans in Australia 1839-1945,* [xix] Charles Meyer lists four main reasons for German emigration: religion, economics, politics and social conditions. These four main reasons were not all-important factors at the same time, nor should they be considered to operate independently of one another (often at least two of the reasons drove a person or group to emigrate). People's reasons for migrating are also complicated because often both "push" and "pull" factors play a role. Examples of "push" factors (circumstances that made people want to leave Europe) were crop failures, rising prices, and the desire to avoid forced service in the army. Examples of "pull" factors (attractions to remain in Germany) were family relationships, fear of the unknown, potential seasickness, leaving friends, etc.

I suspect these reasons applied for the German, indeed European, emigrants who were attracted to leave as they heard of the New Zealand Vogel Scheme 1871-76 from Herr Wilhelm Kirchner's emigration agents. I edit here some of the points Meyer makes.

Religion

During the 1870s German Catholics were disadvantaged and their leaders including Bishops were imprisoned as Bismarck launched an anti-Catholic *Kulturkampf* [xx] (culture struggle) in Prussia in 1871.This was partly motivated by Bismarck's fear that Pope Pius IX and his successors would use papal infallibility to achieve the,

papal desire for international political hegemony.... The result was the Kulturkampf, which, with its largely Prussian measures, complemented by similar actions in several other German states, sought to curb the clerical danger by legislation restricting the Catholic church's political power. A goal was to end the pope's control over the bishops in each state, but the project went nowhere.

In 1875 Bismarck accelerated the *Kulturkampf.* In its wake, all Prussian bishops and many priests were imprisoned or exiled, including the local Bishop Konrad Martin of Paderborn. Prussia's population had greatly expanded in the 1860s and was now one-third Catholic. Bismarck believed that the Pope and Bishops held too much power over the German Catholics and was further concerned about the emergence of the Catholic Centre Party, organised in 1870. With support from the anticlerical National Liberal Party, which had become Bismarck's chief ally in the Reichstag, he abolished the Catholic Department of the Prussian Ministry of Culture. That left the Catholics without a voice in high circles. Moreover, in 1872, the Jesuits were expelled from Germany. In 1873, more anti-Catholic laws allowed the Prussian government to supervise the education of the Roman Catholic clergy and curtailed the disciplinary powers of the Church. In 1875, civil ceremonies were required for weddings. Hitherto, weddings in churches were civilly recognized.

The Catholics reacted by organizing themselves and strengthening the Centre Party. Bismarck a devout, pietistic Protestant (Lutheran), was alarmed that secularists and socialists were using the *Kulturkampf* to attack all religion. He abandoned it in 1878 to preserve his remaining political capital since he now needed the (Catholic) Centre Party votes in his new battle against socialism. Pius IX died that year, replaced by the more pragmatic Pope Leo XIII who negotiated away most of the anti-Catholic laws. The Pope kept control of the selection of bishops, and Catholics for the most part supported unification and most of Bismarck's policies. However, they never forgot his culture war and preached Catholic solidarity to present organized resistance should it ever be resumed.

Economics

When the wars against Napoleon ended in 1815, the war economy for certain products also collapsed and competition from cheaper British products grew when they could be sold again in Europe (Napoleon had cut England off commercially from the continent). Masses of soldiers were allowed to leave the German armies and went back to their rural home villages, and soon there was not enough good farmland and work for the whole population, especially in Prussia and the southwestern German states. Prices started to rise.

During the years when Prussia was at war with Denmark, Austria and France (1864-1871) and during the uncertain period in the few years that followed, many Germans left Europe. As peace became permanent, emigration numbers fell.

The newly united Germany (Second German Empire, 1871) transformed itself from basically an agricultural nation into an industrial nation. New technology meant that wealthy people now put their money into industry instead of unprofitable agriculture. There was mass migration within Germany that must have been quite unsettling for those of a more conservative inclination. The movement of the Möllers from Beckum and the Alves from Hückeswagen respectively, to Gelsenkirchen which was amid the emerging industrial heart of Germany are cases in point. This massive social change and dislocation resulted in a mixing of the Prussian and German populace in a way unprecedented. These two families are typical and symptomatic of what was happening in the Ruhr Valley from 1871 through 1875 and beyond.

Politics

It can be said that Germans who left Europe to avoid compulsory army service emigrated for political reasons. Whether he was a reservist or an active soldier during Bismarck's military conquests we do not know but, we do know that the threat of involvement in military action would have not made Carl Alve feel particularly secure, especially as he became a husband and father. In January 1871 Carl turned twenty-two years old. Whether he was still living in Hückeswagen, or he had migrated to Gelsenkirchen, he was a prime candidate for conscription and mobilization as the Prussian army fought the Franco-Prussian war of 1870-71. Against this backdrop Carl must have wondered when and where the next war would be and, if he wanted to be part of the German military machine in the future.

Social Conditions

Another reason for emigration was the decline of people's security as a result of social or economic changes. And if these people could not come to terms with this change in their social situation, they emigrated. The category of emigrants motivated by social reasons also includes people whose action was somewhat "speculative"; they may or may not have had a pretty good life back home in the German speaking countries, yet they were curious to see if they could have it even better in a country like Australia or Aotearoa New Zealand – a bit of adventure. Mark Dunnick comments on reasons for European emigration in the 1870s, [xxi]

> *Decisions to migrate were made on a personal level and were influenced by a range of different social factors. Religious differences, political repression and family circumstances all contributed to individual choices. Many European countries conscripted young men into military service, and families were reluctant to lose a son for several years or even permanently. Most migrants had a specific destination in mind, often following friends or relatives who had made the journey earlier.*

Once the decision to migrate overseas had been made, potential migrants had to travel to a port and buy a ticket to their destination. For Northern Europeans, these ports were Hamburg or Bremerhaven. Beginning in the late 1860s, Hamburg shipping lines ran weekly services to New York, and each ship carried several hundred people. From 1870, steamships replaced sailing ships on most routes, with 173 steamships operating in the Atlantic in 1873. Regular steamship services required organised sales and marketing operations. The steamship companies established permanent ticket agencies staffed by professional emigration agents in major European cities. These professionals each had a network of sub-agents who distributed information and advertisements outside of the cities. The sub-agents were usually shopkeepers, publicans or farmers with a regular job and income, who earned a small commission if they made a ticket sale. Long distance voyages to Australia and New Zealand were among the few routes that remained profitable for sailing ships propelled by trade winds, which did not require fuel stops.

The Push Factors

For the Alves there were both push (go) and pull (stay) factors which we can summarise as:

1. They were Catholics at a time when the *Kulturkampf* persecutions were very real and threatening for them. I suspect for Theresia especially, who had spent time in a Gelsenkirchen Catholic orphanage, and who was quite devout, the state control of Catholicism was ugly and deeply disturbing.

2. Having witnessed three Prussian wars 1864-71 and being of conscription age, whether he participated in any of these wars, Carl likely had no desire to be called up to participate in another war. Like many, especially Danes in northwestern Germany, he may have chosen to emigrate to be free of the possibility of call up. The local police vetted potential emigrants who were dodging conscription. It seems Carl passed their checks. Again, I suggest he had most likely completed his military service.

3. As poor people, albeit Carl was a coalminer and perhaps felt that was poverty, the prospect of improving his lot in Canada, the USA or Aotearoa New Zealand was a very attractive position. He had lived long enough to know that employment in Germany was fickle and likely to perpetuate his and his family's poverty.

4. Theresia grew up, at least for a few years, in an orphanage. What did that mean for her? We know she had a close relationship with her sister Catharina, who emigrated to the USA around the same time as Theresia left for Aotearoa New Zealand. Although her brother Gerhard, who may have introduced her to Carl, was at hand it is unlikely she had close family connections otherwise holding her back. Hers was a fractured family which probably meant emotionally there was little holding her familywise to stay in the Ruhr or, in Germany.

5. With baby Mary expected and born (December 1874) before leaving, Theresia and Carl saw and responded to the publicity of the seasoned immigrant agent Wilhelm Kirchner. It promised them a bright future in a faraway land they could travel to for

free if they worked for the Government of Aotearoa New Zealand for a few years. While they would have known little about Aotearoa New Zealand, its people or the work they were going to, they were promised that in no time they would have land of their own, as Rolf Panny pointed out above. Land to farm on deferred payment would be theirs while they enjoyed things that would have been a pipedream in the Germany they would leave behind. It seems there might have been a similar opportunity to emigrate to Canada which required a much shorter sea voyage around the same time. Why the Alves ended up in Aotearoa New Zealand may forever be a mystery. Perhaps the Antipodean deal was judged to be more fiscally prudent; or maybe they just missed the boat that was heading for Canada!

The Pull Factors

1. Carl Alve's younger sister Anna Maria married within a month of Carl, Theresia and Mary emigrating. How did Carl feel about leaving his more intact family behind? Anna Maria – her new husband Carl and his godson Friedrich Carl – Ewald his brother and Rosa his older sister? A difficult choice maybe, albeit his parents had passed it seems.

2. Theresia had a more fractured family, although her older sister Catharina had spent time in the orphanage with her. Perhaps together the sisters had mused about emigration and the possible separation it might mean for them. Interestingly, it was Catharina's descendants in the USA who maintained correspondence with Alve descendants in Aotearoa New Zealand and vice versa. We have no record of correspondence between Carl's German family and their overseas cousins. Theresia would be leaving also her brother Gerhard and the sense of family he represented. The fact that her parents were dead, it seems, meant that the big pull, had they been alive, was minimal. Anyway, they had abandoned her to the orphanage for whatever reason! We also note here that Theresia's elder brother Gerhard, while living north, was likely in touch. He was married with three children born before Theresia and Carl married. She was leaving them behind.

3. A one-hundred-day journey on a small sailing ship to about as far away as you could go must have been daunting to say the least. The privations of a long sea voyage with a young child must have been carefully weighed up as they explored emigration. Child mortality and sickness were common on emigrant ships, as Carl's sister Anna discovered as she emigrated to U.S.A. and lost her daughter on the way! It is probable

they knew this.

The Vogel Immigrants

In 1870 Colonial Treasurer Julius Vogel unveiled an ambitious Public Works and Immigration scheme aimed at boosting the population of Aotearoa New Zealand, building infrastructure and centralising the state and the economy. The scheme would transform the country, with the settler population nearly doubling within a decade. Almost one hundred thousand assisted immigrants arrived in Aotearoa New Zealand between 1870 and 1880. Amongst these were seven thousand Continental European assisted immigrants recruited between 1871 and 1876 and these included a high proportion of young families and married couples. These migrant families made a much more significant contribution to the nineteenth century colonial population than earlier continental European migrants in Aotearoa New Zealand who were mostly single men. These Vogel immigrants played an important part in the transformation of colonial Aotearoa New Zealand. Mass immigration and public works pushed settlements, roads and railways into regions where the government previously had little control or reach, and in 1876 the provincial governments were abolished and replaced by a more centralised state, and a sub-system of local counties. The new railway system symbolised nineteenth century industrial capitalism, representing modernity and progress in the eyes of the colonists. The state funded national railway system planned by Vogel also accelerated the alienation of Māori land, the clearance of forests and the opening of remote areas to Pākehā settlement. As historian Donald Akenson [xxii] points out,

> *The better life for Europe's migrants was paid for in part by a worse life for those they dispossessed, and historians of migration and colonisation need to keep this in mind...*

Like most of the Vogel assisted immigrants and their children, the Alves probably had no knowledge of the *Te Tireti* (Treaty of Waitangi) the colonial government negotiated at Waitangi on 6th February 1840 with Aotearoa New Zealand *tangata whenua* (Māori people of the land), and subsequently affirmed by the signatures of several Māori *Rangatira* (Chiefs) up and down the land. It is likely the immigrants rarely considered the Māori people who were dispossessed of *mana* (moral authority, prestige) and *hauora* (wellbeing). Nor would they have anticipated the sickness and death occasioned by diseases they were not immune to. The colonial infra-structure project they helped to build was a disaster for Māori! Settlers and government policy relentlessly pressured Māori to sell their remaining land. Māori continued to resist land loss and retain their autonomy as best they could, but the colonial state continued to grow stronger. By 1901, as the Alves crossed the Tararua Range to farm at Rangitāne, the Pākehā population reached 772,719 while the Māori population had dropped to 43,112 people, the lowest number since records began.

The Journey to New Zealand

I am indebted to the Te Ara Encyclopedia of New Zealand for this information. I have re-worked and edited it to make it more specific for the Gutenburg sailing. [xxiii] In addition to this information the Te Ara website above has other associated information which makes for interesting and informative reading, such as:

- Departure to landing
- Cabin and steerage
- Life on board
- Sickness at sea
- Personal accounts: 1840–1899

Europeans who decided to make a new home in Aotearoa New Zealand embarked on the longest journey of migration in human history. In the eighteen seventies this voyage was usually made by sailing ship. Not only was the passage long and comparatively expensive, but it was also miserable and dangerous... the journey to New Zealand took from 75 to 120 days and cost at least £15. Most Vogel immigrants, including the Alves, had this amount paid by the New Zealand government.

Those promoting emigration to New Zealand had a particular reason to see that standards were maintained: on such a long voyage, bad rations and poor conditions would have led to disease and death. To prevent the passage to New Zealand becoming notorious, the New Zealand provincial and central governments insisted on even higher standards than those of the British on the Atlantic and other sailings. Reports of the dreadful conditions on board, from those who had made it to the other side of the world, put many people off doing likewise. In the early 1870s a Wellington immigration officer informed the agent general in London that,

> *... letters written home by immigrants who have been made miserable throughout the passage by causes entirely remediable, do more to retard emigration than all the costly advertisements, peripatetic lecturers, and highly paid agents do to advance it.*

Between 1839 and the 1890s, several hundred sailing ships brought tens of thousands of immigrants from Europe to New Zealand. In the 1840s ships were generally around 500 to 600 tons and carried between 100 and 250 passengers. By the 1880s they could weigh over 2,000 tons and carry up to 500 passengers. By these standards the Gutenburg which transported the Alves was a relatively small sailing ship at around 700 tons carrying less than 200 passengers when she sailed to Wellington in 1876.

A route to transport convicts from Europe to Australia was pionéered in the late eighteenth century. This took ships south-west down the north Atlantic, often as far west as Brazil, then south-east to Cape Town. The 'easting' to Australia from Cape Town was roughly along the 39th parallel. By the 1840s ships bound for New Zealand were following a similar route across the Atlantic (though seldom reaching Brazil), then swinging wide round the Cape of Good Hope into the roaring forties – westerly winds that moved ships along at great speed. Vessels sailed as far south as their captains dared, to benefit from stronger winds, but there was a risk of violent storms and icebergs. Indeed, as the captains report for the Gutenburg sailing indicates, this ship came within two miles of icebergs in the southern Indian ocean!

In 1850, when the Charlotte Jane went as far south as 52° 36', the Lyttleton Times criticised its captain for inflicting miseries on passengers in the interests of making a fast passage. Immigrants were subjected to a great variety of conditions en route. Storms in the English Channel or the Bay of Biscay were followed by pleasant sailing in the trade winds. In the equatorial doldrums, awnings were often raised over the decks to provide shade from the incessant sun. Storms were encountered again in the Southern Ocean or Tasman Sea, sending ships tumbling and rolling.

The Gutenburg Emigrant Ship

Alve descendant forbears travelled on the Gutenburg for three plus months when they emigrated from Germany to Aotearoa New Zealand in 1875/76. Carl Alves (sic) with his wife Theresia and daughter Mary travelled along with one hundred and sixty-four passengers. Amongst these was Heinrich with Dorothea Schormann with their children Friederich and Maria, and Heinrich (Neins in the passenger list) Wilhelm Carl Briesemann, the only fare paying passenger on the ship. See notes below. The Gutenburg sailed 18 December 1875. This was after the Vogel Scheme agreement between Kirchner & Slomann with the NZ Government had expired on 14 November 1875. In effect it was one of the last three Vogel immigration scheme (1871-1876) ships to sail.

It was planned that the emigrants would embark from Hamburg on 15 December, but the river Elbe was frozen over, so they were taken over-land to Bremerhaven to board her, while the ship was towed through the ice.

Figure 20 - The emigrant memorial at Bremmerhaven.

It is unclear why some family members understood that the Alves travelled to New Zealand on the ship Humboldt. It may be that they had earlier booked passage on the Humboldt which left Hamburg for Wellington during October 1874. If this was the situation, Maria would have been heavily pregnant with Mary who would have been born on the ship two months later. It is possible that either they decided against leaving then because of the advanced pregnancy, or they were not permitted to leave.

Their Gutenburg ticket number was *75* and the surname indicated is *Alves*. Carl aged 27 and Marie aged 20 are described as married man and woman from Prussia. Carl's occupation is recorded as *farm labourer (ackerslauten)* and their daughter Anna as *aged 1½*. See the transcript of the full passenger list in Appendix 3. They were in the company of 164 emigrant passengers including 11 boys, 18 girls and 4 infants. Nationalities of the passengers were Germany - 71; Italy - 48; Norway - 18; Denmark - 15; Sweden - 1; Austria - 1 Switzerland - 0.

Ticket number *76* on the Gutenburg was held by Heinrich (33) and Dorothea (27) Schormann and their children Friedrich (6) and Marie (1½). They too were from Prussia and Heinrich is also described as a *farm labourer*. It was Hermann Heinrich Schormann who subsequently, with Carl Alve, jointly purchased land on Alfredton Road, Eketāhuna in 1880 - see below.

Details of the journey on the Gutenburg are recorded in various documents held at the National Archives in Wellington. These note that the ship left Bremerhaven on 18 December 1875.

This was the second journey of the Gutenburg to New Zealand. She had earlier discharged 137 immigrants from Europe at Lyttelton, *Otautahi* during October 1874. The *Lyttelton Times* on that occasion had described her as a "fine iron clipper-built ship". Captain Buckwoldt was her master on that journey also.

For over thirty years I searched for an image of the Gutenburg sailing ship without success. It seemed like every *Vogel* immigrant ship had a picture accessible online, except the Gutenburg. In July 2023 I posted on *wrecksite.eu* asking if anyone knew of an image of the Gutenburg. I was advised that there was an image of the Edinburgh (the original name of the Gutenburg when she was built in Tyneside in 1862) in Hobart, but this was a wooden hulled ship built later. However, this post prompted me to look further at shipping around Australia and I discovered the image below. This photo was taken in March 1867 at Port Adelaide where a new slipway, *Fletcher's Dunnekier Patent Slip,* had just been constructed and our Gutenburg (then named the Edinburgh) was the first ship to be inspected, cleaned and repaired there. The opening of the Fletchers' Slip was a momentous event in South Australia for it marked the opening of the biggest patent slip in Australia at the time. The newspaper report of this event highlights this. [xxiv]

This Slip is not dissimilar to the one built a few years later in Evans Bay, Wellington that was even larger than the one built in Adelaide. It seems that the pending opening of the Suez Canal (1869), plans for a Panama Canal (delayed to 1914) and the sailing of more ships into the Pacific Ocean from the United Kingdom and Europe was part of the motivation for more slipways being constructed in Australasia at this time. However, the size of ships began to increase so much, that slipways gave way to *dry docks* that could better handle them as they needed cleaning, repair and painting. A feature of the Evans Bay slipway was the need for the coastal road closure when ships were hauled up the slipway from the Bay. Despite this it continued in use until 1985, in latter days servicing Cook Strait ferries! [xxv]

As noted below in the description of the *Gutenburg* (formerly the Edinburgh), the ship sank on 17 January 1897 when owned by another company (JJ Wallis & Son) after the Slomans. You can view details of the shipwreck here. [xxvi]

Figure 21 - The Edinburgh (later the Gutenburg) was the first vessel on Fletcher's Dunnikier Slip, Port Adelaide 12 March 1867. State Library of South Australia, B 3456, PRG 1218/3 or OH 456/1.

Details of this ship:

Name:	**EDINBURGH**
Type:	Sailing Ship
Keel:	18/08/1862
Launched:	23/11/1862
Completed:	27/12/1862
Builder:	J Wigham Richardson & Co
Yard:	Neptune, Low Walker
Yard Number:	13

Dimensions: 698grt, 691nrt, 880dwt, 172.6 x 29.3 x 18.8ft
Engines: None
Engines by: n/a
Propulsion: Sail
Construction: Iron
Reg Number: 45758

History:

1862	Levi & Co (Thos Aggs & Co), London
1868	RM Sloman, Hamburg; renamed GUTENBURG
1891	JJ Wallis & Son
17/01/1897	Wrecked

Comments: Built for Indian and China trades
Contract price £10,845. Profit £733-8s-5d
Wrecked on Ran (or Run) Island (Banda Sea, Indonesia)
Final passage from New York to Macassar (Capetown)
Carrying a cargo of cased petroleum when wrecked

The Schormann Family

Figure 22 - Heinrich & Dorothea Schormann.

The Gutenburg Passenger list has these two entries – see Appendix Three,

75 ALVES Carl MM 27 Prussia Farm Lab. Marie MW 20 Anna G1½
76 SCHORMANN Heinrich MM 33 Prussia Farm Lab. Dorothea MW 27 Friedrich B 6 Marie G 1

The proximity on the passenger list of the Alves and Schormanns, reinforces the notion that they knew each other (perhaps well) before they embarked on the Gutenburg to come to Aotearoa New Zealand. Perhaps they obtained their tickets together. The Schormanns lived in the Gelsenkirchen area where their daughter Maria Gertrud Schormann was born at Katernberg, (near) Essen, Germany. She was born 3 August 1874 and christened 23 August 1874. She was just a few months older than Carl's and Theresia's daughter Mary. They had an older child, Friedrich, who was aged six when they left for Aotearoa New Zealand.

H. Heinrich Schormann was born at Eickum, Herford in Westphalia on 4 February 1842. He died while living on the Managaoranga Road, Eketāhuna property he farmed after his partnership with the Alves on the farm at Alfredton Road, Eketāhuna. He was buried on 30 March 1905 in the *Mangaoranga Cemetery, Eketāhuna*. His parents were: Johann Christian Schormann and Hanne Catharine Giesselmann. His wife, Dorothy Louisa Schormann (born Joseph), died on 3 October 1910 in *Forty Mile Bush* (probably the farm mentioned above) and is buried alongside her husband. Together Heinrich and Dorothy had at least seven children, the first two were born in Germany and the others in Aotearoa New Zealand:

> *Friedrich H. Schormann (1869-1947)*
> *Marie Gertrud Scharnwebber (née Schormann) (1874-1949)*
> ====
> *Hermann Schormann (1876-1942) – (see comment below)*
> *Emma Hanson (née Schormann) (1879-1943)*
> *William Schormann (1880-1911)*
> *Albert Schormann (1887-1970)*
> *John (Jack) Christian Schormann (1889-1964)*
> *Frederick Schormann (1899-1973) – possibly their grandson from son Friedrich H.*

Hermann (Jnr) Schormann's birth, if it was on 19 April 1876 as some genealogists suggest, was within a month of the Schormanns arriving in Wellington after their hundred-day voyage from Germany. Hence Dorothea, Hermann's mum, was pregnant before and during the sea voyage to Aotearoa New Zealand.

Heinrich Briesemann

Heinrich Wilhelm Carl Briesemann (1850-1917) was the only fare paying passenger aboard the Gutenburg ship when it sailed, with the Alve family aboard, from Bremerhaven to Wellington, New Zealand. He hailed from Wismar, Mecklenburg and was the younger of three sons born to Franz Joachim and Antonie (née Taddel) Briesemann. Heinrich's brothers were Franz (a dealer in fine arts and other collectibles) and Karl a medical doctor who died young in 1870 of an illness contracted through his medical work. This may or may not have related to the Franco-Prussian war happening at the time of his death.

Figure 23 - Trevor Brieseman with his daughter Alison in Tawa.

Heinrich fought in the Franco-Prussian war (1870-71) and suffered as a result. It is unknown if he had physical wounds, but psychologically it seems the war took its toll on his health – perhaps PTSD in modern day parlance? It seems he became an embarrassment to his family before being encouraged to emigrate.

Heinrich's elder brother Franz bought a large manor house (*schloss*) which continued as his home until his death in 1894. This *schloss*, Brookhausen is seven kilometers north northwest of Schwaan near Benitz. In recent years it has been restored. An article about this property concludes,

> *"The community and the people of Brookhüsen, who feared and fought for their manor house for so long, can now be proud of their beautiful 'castle', which had been left to decay for so long and which is now a real feast for the eyes." [xxvii]*

Franz bequeathed his collection of outstanding paintings from the sixteenth to eighteenth centuries by Italian, French and Dutch masters to his native town of Wismar where his father had been *Burgermeister* (Mayor). The collection is part of the City History Museum; some pictures can also be found in the town hall of Wismar.

It is likely that Heinrich Briesemann (a single man at the time) and the Alves met during their voyage to Aotearoa New Zealand aboard the Gutenburg, despite their difference in social status – he was the only paying passenger aboard the ship. Nothing is recorded of any interaction they may have had. Upon arrival in Wellington (March 1876) the Alves moved to Featherston and Heinrich to Midhirst, Stratford and they seemingly had no further contact. Heinrich subsequently married Rose Judith Jane Wheeler from Bath in England in October 1895 at Stratford and they had two sons: Franz (1899-1973) and Wilhelm (1903-1972). Heinrich died in 1917. Rose survived him until 1937.

One of their sons, Franz married Ivy and they subsequently parented four children: Ethel (Australia), Alan Francis OBE, JP, Trevor, Wellington and Dr. Melvin Athol who became a medical officer of health in Christchurch. Many of the family were active Salvation Army officers. Trevor was a corps officer and Melvin did medical missionary work in India. Trevor lives in Tawa, Wellington with his daughter Alison near where I live. We have exchanged stories in the writing of this extract about Heinrich Briesemann – his family and his descendants.

Wilhelm Kirchner – Emigration Agent

Ludwig Wilhelm Kirchner (1814 Frankfurt - 1893 Wiesbaden) first emigrated to Australia in 1839 and returned to Germany in 1848 to work as an immigration agent for the New South Wales government. He arranged the publication and distribution of a promotional booklet titled, *Australien und seine Vortheile für Auswanderer* (Australia and its Advantages for Emigrants). He based himself at his mother's house in Frankfurt am Main, arranged the publication and distribution of his promotional booklet, and put-up advertisements and posters in towns and villages all over the Rhine regions. There was a big shortage of labour in New South Wales at the time; convict transportation had finished in 1841. The NSW state government authorised him to offer subsidised tickets to migrants. They would be contracted to work for a set number of years for landowners who had given commitments to Kirchner. He recruited approximately 4,000 German emigrants, many of whom worked in vineyards on the outskirts of Sydney and in the Hunter Valley.

Figure 24 - Wilhelm Kirchner - German Emigration Agent.

Kirchner's work as immigration agent was very successful for New South Wales, and he returned to Australia in 1851, where he was appointed Sydney Consul for Hamburg and for Prussia, and his businesses flourished.

In addition to promoting mainland Australia as a place for European immigrants to settle, Kirchner sponsored several Germans into Tasmania during 1855, including my Wagner grandmother's forbears Philip and Caroline Wagner from around Wiesbaden and Frankfurt, their parents and their siblings. These immigrants provided a labour force for colonists in Tasmania. The Tasmanian Wagners settled in Woodsdale and the Midlands area initially, and later spread throughout the Island. In 2022 I contributed to Michael G. Watt's research about Germans who settled in the northwest Tasmanian Fingal Valley. These settlers included some related and connected to the Wagners. Commenting on Kirchner's involvement in Tasmanian German immigration Watt notes, [xxviii]

> *Nearly all emigration from Germany to eastern Australia, which occurred between 1850 and the mid-1860s, coincided with a period of economic recession in Germany, poor harvests and political unrest in central Europe. Overpopulation along with lack of agrarian reform made it increasingly difficult for small farmers and agricultural labourers, as well as artisans in the cities and towns, to maintain their lifestyles… Later they came from Saxony, Pomerania and the Danish border area.*

While other immigration agents began recruiting European emigrants for the Aotearoa New Zealand Vogel immigration scheme in the early 1870s, the experienced Kirchner was contracted to take over this work when earlier agents did not perform to expectation. German social and political circumstances had changed, and the task of recruitment was difficult with the effect that the Vogel Scheme came to a premature and messy end at the beginning of 1876, just before the Gutenburg (and Alve) immigrants arrived. As we shall see, this did not affect the Alves nor their fellow immigrants, but it would affect the last shipload who came to Aotearoa New Zealand aboard the Fritz Reuter to Port Nicholson later in 1876.

Messy End to the Vogel Immigration Scheme

There was a dispute between the Aotearoa New Zealand government (represented by Dr Featherston, Consul General based in London) and the German immigration agent Kirchner and ship owner Sloman about the terms of the contract that allowed for 4,000 Europeans to be brought to Aotearoa New Zealand during the latter part of the Vogel immigration scheme. An issue contributing to the end of the Vogel scheme related to changing conditions in Europe and particularly in Germany as that land recovered from its wars. Berry writes, [xxix]

> *In the light of the N.Z. Agent General's concern about low German emigration numbers, the German government tightened its restrictions on emigration and foreign agents were expelled. Opposition to emigration originated with the Franco-Prussian war, to conserve manpower...* (and quoting N.Z. government correspondence) *Many Germans were wanting to emigrate, especially from South Germany, the Rhinelands (west of the Rhine) and Alsace-Lorraine (Northwest France). The United States was experiencing a depression in 1873 and 1874. If more information could be spread in Germany about New Zealand, and the way the government helped people to get there, many immigrants could be obtained, despite restrictions by the German authorities.*

An outcome was that it became harder to recruit prospective emigrants to fill the Vogel scheme quotas. The scheme ended prematurely in November 1875. The Gutenburg sailed 18 December 1875 which seems not to have been an issue. However, the ship Fritz Reuter did not sail until April 1876. The immigration agents argued that their recruitment and preparatory processes began much earlier, albeit the immigrants did not leave until well after the cutoff date!

While there had been correspondence between Dr Featherston, Kirchner and Sloman, Featherston categorically said no more Europeans to Aotearoa New Zealand in February 1876 by which time many people had been recruited as emigrants. Part of the issue it seems, while not wanting to disparage him, Dr Featherston was very ill at the time. He died in London 19 June 1876.

The Fritz Reuter sailed from Hamburg on 11 April 1876 and arrived in Wellington on 4 August 1876. It took 110 days to arrive in Wellington, New Zealand. Captain Peyn was in command. There were 420 statue adults with crew in addition. More than 260 Poles made up half of the passengers, the largest number of Poles who had arrived in the colony at any one time. Scandinavians, Germans and Italians made up the balance. Immigration officials would typically have counted the Fritz Reuter passengers as *statute adults,* but immigration officials did not count them this time. These *foreigners* arrived apparently against the express order of the colonial government, a government that had bluntly stopped *foreign* immigration at the end of 1875, although not clearly communicating this to the European agents who continued to recruit emigrants. Perhaps the European agents did not want to hear the news and chose to ignore it in the case of the Fritz Reuter!

The day after they arrived in Wellington the local paper, *the Evening Post*, missing (or ignoring) the fact that all settlers in Aotearoa New Zealand were foreign immigrants, bluntly wrote,

> *... She brings no Government immigrants but nearly 500 souls on board, equal to 420 statute adults, who were ready to come out when orders were given to discontinue the shipment of foreign immigrants. They were therefore forwarded independently of the Government and probably will be landed on Monday next. Their general health has been excellent during the voyage. Eleven deaths occurred, viz., 1 adult, 4 children, and 6 infants under 12 months old. She is consigned to Messrs. Krull and Co.*

For more detailed information about this messy end to the Vogel Scheme visit:

- *IMMIGRATION TO NEW ZEALAND. (LETTERS FROM THE AGENT-GENERAL.) 1877* Presented to both Houses of the General Assembly by Command of His Excellency. Schedule of Correspondence. [xxx] This includes extensive correspondence between the Aotearoa New Zealand Government, Kirchner and Sloman.
- Doctor Mark E. Dunnick, whose ancestors were Polish Vogel Immigrants, the Zdunek family, who came to Canterbury on the Friedeburg in 1872. He has written a PhD thesis on the Vogel Immigration Scheme including this *messy end.* [xxxi]
- A good summary by Barbara Scrivens (2018) of the Vogel Immigration Scheme and its key players from the perspective of a descendent of the Fritz Reuter immigrants. [xxxii]

In passing, I note that Olga Purdom (daughter of Carolena Purdom née Alve) married Jack Palenski whose father Axubold Karl Herman Palenski was a two-year-old child aboard the *Fritz Reuter* when it arrived in New Zealand on 4 August 1876.

And here is another Reference [xxxiii] which surveys the causes and effects of emigration from Germany (1870s–1880s). Between Bismarck's appointment as Prussian minister president in 1862 and his departure from office in 1890, almost three million Germans left their country in search of a better life abroad. Many of them went to the United States and nearly ten thousand found their way to New Zealand.

AOTEAROA
NEW ZEALAND

Chapter Six: Wellington & Featherston 1876-1881

Landfall Port Nicholson

The Gutenburg arrived at Port Nicholson, Wellington on 23 March 1876. *The New Zealand Times* edition of 24 March 1876 reported on the voyage as follows,

> *The German ship Gutenburg, Captain Bockwoldt, arrived in harbour yesterday from Hamburg. She left Bremmerhaven on the 18th of December and met with a succession of W. and S.W. winds till the 27th. The following day, as a consequence of thick foggy weather, anchored close to the Varne lightship. The weather cleared up on the 29th, when she weighed, and beat down Channel, which she cleared on the 2nd January. Had southerly winds until the 8th, when she fell in with the N.E. trades. Sighted San Antonio Island on the 16th; crossed the equator on the 24th, and experienced southerly winds to the 27th, veering to the S.E., continuing to the 5th of February, when it shifted to the N.E., in lat. 30 S. and long. 28 W., with fog. On February 23rd she passed a number of icebergs at a distance of about 2 miles. On the 25th the steward, Emiel Bargman, died from brain fever. Had a continuation of N.E. winds to Banks peninsula, which she made on the 12th inst. Passed Cape Campbell on the 22nd in the evening, when the S.W. wind sprang up, which brought her into port. She comes into port a clean ship, there being no sickness of any kind on board. One death and one birth on the voyage. She has on board one saloon passenger and 165 souls, equal to 144 statute adults, under charge of Dr. Evers, surgeon-superintendent. Her cargo consists of 300 tons of coal for Messers Johnston and Co., Messers Krull and Co., being the agents.*

The report of the Surgeon-Superintendent, Dr Evers, includes these comments on the voyage,

> *The single women were locked up each evening from sunset to sunrise... The greater part of the Italian immigrants were very odd fellows... they began to quarrel with their fellow emigrants as well as with the officers and crew. They showed so little cleanness... they refused to follow the regulations.*

The "Times" on 25 March 1876 reported that it was from aboard the *Manawatū* that Carl and Theresia, with Mary, finally stepped on to New Zealand soil,

> *The P.S. Manawatū, Captain Harvey, left Wanganui at 8.45p.m. of the 23rd, crossed the bar at 9.30, and arrived alongside the wharf at 10.20a.m. yesterday. Experienced fresh N.W. winds to arrival. Had a very heavy sea in crossing the bar. Passed a barque and schooner beating through the Strait. After landing passengers and discharging cargo, she*

> *proceeded to the German ship Gutenburg, and brought all the immigrants with luggage to the wharf...*

It is an interesting co-incidence that it was from aboard the Manawatū that the Alves stepped onto Aotearoa New Zealand land given that from 1900 southern Manawatū was home to them and many of their descendants, even to the present. The immigration commissioners reported upon the ship's arrival,

> *On inspecting the immigrants, we found that generally they were a healthy and robust body of people except for the Italians many of whom were undersized and, in our opinion, unfitted for the laborious work required of immigrants introduced to this Colony.*

After a voyage lasting 99 days aboard the *Gutenburg* Carl, Theresia and Mary spent an unknown period in quarantine and in immigration barracks in Wellington, before they made their way over the Remutaka Hills by bullock wagon to Featherston.

Carl & Theresia with Mary were living in Featherston when Charles William was born during December 1876 nearly nine months after their arrival. Information about his birth was supplied to the registrar at Featherston by a settler named James G. Cox.

Their third child, Theresia Veronika, was born in October 1878 at Kaiwaiwai (near Featherston). Anna, their fourth, was born also at Featherston nearly two years later in August 1880. Both their birth certificates record Carl as a labourer during this period. Around the time of Anna's birth, Carl moved north to begin clearing land he had purchased, and to start building a house for the family.

The Remutaka Railway and the Line North 1876-1881

Carl Alve's first work in New Zealand was on the construction of the Remutaka Incline Railway from Wellington into the Wairarapa. Surveyed by John Rochfort in 1870–71, the railway from Wellington as far as Kaitoke opened on 1 January 1878 and was extended to Featherston on 12 October 1878. This work may have involved him in some of the tunnelling work associated with the Mangaroa-Featherston section of the line. Having worked in coal mines, such work would not have been foreign to him. Writing about this section of the line, Bagnall in *Wairarapa: An Historical Excursion* noted,

> *The tunnel was not pierced until March 1877, the two faces being a mere seven inches out at the junction .... unskilled labourers were paid 9s. to 10s. per day for eight hours.*

Figure 25 - Featherston in the mid-1870s.

The line to Featherston, including the Remutaka Incline, was opened about two and a half years after the family arrived there. It had very steep grades over the Remutaka Range of 1 in 40 on the Wellington side and 1 in 15 on the Remutaka Incline (Summit – Cross Creek) on the Wairarapa side, which required Fell locomotives and brake vans using a raised centre rail.

Railway construction into the Wairarapa continued, Carl working on it to support his growing family, and to save for the purchase of land. Bagnall continues, [xxxiv]

> *... the railway's uncoiling over the plain henceforward was comparatively rapid. The Masterton opening was in November 1880, the Woodside to Greytown climax having been quietly reached the preceding May.*

This railway Remutaka Incline line was closed on 30 October 1955, when a new 8.8 km tunnel between Upper Hutt and Featherston that bypassed it was opened. For seventy-seven years this earlier, innovative solution to crossing the Remutaka Range between the Hutt Valley and Featherston operated and is celebrated at the Fell Locomotive Museum at Featherston.

Application for Land

Early in 1880 Carl applied for a grant of 117 acres of land with Hermann Schormann, whom he had accompanied aboard the Gutenburg while emigrating to New Zealand - see above. This land was in Alfredton Road near Eketāhuna amid the *German Settlement.*

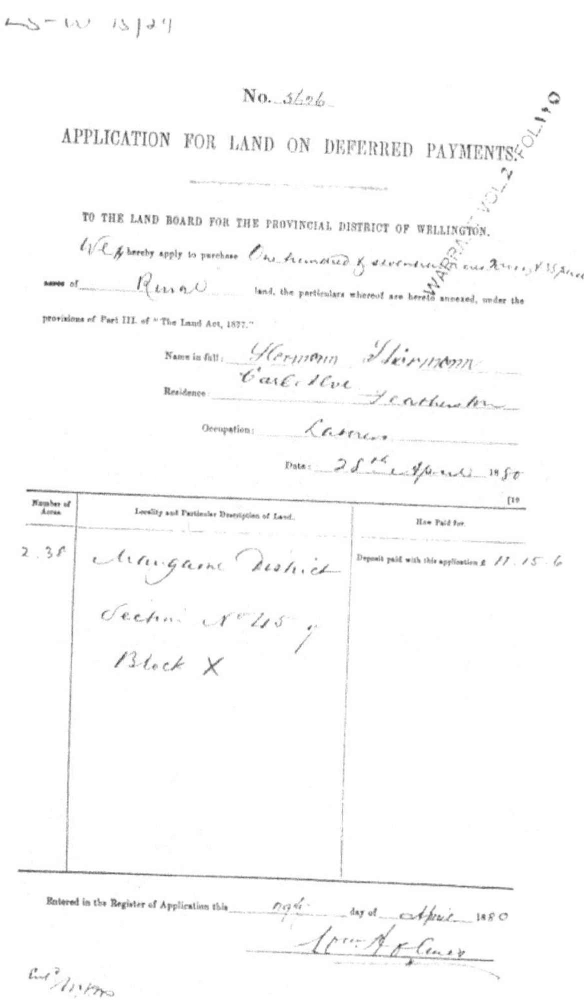

Figure 26 - Hermann Schormann and Carl Alve were granted land jointly, on deferred payment, in 1880. This is their completed application form for the land grant.

A footnote (p.16) in Irene Adcock's, *A Goodly Heritage* [xxxv] indicates that several German families settled in this area about 1880. These included Messers Fritz Hanker, Rhode, Schormann, Alve and von Reden. They took up land on the line of what is now the Alfredton Road from Eketāhuna. Recent research indicates that another German, Franz H. Scharnweber, also settled and farmed in this area at Pleckville, a little further East towards Alfredton from where the Alves and Schormanns settled. In fact, Scharnweber arrived in Wellington as a Vogel immigrant aboard the Terpsichore, arriving a week before the Alves and Schormanns.

In addition to the Bayliss brothers, another settler in the same area was the redoubtable Scot, Alexander Anderson. Both Frederick von Reden and Alexander Anderson would become Justices of the Peace later in the 1880's and be prominent in local government.

The land granted to Alve and Schormann is shaded on the map below. It is currently (2023) owned by the Woodhouse family who farm a block about five times the size of that settled in 1880. It is currently identified as 292 Alfredton Road.

Figure 27 – Southern section of the block purchased by Carl Alve and Hermann Schormann in April 1880. Woolshed bottom centre and House bottom left. Mangaone Survey District Block X Section 45 when purchased.

We know little of the Schormann family's early movements in New Zealand; Hermann may have worked with Carl Alve for the railways completing the Remutaka line, before farming with Carl.

The land settled by Carl Alve and Hermann Schormann was amid an area settled predominantly by Scandanavians. It was officially described as being in the *Mangaone District Section No. 45 in Block X*. The deposit made with the application on 29 April 1880 was £11-15-6. Payments on the land are recorded until 9th January 1891 - ten years being the normal term during which deferred payments were made. It seems that Carl and Hermann Schormann may have taken separate titles to the land soon after they were allotted it, dividing it in half. *A Return of the Freeholders of New Zealand, 1882* has the following entry,

> *Alve, Charles, Settler, Mangaone, owning 58 acres of land valued at 140 pounds in Wairarapa West County.*

The record of title currently dates from 1969 and clearly includes this original block. [xxxvi] I have not accessed earlier land records which may indicate early transfers, after Carl and Hermann acquired this land.

Chapter Seven: The Eketāhuna Farm 1880-1896

Mellemskov/Eketāhuna

As has been discussed earlier, in the early 1870's Sir Julius Vogel initiated a new colonisation scheme to essentially open the hinterland of the country beyond the coastal settlements by clearing the bush and building new roads, bridges and railway lines. And with that would come people and homes. In 1873 European settlers began to arrive in New Zealand, the majority being Scandinavian, and they began working on this Scheme. On the 4 March 1873 the *Forfarshire* arrived in the Port of Wellington. After a brief rest at the immigration barracks a group of mostly Swedish made their way over the Remutakas to Kopuaranga north of Masterton where a camp had been established earlier by the Scandinavians. These people were mostly Danish, Norwegian and some Germans. The living conditions in the temporary camp were extremely crowded, primitive and very unhygienic. But they stayed for the promise of new homes in the Eketāhuna Block thirty-five kilometres north. They just had to wait until the land had been surveyed.

Once settled they re-named their new home Mellemskov which means *Heart of the Forest*. However, by the late 1870s the name had reverted to the Māori name Eketāhuna [xxxvii] which means *to run aground on a sandbank,* so named by the *tāngata whenua* to describe the location where their *waka* (canoe) could not travel any further up the Makakahi River, which runs through the township.

Move to Eketāhuna

It is unknown when the family joined Carl in Alfredton Road, but they were there when Carolena was born in August 1882. As well as clearing and working on his newly acquired land Carl was also employed in clearing the Forty Mile Bush which ran north into Southern Hawkes Bay. The settlers in this area subsisted on earnings from contract bush-felling, which often took them far from their homes.

A glimpse of the difficult situation faced by these settlers is given in this extract (p.271) from, *Wairarapa: An Historical Excursion,* [xxxviii]

> *Something of the problems of the deferred payment settlers in the Mangaone on the still unfinished road to Alfredton comes through to us in a petition signed by Frederick Von Reden* (an Alve neighbour) *and eleven others in July 1882. The men who had bought their land three years earlier were struggling to keep their engagements with the Government. The heavily bushed country which they had accepted at two pounds per acre was taking 'a great amount of labour and expense before we can make it*

Figure 28 - Horse teams carting sawn timber to Eketāhuna Railway Station in the 1880s.

remunerative'. They were finding it almost impossible to pay this high price for unimproved sections.

'Most of us had saved a little money in previous years before we took the land, and this has helped us so far in keeping up payment.' This had now gone, and they were at a loss to find the cash to keep up future payments. A man with a hundred-acre section had to pay 20 pound a year rent and effect improvements to the value of 10%. Their only opportunity for employment they claimed was 30 miles or more away from home and even then 'after he has worked for a month and paid for his own and his family's provisions there is very little left to enable him to work his own land and meet his ... payment.'

Carl Alve was most likely a signatory to the above-mentioned petition.

Naturalisation

On 10 March 1886 Carl wrote to the Honourable T.A. Buckley, Colonial Secretary, asking to be naturalised. He indicated that he had been in Aotearoa New Zealand for ten years, five of which had been in Eastern Wairarapa. He signed himself, *Charles Alve*. A local J.P., Alexander Anderson, a neighbour mentioned above, witnessed and probably wrote his letter. He subsequently signed an Oath of Allegiance on 5 May 1886 and was naturalised on 18th May. New Zealand citizenship was automatically conferred on Theresia and Mary also. The Alve family were now Kiwis!

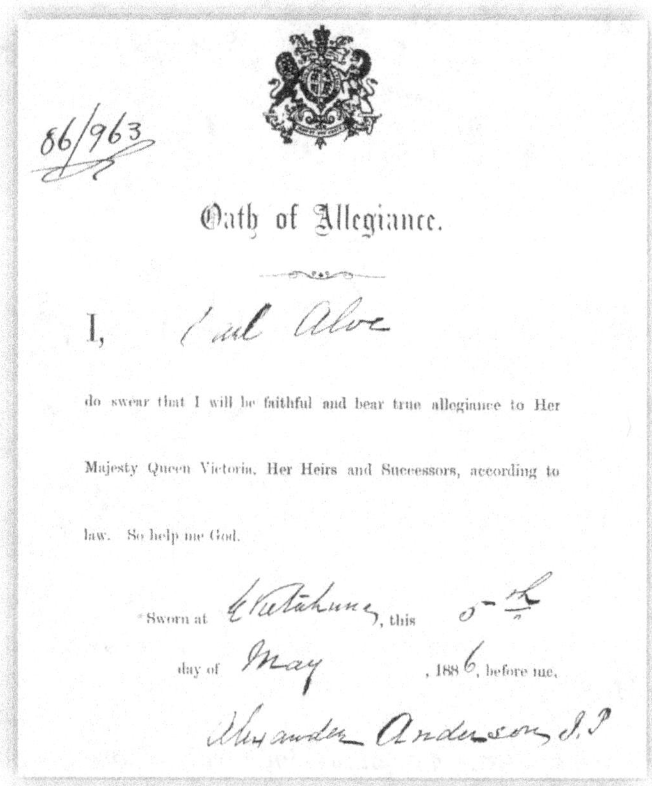

Figure 29 - Carl Alve's Oath of Allegiance as a British Subject dated 5th May 1886.

Life in Eketāhuna

The first-generation Aotearoa New Zealand Alve family continued to arrive at regular intervals during their Eketāhuna years.

Carolena	August 1882
Elizabeth	December 1884
Alfred Ernest	December 1887
Henry Wilhelm	October 1889
Edward Otto	January 1891
Rosa Ellen	January 1893
Emma Ida	May 1896

The circumstances of Alfred's birth indicate that these were pioneering days. He was born when no one was present to assist Theresia in childbirth. The family arrived home to discover his birth and Theresia rested, after having cleaned him and put him into his crib. It is also noted that

Edward was born on his father, Carl's, 42nd birthday, and that Rosa was born on New Year's Day in 1893.

The first Alve death in New Zealand occurred on 10 May 1896 as the family prepared to leave their Eketāhuna farm. Emma, who was born prematurely, lived for less than a day after her birth on 9 May. We know little more than that, other than she was buried in the Early Settlers Cemetery on the edge of Eketāhuna along Alfredton Road. This graveyard is now just a vacant paddock with a cairn noting the names of some buried there, but not Emma. A headstone for Emma was placed on her sister Rosa's grave at Featherston during 2024.

Most of the Alve children attended the Eketāhuna school. A detailed file about the early days of the community and the school, with some mention of the children attending, is contained in a PDF file [xxxix] which includes interesting Eketāhuna social history.

There follows an early report on some of the community challenges as schooling began in Eketāhuna,

3rd December 1884

In its recent issue the Weekly Star, Masterton paper, published an article in which some very hard things were said concerning the Wellington Education Board on account of its alleged neglect of the Eketāhuna State School. If our contemporary be correct in his statements a case demanding immediate attention is disclosed. The children are said to be crowded together in a shocking manner; the roof lets in the rain like a sieve; there is a great want of school apparatus; and there is no proper residence for the teacher. According to the same authority the expenditure required to put matters on a very much better footing would be comparatively small.

The Alves farming partner, Hermann Schormann for a short time in the early 1880s was an elected member of the Eketāhuna School Committee. The following extract, reporting on a school concert, presents a great introduction to several of the district residents. There is no indication the Alves were present at this concert albeit it was very well attended. We do note however that their neighbours, the von Redens, were very much in the centre of the entertainment provided. Note the sprinkling of German and Scandanavian names in these reports.

23rd August 1886 EKETĀHUNA SCHOOL CONCERT

Friday last will long be remembered in Eketāhuna as an important day in the history of that rising township, not only as an event, marking the progress of the district, but to show the close alliance and good feeling existing, between the town and country districts, and desire of assisting, in matters social, as well as in the business and general advancement of each other when the concert was first mooted to clear off the little debts of the school-committee.

It was only expected to be a purely local affair, but as the idea became known it increased in proportion, and offers of assistance came from Masterton, Alfredton, and Pahiatua, the outcome of which was that the programme of Friday evening last would have been received as a creditable production by an audience in a large town. The schoolroom, which has recently been enlarged, was specially fitted up for the occasion, having seating accommodation for about one hundred and fifty persons, and when the Chairman, Mr. A. Anderson, announced the opening item the whole of the seats were occupied there being many visitors from Pahiatua and Alfredton.

The opening overture, "Zampa," was creditably performed on the piano by Miss Reid and Mr. Keisenberg, the audience being quite enthusiastic in the bestowal of their applause at its conclusion. "Hunting Tower", a vocal duet by Mr. and Mrs. Von Reden, fully deserved the hearty reception accorded to it, as the rendering first class in time and tune. Mr. Wickerson had to respond for his rendition of the "Little Hero," giving "Carriasma" on the recall. Mr. G. Armstrong kept the audience amused during the recital of "Father Phill's Subscription 'List'" which illustrated the humourous manner in which a priest made his congregation feel a sense of their duties towards the church. "Won't you buy my pretty flowers" was very sweetly sung by Mrs. Beckman, being assisted in the chorus by Miss Reid, who possesses a very telling alto voice. A duet, "All's-Well," by Messrs. Wickerson and Papworth was followed by a song "Come under my Plaidie," in which Mr. Miller captivated the assembly by recounting a love adventure of a young Scotch Lass, with a lover of three score years and ten; in response to an encore, he treated the audience with another Scotch ditty. Messrs. Keisenberg, Papworth, and Bently, had to respond to an imperative demand for their musical selections on the piano, double bass, and cornet. The "Jay" episode from Mark Twain's "Tramp abroad," was the subject of a reading capitally given by Mr. Shelton, the local Schoolmaster, who appears to possess exceptional elocutionary powers. A Scotch "Hornpipe," by Mr. G. Goddard, which showed, "There is life to the old boy yet," brought the first part of the programme to a finish.

The second part opened with a piano duet " Pretty Brides," by Miss Reid, and Miss Von Reden, which was greeted with a well merited round of applause. Mr. Wickeson next sang, "Thou, art a ?" and was followed by Mrs. Neilson and Miss Reid who rendered the duet "Juanita" in capital style, eliciting a very complimentary reception from the audience. A humorous reading by Mr. Greville, who treated the company to some farfetched sailor yarns, preceded the song "Jacks yarn," which was given with such Spirit and effect by Mr. G. Armstrong, that he was compelled to pay the penalty of pleasing the audience by singing the "White Squall." Mr. Edge was the next aspirant to vocal honors, and the manner in which he sang "The Bloom is on the Rye," clearly showed he was possessed of both voice and style, the audience testifying their appreciation in a prolonged round of applause. Messrs. Keisenberg, Papworth and Bently were again successful in a musical selection, having to appear twice, to satisfy the desire of their admirers. Mr. Von Reden introduced a novelty in the vocal selections by singing the, "Watch on the Rhine" in German, the spirited manner in which this great national song was given and fairly roused the enthusiasm of the audience. In response to a request, Mr. Armstrong sang "The Scout," which brought a most successful programme to a close. The accompaniments were played by Miss Reid and Mr. Keisenberg and when it is said that there was not a single hitch in the somewhat lengthy programme, it will be a sufficient proof that they were successful at the piano.

The Chairman proposed a hearty vote of thanks to the ladies and gentlemen who assisted in the evening's amusement, especially to those who had come from a distance. He was glad that the Eketāhuna people appreciated the efforts of their visitors by giving them such a hearty reception. This was seconded by Mr. McCardle, who in dwelling on the progress of the district, spoke of the great benefits to be derived in holding these pleasant gatherings. He hoped they would soon see their way clear to erect a hall, so that meetings of every description could be held in it, without having to encroach on the school room. The vote of thanks having been carried by acclamation the room was cleared, and about two hours' dancing was indulged in, the persistent manner in which both old and young kept the floor, spoke of the thoroughness of the enjoyment, and the utter disregard of the future effects of such vigorous exercise. Those that did not join in the light fantastic, lingered behind to hear the music, and when the last dance was finished, they all declared it was the jolliest evening they had spent in Eketāhuna.

The Masterton contingent - express themselves highly pleased with the reception given them, very flatteringly to the hospitality of Mr. and Mrs. Jones, of the Temperance Hotel, who did all in their power to make the stay a pleasant one for them. To enable the visitors to return home by the morning luggage train which leaves Mauriceville at half-past seven, breakfast was prepared at four o'clock, and a start made at half past four. But owing to the heavy state of the roads, the station was not reached till half-past eight, consequently they had to ruralise there until the usual down train at 2 o'clock conveyed them to their destination.

The Eketāhuna School file includes reference to the attendance of various of the Alve children including Mary, Anna, Carolena and Elizabeth, but not Theresia nor Charlie, albeit lists for every year are not there. Mention is also made of Catherine Wallace (who would become Charlie's wife), members of her family and various of the Schormann children. On page ten the following report on student progress is offered. Alve, Wallace and Schormann children are underlined.

12th May 1886

The following is the result of the examination of the public school at Eketāhuna on Friday last. Our correspondent says Mr. Lee, the Inspector, spoke very highly of the appearance of the children, and the way they passed the examination, and commented on the difference on the whole to what it was six years ago.

Total on roll 58; presented, 57; passed, 52; failed, 4; exempt 1 (insufficient attendance).

Standard V. Presented, 1; passed, 1; George Neilson.

Standard IV. Presented, 2; passed, 2; Martin Neilson, Matilda Anderson.

Standard III. Presented, 13; passed 9; Mabel Bayliss, Ellen Hodder, Laura Frederickson, John Tonner, Albert Anderson, Oscar Neilson, Maud Jones, Christina Often, Maren Thomasen.

Standard II. Presented, 10; passed, 9; exempt 1; Daniel Bayliss, Walter Jones, <u>Herman Scorman</u>, <u>Mary Alve</u>, Louisa Jacobsen, Emma Murrell, Edith Neilsen, Hilma Neilsen, Minnie Neilsen.

Standard I. Presented, 10; passed, 10; Willian McLennan, Herbert Murrell, Otto Rolde, Arthur Selby, John Selby, Percy Waterson, Jane Andersen, Hilma Fredericksen, Laura Jessen, Eliza Tonner.

Preparatory I. (17), II. (4); total, 21. All fully satisfied the examiner.

Seven years later the Eketāhuna School examinations were reported thus:

20th April 1893

The Eketāhuna school was examined on Tuesday find Wednesday, April 11th and 12th, by Mr. Fleming, Inspector. The following is a list of those who passed.

Standard VII. Walter Jones, James Nelson. Gertrude Toohill.

Standard VI. Alfred Bayliss, Alfred Fredericksen, Theodore Hansen, Annie Neilson.

Standard V. Charles Aulin, James Clayson, John Hodges, John W. Jensen, George McAnulty, George Neilson, Neils Sorensen, Ada Brenmuhl, Olive M. Jones, Annie Lund, Hilda Olsen, Clara Parsons, Agnes Toohill, <u>Catherine Wallace</u>.

Standard IV. Victor Anderson, Bryce Clayson, Henry Fulton, Alexander Jacobsen, John Neilson, <u>William Schorman</u>, Elizabeth Bayliss, Florence Fogden, Alma Hansen, Mabel Lucas, Alma Neilson, Alice Sparksman.

Standard III. Francis Brenmuhl, Thomas Edwards, Henry Edwards, Robert Hagen? Henry Frederickson, William Fulton, Thomas Hodges, William Johnson, John Kelliher, Samuel Lowe, John McAnulty, Ernest Murrell, Ivor Parsons, Archibald Smith, Jesse Smith, Neils Thomsen, <u>George Wallace</u>, <u>Anna Alve</u>, Alice Anderson, Margaret Cruickshank, Annie Fogden, Emma Fredericksen, Ada Funnell, Amelia Hansen, Maud Kibblewhite, Emily Maddock

Standard II. William Bennett George Edwards, Robert Funnell, Arthur Hunter, Charles Maddock, Ernest Neilson, Carl Olsen, Christian Sorensen, Carl Syversen, Norman Waldin, <u>Caroline Alve</u>, Amy Andersen, Josephine Brenmuhl, Nellie Bright, Catherine Goggin, Sarah Lowe, Susannah Maddock, Elizabeth R? Toohill.

Standard I. Walter Bright, Jos, Cameron, Andrew Clark, Malcolm Cruikshank, William Cruikshank, James Fulton, Patrick Goggin, Coleridge Hyde, Augustus Kelliher, John Neilson, George Robinson, Herbert Sparksman, John Walked, <u>Elizabeth Alve</u>, Ada Bayliss, Edith Fogden, Annie Fredericksen, Gertrude Funnell, Elizabeth Hodges, Jane Neilson, Mary Olsen, Johanna Olsen, Eda Rhode.

An interesting anecdote relating to the Alve days in Eketāhuna is provided by Colin Alve's wife Margaret (née Gillanders). In a letter to the author written in 1978 she noted,

It is a coincidence that my mother's parents lived in Eketāhuna at the same time as your great grandparents. As a little girl, my mother was sent to get eggs from the Alves. Your great grandmother (Theresia Alve) kept geese and my mother was terrified of the big gander which would hiss at her. Your great grannie would shoo it away in German. The Alves and the Haycocks (mum) both shifted to the Manawatū (in 1902) and lost touch! (at least for a time!)

Figure 30 - Boys at the Eketāhuna School 1896.
Henry and Alfred Alve are 4th and 6th from left in the back row.

Catholicism

Irene Adcock's history of Eketāhuna and Districts [xl] gives us some insight into the religious
history of Eketāhuna. The Alves were Catholics and would have been involved in the beginnings
of organised religion in Eketāhuna. Adcock (p.104) comments,

> *In the early nineties, by which time a fair sprinkling of British stock had joined the*
> *Scandanavians - and the half dozen German families in Alfredton Road - clergymen from*
> *several denominations were visiting the Eketāhuna area to administer to the need of their*
> *parishioners.... According to some reports the first services of the Roman Catholic*
> *Church were held in the Eketāhuna schoolhouse. Father Vincent McGlone in his history*
> *of the Catholic Church in the Wairarapa district records that, "At Eketāhuna Mass was*
> *said in the beginning at Mr Kelliher's Club Hotel. He was an Irishman and always*
> *welcomed the priest"; the priest at the time being Father John McKenna of Masterton.*
> *With his brother, Father Thomas McKenna, the curate of Masterton, this priest devoted*
> *much of his time to the Bush district.*

Anecdotes have been passed down about Carl Alve's uneasy relationship with the Catholic
Church and its Priests. One suggests that he was at one time castigated from the pulpit for giving
only 10 shillings to the Church, which was, supposedly, less than generous. On another occasion
it is suggested that the Priest asked for, and took, a cooked leg of mutton when there was no

money in the house for his collection. In Theresia's biography in Appendix 1 mention is made of another occasion when money was an issue at the baptism of one of the Alve children.

In the Wairarapa, during the Alve years there, the cost of extending the Church into new communities was no doubt considerable and consequent appeals to the faithful would have seemed heavy. Compared with Germany where it had been long and well established, the pioneer Church in New Zealand inevitably would have appeared, and felt, very different. For a German family language will have been an additional barrier, albeit the mass said or chanted in Latin would have been familiar. We can well imagine Theresia lamenting the religious changes, in fact there are anecdotes that she did note how different the church in Eketāhuna was from that of Pfarrer Schulte in Gelsenkirchen, which was more established and resourced in the heady days of massive population growth associated with the growing mining and steel industries there. Notwithstanding these tensions, the services of the Catholic Church and its Priests were called on by the family when Emma and Rosa died in 1886, through Anna's death in 1906 and Carl's in 1910 when they were buried in the Catholic section of the Palmerston North Cemetery, and beyond.

Economic Depression

The 1880s and 1890s have come to be known as the long depression in New Zealand. In the winters there was visible hardship and distress. Those who had immigrated in the 1870s sent fewer positive messages home, and free passages were ended. Fewer new settlers arrived, and people began to leave. The Te Ara Encyclopedia of New Zealand describes this period. [xli]

> *The long depression from the late 1870s through to the early 1890s was an accident waiting to happen. It is argued that the underlying sluggishness of the 1870s was obscured by unsustainable borrowing.*
>
> *The slump was precipitated by the collapse of the City Bank of Glasgow in 1878. This led to a credit contraction in the City of London, then the centre of the world's financial system, which reduced the credit available to New Zealand. With many activities dependent upon credit and landowners heavily over-borrowed, a credit shortage compounded the effects of a falling wool price.*
>
> *There was much hardship, with 'sweating' (exploitative labour conditions) in the factories, a lack of jobs for rural workers, and farmers going bankrupt. Harry Atkinson, the dominant colonial treasurer during these years, got a reputation for cutting government expenditure. However, he had little choice but to retrench because he could not easily borrow when revenue was less than planned spending.*

Atkinson's careful management of the national finances set the economy up for the long boom, which began in the mid-1890s.

Another indicator of the difficulties the Alves faced on Alfredton Road was an 1893 bush fire that affected them and their neighbours.

A large amount of damage has been done to property along the Alfredton Road through bush fires. The high winds prevailing carried the fire across the road into Mr von Reden's paddock, lighting his grass. The fire spread very rapidly, burning down a large quantity of fencing. From there the fire spread to Alve's section and completely destroyed the orchard, the whole of the fruit trees – 50 in number – that had taken years to rear, being destroyed in a few minutes. Fortunately, a heavy rain storm came on and prevented further damage. [xlii]

The Alves farmed the Eketāhuna land until the winter of 1896 when they moved south to Featherston to share milk at Donalds Dairies where they supplied the Tarureka milk factory. As noted earlier, farming profitably on the Eketāhuna land was difficult from the outset and caught up with Carl and Maria at this stage, prompting them to leave their Eketāhuna land.

The Schormann and Scharnweber Families

Perhaps the Alves sold their Eketāhuna land to the Schormanns (or not). I do know that during the early 1890s the Schormanns owned land nearby on the Mangaoranga Road to the south – Block X Sections Pt.51 & 54 of the Mangaone Survey District. Both Hermann (1905) and Dorothea (1909) died during the first decade of the twentieth century and are buried in nearby the Mangaoranga cemetery. There was an estate clearing sale at the above property in October 1910 mentioning the sale of cows and pigs, but not the land. [xliii] I conclude this chapter by reviewing subsequent contact with and awareness about the descendants of Hermann and Dorothea. The picture below indicates contact between the families continued well into the twentieth century.

Maria Gertrud Schormann (the Schormann's daughter who was born in Germany) married Franz Heinrich Scharnweber (1851-1924) around 1890. Franz had come from Germany to Aotearoa New Zealand aboard the Terpsichore which arrived in Wellington in March 1876, just a few days before the arrival of the Gutenburg. Franz acquired land on the Alfredton Road east of the Alve-Schormann original block at "Pleckville" before he married Maria Gertrud.

Their first child was Herman Henry Schwarnweber who was born at Eketāhuna in 1892 and had two marriages:
1. Ellen Jane Nagel (1918 in Eketāhuna) to whom was born two children – Mavis Rolls and Francis Henry (Curly) Scharnweber.

2. Olive Martha Kay (1947 in Masterton).

Figure 31 - Maria Gertrud Scharnweber (née Schormann), Theresa Alve and Janey Welsh (née Scharnweber) possibly around the time of Maria Theresia Alve's death on 30 April 1942.

Their second son, Frederick Wilhelm, was born 1894 and he died aged fifteen on 6 November 1909. Frederick is buried near his grandparents, Hermann and Dorothea, at the Mangaoronga cemetery, just out of Eketahuna to the south.

Maria and Franz Scharnweber also had two girls:
1. Janey Welsh (1892-1972) – see picture above, and
2. Dorothy Shearer (1897-1986).

It seems that the Scharnweber family lived in the Eketāhuna area farming before moving to Akura Road, Masterton in the early 1900s. Roger Daniel (who commented June 2023) lived with his brother Michael on Akura Road opposite its junction with Ngaumutawa Road from 1929 through to around 1950. Roger recalls that the Scharnwebers lived across Akura Road on the corner, within site of the Daniel house. During that period, he recalls that an elderly Maria Scharnweber lived there with her son Henry and family. She died 6 April 1949, perhaps while

Figure 32 - The Mangaoranga Cemetery, Eketāhuna where Hermann (1905) and Dorothea
Schormann (1909) are buried, as is their grandson Frederick William Scharnweber.

still living there. Roger also remembers schooling with Esmé Shearer (and her sister) whose
mother was Dorothy Shearer née Scharnweber.

The second Schormann daughter, Emma (1879-1943) married Henry Hanson in 1899. They are
both buried at Eketāhuna. They had at least six children and many remain in the Wairarapa. I
have had recent contact with Emma's great granddaughter Kristine Hansen, a genealogist, who
was born in Eketāhuna and who now lives in Dannevirke.

Dorothea's and Hermann's grandson (he may be the younger son) Frederick Henry Schormann
(1898-1973) married Louisa Adele Farrow (1898-1960) who was a first cousin of Catherine Alve
(née Wallace) through their Pawson mothers Jane and Ellen respectively, who were sisters.
Frederick and Adele farmed at Putara Road, west of Eketāhuna.

Chapter Eight: Return to Featherston 1896

Figure 33 - The Donalds' Tarureka Estate Featherston in the 1890s.

Having gained some experience dairy farming at Eketāhuna, Carl and family were equipped to become dairy farm sharemilkers for the Donald family who ran a few farms around Featherston at the end of the nineteenth century. These were known as Donalds' Dairies.

Rosa's Death

Rosa, perhaps named after her father Carl's older sister, died 21 August 1896 at Featherston of diphtheria. She was three and a half years of age. Her death came soon after the family moved from their Eketāhuna farm to work for Donald Dairies in Featherston. And it added to a distressing year in which her younger sister Emma had died soon after her birth in May. Later that year older sister Theresia (aged eighteen) contracted life-threatening hydatids that required surgery and a long stay in Wellington hospital.

Figure 34 - 'At Rest' Remembering Emma, Rosa and Anna.

If 1896 had been for the Alves an *annus horribilis*, the following year was much more palatable as Clara was born healthy and well on 25 July and, romance was in the air again. This time it was Mary who fell in love with George Busch from North Canterbury. So, 1898 had Theresia and Carl thinking again about a wedding, across the world from where they had celebrated their own, a quarter of a century before.

Tarureka Dairy Operation

Figure 35 - The Donalds' Tarureka Dairy Factory on the edge of Featherston was supplied by the Alves 1896-1902.

James Donald (1829-1899) who employed Carl sharemilking, had his own butter factory named "Tarureka", which was established in 1882. Bagnall's *Wairarapa: An Historical Excursion* notes,

> *By 1889 there were a total of four "dairies" each milking 125 cows, mostly Red Danes, supplying it. Each dairy had its own brake capable of carrying forty cans of milk to the factory. The dairies were all run by sharemilkers who were responsible for the feeding out of hay, milking of the cows and delivering the milk to the factory. Here the milk was weighed and a tally kept in order to pay the sharemilkers their agreed share on the 15th of every month. Tarureka was equipped at first with a 90 gallon capacity separator, but by 1901 two 400 gallon separators were processing the milk from the 600 cows. Five hands were employed in the factory while on the farms some fifty persons were employed in all.*

While the Alves did not join this operation until the winter of 1896, the above image and description indicate what sharemilking for the Donalds might have looked and felt like.

Mary's Wedding

Despite the privations and hardships they had experienced at Eketāhuna, the nineteenth century ended for the Alves on an optimistic note. George and Mary were married on 27 December 1898, at her parents' Kaiwaiwai residence in South Featherston. This Tuesday wedding brought all the family together, and some of the Busch family, for the first Alve family wedding in New Zealand. The first for this family since Theresia and Carl had married in Gelsenkirchen on Valentine's Day 1874, nearly twenty-five years before. I have not sighted Mary and George's wedding certificate to discover who married them and who the formal witnesses to the wedding were. I will leave this search to a future family historian.

Figure 36 - The Wedding of Anna Maria (Mary) Alve and George Busch at the Alve residence, Kaiwaiwai.
All the Alves with the bridal party and some of the Busch family, I suspect.
L-R: Busch F, Busch M, Carolena, Alfred (sitting front), Charlie, Anna, Theresia, George Busch, Mary Busch, Busch M, Henry (sitting front), Carl, Busch M, Maria Theresia, Clara (on M.T. lap), Eddie (sitting front), Elizabeth, Sarah Busch, Busch F.

George found employment as a shepherd/manager at Oporua during 1899 and in July 1900 their first child, William (Bill) Busch was born to begin the second generation of the Alve Whānau in New Zealand.

Rangitāne Land Purchase

The Alves' Featherston stay was quite short as the opportunity came for Carl and Theresia to purchase land in the Manawatū across the Tararua Range from Featherston as the national financial depression lifted and more prosperous times arrived. They bought a 111-acre block of land from Mr Bruce Beale, a solicitor from Palmerston North. Mr Beale as a First Lieutenant and then Captain subsequently served in the ninth contingent sent to the Boer war in 1902. According to Henry Alve, they paid seven pounds ten shillings per acre for this land which was standing bush on the banks of the Manawatū River. Another report suggests that the price was five pounds per acre. Much more than the two shillings and sixpence that one of the Half Crown Bend traditions might suggest was paid to Māori by the first pākehā purchaser – see next chapter.

The scene was set for the family to start yet another adventure with Carl, Theresia and the two younger children, Eddie and Clara, being the advanced party who began occupying and clearing this land as the centuries changed from nineteenth to twentieth. Others of the family stayed back in Featherston attending school and/or continuing work with the Donalds to maintain the family income flow.

Chapter Nine: Rangitāne 1900-1910

Carl & Theresia, with their two youngest children Eddie & Clara moved, late in 1900, to Rangitāne in the Manawatū to occupy newly purchased and Māori-lease land. Others of the family stayed behind at Featherston sharemilking at Donald's Dairy to help pay off the new farm or, in the case of the younger children Alfred and Henry, to continue their schooling at Kaiwaiwai. The site where the Alve family built their initial shelter, a slab whare, which progressively became a six-bedroom homestead, was a little upstream from the Ngāwhakaraua jetty.

The Rangitāne farm was adjacent to the Ngāwhakaraua Māori settlement. The Ngāwhakaraua bend in the Manawatū River was an important centre for early travelers to Palmerston North in the period 1840-1873. The river was navigable from Foxton to this point. History records that in 1840 Jack Duff, a trader, left his whaleboat here and continued upstream by canoe. Charles Kettle, the early surveyor, camped near here in 1846 during his journey upriver. In 1866 a jetty was built here to connect with the end of the last straight stretch of the road from Palmerston North to Ngāwhakaraua. In the early 1870's the small steam launch, "Pionéer" unloaded many of the stores and people destined for the fledgling settlement that became known as Palmerston North.

By 1870 there was a dry weather track connecting Foxton with Palmerston North and in 1871 a wooden railed tramway with carriages drawn by horses was being constructed from the new settlement of Palmerston as far as Ngāwhakaraua. This was extended and finally reached Foxton in 1873. Subsequently the jetty was little used and fell into disrepair. By 1876 the line was completely ballasted; iron had replaced the wooden rails and steam engines replaced the horses. The Rangitāne station on this line was a stone's throw northwest from the Ngāwhakaraua jetty and the Alve house and was close to the boundary of the initial Alve farm. Of the eight railway stations on its 31km line - Motuiti, Himatangi, Bainesse, Oroua Bridge (present day Rangiotū), Rangitāne, Tiakitahuna, Karere and Longburn – half included Rangitāne Māori settlements.

The Māori settlement of Ngāwhakaraua was occupied by several of the Rangitāne (and possibly Ngāti Raukawa) people. They had moved upstream from the Puketotara Pa to Oroua Bridge (built 1867) and on to Ngāwhakaraua where the principal buildings were a meeting house and a very fine church. This settlement adjacent the Alve farm was occupied when the family arrived in 1900 and continued into the 1920's when its residents moved to the Rangiotū settlement adjacent the Oroua River and bridge where the "Te Rangimarie" meeting house on the marae is cherished by the Te Awe Awe family.

The Duries record some of the Māori history (mid to late 1800's) of this area in, *The Rangimarie Narrative* – a submission to the Waitangi Tribunal (pp.76-81) in December 2019. [xliv] In this document the transition from Māori to Pākehā land ownership and associated (de)privation for local Māori is tellingly recorded and lamented. In the process, the Alves benefited from their arrival at Rangitāne from the Wairarapa in 1900 as they gained ownership and lease of land that once was the possession of Māori – principally the Rangitāne tribe.

PART D: NGA WHENUA PĀPĀTUPU O TE RANGIOTŪ RĀUA KO TE AWEAWE

217. We begin this section with an overview of the changing scene for Ngāti Raukawa and Rangitāne and will then address the same in more detail. The peace held fast as the land in the Oroua valley and south along the Manawatū river was jointly held by Ngāti Raukawa and Rangitāne. However, neither Ngāti Raukawa nor Rangitāne was able to hold the land against the Government. Within 40 years of the Treaty of Waitangi, none of the land was held under the authority of the rangatira. All that can be said is that some members of Ngāti Raukawa and Rangitāne, but not others, retained fractionated shares in disbursed allotments that were mostly small.

218. The occupational pattern also changed as the hapū left their traditional, riverside pa and papakainga to relocate alongside the roads and railways that were the mainstay of the settler economy. Individual survival depended less and less on the customary economy of reciprocal gift giving which served also to maintain relationships between hapū. The tribal economy could not be maintained as no resources remained in tribal ownership. With the loss of the land and the destruction of the natural environment, the pristine forests, swamps, and rivers, there were also significant losses in Māori spiritual capacity and wellness...

... 222. Along the river Māori were raising pigs and growing potatoes, wheat, maize, kumara and flax for sale locally and for Wellington, transported by schooner from Te Awahou.

223. The principal Rangitāne settlements at this time were at Hotuiti (between Foxton and Shannon), Tokomaru (near the convergence of the Tokomaru and Manawatū rivers), Te Pararema (adjacent to Tokomaru), Paparewa (Shannon), Raewera, Puketotara, Tuwhakatupua, Rewarewa and Tiaki Tahuna. These were mainly fortified pā with associated papakainga. The further settlements of Ngāwhakaraua, Rangitāne, and Opiki may have developed later, in about the 1860s, as also did Rangiotū.

224. Māori also established churches in the district. Puketotara, which was the largest Rangitāne settlement, boasted to have built the first church in European style, ahead of the famed church of Rangiātea at Ōtaki which was erected at the direction of Te Rauparaha. Puketotara papakainga had since shifted to Rangiotū and all that remains of the old church, which was destroyed in a fire, is the bell which is still held at Te Rangimarie marae.

Wiremu Te Awe Awe noted in the 1960s that the church from Puketotara was relocated to Ngāwhakaraua. It was there it was destroyed by fire and the bell mentioned here relocated to Te

Rangimarie where it was with Te Awe Awe descendants at the Rangiotū, Te Rangimarie marae in 2023 when I sighted it.

The Rangimarie Narrative continues,

> *Ngāti Raukawa established a major church at Moutoa, part of which was later re-erected downstream at the Ngāti Whakatere marae of Poutu, and which still survives.*

> *225. The relocation of Māori settlements began with the sale of the Ahuaturanga block and the transport of settlers by steamer to the closest point to that block that was safe for steamer navigation, on a bend beside the papakainga Ngāwhakaraua. Māori from downriver relocated there and a large papakainga was established with a substantial wharerunanga and wharepuni, able to accommodate travellers. The steamer which brought in the settlers was the Pionéer. A dry weather road was developed to take settlers from Ngāwhakaraua to Karere, and later, further on to papaioea waerenga, or clearing, which became Palmerston North. The dry-weather road became called for the steamer, and in a euphemism for the road, it was named Pionéer Highway. Later a wooden railway with a horse drawn carriage was established.*

> *226. Further relocations followed. A similar settlement called Rangitāne was established further down from the bend in Pionéer Highway, on a track to the Oroua river that would later become part of the road to Foxton. Tiaki Tahuna was relocated further along Pionéer Highway from its original site on the Manawatū river where it was named for an adjoining sandbank. There it became known to the settlers as Jackeytown. In the same way the bend in the river at Ngāwhakaraua became known to them as 'Half-Crown bend'.*

Ngāwhakaraua was home to a large Rangitāne pā, including the church, Te Ahu-a-Turanga, and meeting house, Kotahitanga. The Māori pā was occupied by several of the Rangitāne people who had moved upstream from the Puketotara pā to Oroua Bridge (built 1867) and on to Ngāwhakaraua. This settlement, adjacent the Alve farm, was occupied when the family arrived in 1900 and continued into the 1920's when most of the residents moved to the Rangiotū settlement adjacent the Oroua River and bridge where the *Te Rangimarie* meeting house on the marae is cherished by the Te Awe Awe family to the present day. A few remained at the Ngāwhakaraua pā site until the 1953 Manawatū river flood inundated the area.

Eddie Alve who leased the Māori land (around seventy acres) on which the Ngāwhakaraua settlement stood after it was vacated reported,

> *There was in the vicinity of 200-300 Māori living in the village when the family arrived. There were two meeting houses, and a really elaborate church where the organist was occasionally Miss Simpson and where 'white' people would attend.*

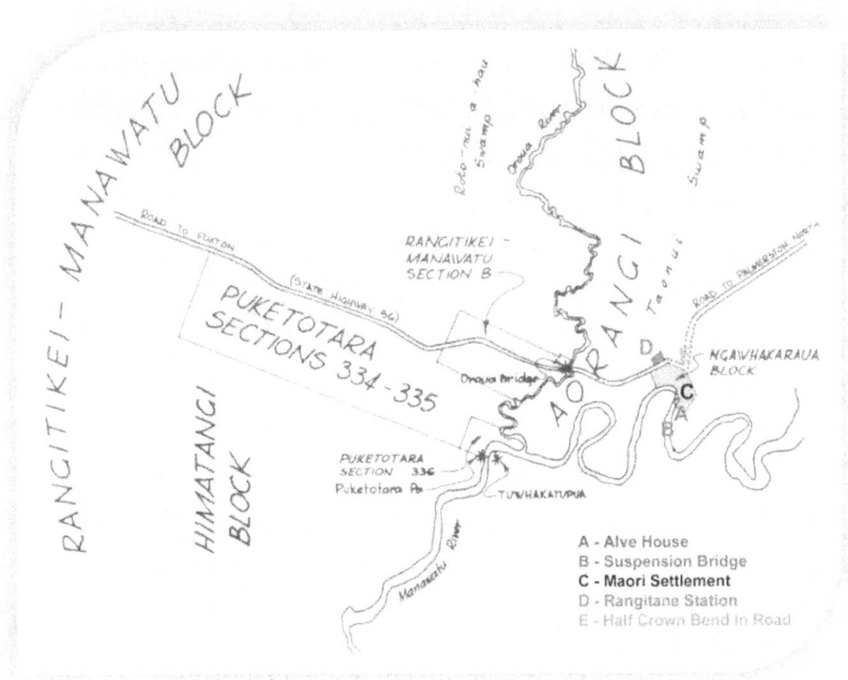

Figure 37 - Alve settlement at Rangitāne.

A Rangitira of the Rangitāne tribe in the 1960's, Mr Wiremu Te Awe Awe (Billy Larkins) noted that,

> *I can recall old settlers there who were very closely associated with the Māoris in the persons of the old Mr and Mrs Alve and their family…. As far as I know they were good neighbours, very neighbourly, they got on very well together.*

Writing in *Suspended Access* Molly Akers [xlv] reflected on the arrival of the Alves at Rangitāne.

> *Late in 1900 the Carl Alve family arrived here from Featherston… Living for a while in a slab whare, they began clearing the bush and growing potatoes. They gradually built up a dairy herd to 104 cows, all hand milked by up to six milkers until machines were introduced in the 1929/30 season.*

The bush that covered the Alve farm has been described as dense,

> *…with its foliage of tōtara, karaka, ngaio, mataī, tī kōuka (cabbage trees), kōwhai, rātā, ponga, ferns, clematis, and nīkau. Additionally, thick tangles of vines covered the trees and made much of the bush impenetrable. The air either sung with bird song or droned with swarms of mosquitoes.*

In a taped interview Merv Eglinton [xlvi] recorded during the 1960s, Eddie Alve commented about the journey to and conditions at Rangitāne,

> *We came up by train. We had a change at Palmerston and got on to the Foxton branch and got off at Rangitāne. In those days there was no road here, we had to go through the Māori pā. There was quite a big pā here at the time and for about twelve months the only place we had to live in was a slab whare. The mosquitoes were terrible. It was just one constant buzz all night long and you had a terrible job to get any sleep at all.... To go to school the only way was to go along the railway line - the road was just a mud pool, a mud track through the middle of the bush.*

According to Henry Alve in the same interview,

> *The original block of 111 acres which was standing bush was bought from the late Mr Bruce Beale a solicitor and barrister of Palmerston North in the spring of 1900. The price was seven pound ten shillings per acre....The family began farming on the original block in November 1902 with a herd of 30 Jersey-Shorthorn heifers....and about six other heifers....and the cow that Mrs Alve had milked earlier....The first milking shed was a four bail lean-to building....This shed did for about four years when Mr Ernie Nash was engaged to build another 12 bail shed with loft and hay barn adjoining.*

The following is extracted from *A History of Rangiotū*, [xlvii] factual amendments in [square brackets],

> *In [April 1902] after the exams were over, Henry joined his parents. One acre of potatoes was planted at the top end of the farm near the river. Most of these were sold to help the family income.... The Simpson family were their neighbours, and during the 1902 [14 June] 'old man' flood, provisions ran low, so Charlie Alve and Bob Simpson went by canoe to Oroua Bridge to get supplies. Luckily for the family, they had no stock except for one cow on the farm. The children sailed about in half a barrel.*

The 1902 flood level is marked on the gauge at the east end of the present Alve Road which indicates that it was only a little lower than the *big daddy* 1953 flood. The map below indicates the catchment area of the Manawatū River. Interestingly, nearly fifty percent of this catchment is east of the Ruahine and Tararua ranges. In fact, the land the Alves farmed near Eketāhuna (1880-1896) is on the southern border of the Manawatū River catchment. This map, from Buick's *Old Manawatū*, outlines the Manawatū River catchment area. [xlviii]

Figure 38 - Manawatū flood levels at Half Crown Bend, Rangitāne near the east end of Alve Road.
The home of Billy Alve, son of Eddie and Ina is at the end of this section of the Toll Bridge Road to Opiki.

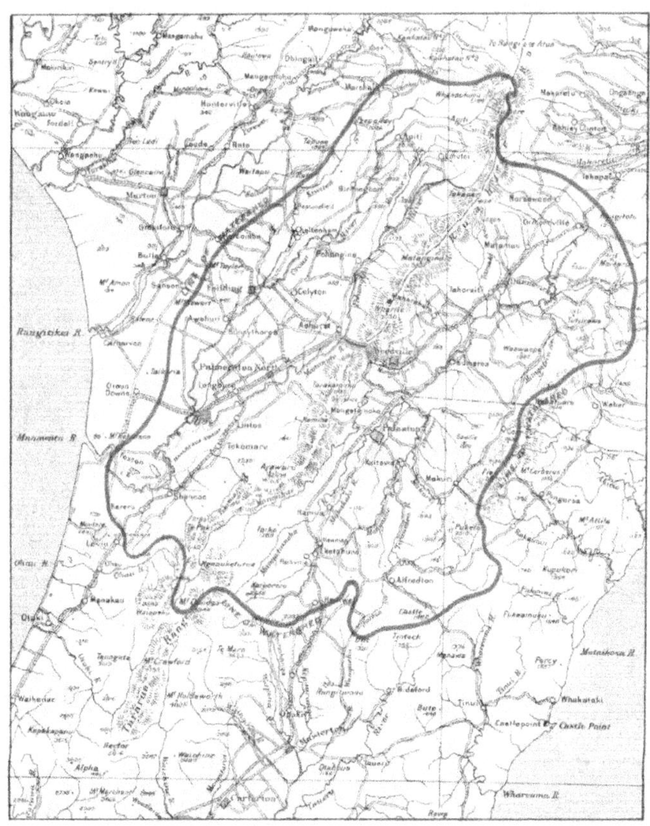

Figure 39 - The Alve Eketāhuna farm (right) and the Rangitane farm (left) are marked by dots.

At the meeting of the Kairanga County Council yesterday afternoon, Mr E. J. Armstrong reported that the works at the Ngawhakarau road were intact, absolutely no damage having been done by the recent flood either to road, bridges or drains, notwithstanding the extremely severe test to which all were subjected. It would prove satisfactory to the Council to find that the designs under which the works were carried out were correct and that the prognostications of failure have not been verified. The flood over the triangular delta between the Manawatu and Oroua rivers, within which the works are situated, was fully two feet higher than the celebrated 1880 flood and covered an area within that delta of about 15.000 acres with from one to sixteen feet of water. The efficiency of the Manawatu and Aorangi Drainage Board's system of drainage was shown in its removal. A large mass of timber floated off adjacent lands stranded upon both the old and newly formed roads. A solid mass of logs and roots, two chains in length, was heaped up on the main drain bridge approach. This bridge had to bear the strain of both timber and the body of flood water which rose four feet above the bridge decking. This is the second occasion on which the bridge has had to resist an abnormal strain, and in both instances successfully and without injury. The same complete immunity from injury applies also to the low level bridges erected under the contract. Crs expressed their gratification at the highly satisfactory nature of the report.

Figure 40 - The Manawatu Standard Newspaper 9 July 1902.

The Alve farm was adjacent to the "Half Crown Bend" in the Palmerston-Himitangi Road; nowadays the eastern junction of Alve Road with S.H.56 to Opiki. There are various theories about the origin of this name each of which, whether true or not, throws some light on the history of the area. Buick in his *Old Manawatū (1903)* [xlix] comments in a footnote,

The precise origin of this term, which is now applied to a bend in the road near the Oroua Bridge, is involved in some doubt, many people believing that it is simply a short and easy way of pronouncing the native name Ngāwhakarau, just as "Jackeytown" has

been substituted for Tiakitahuna. I am, however, informed on very good authority, that it arose when the road was being made, from the fact that a black (sic) cook, who ran a sort of eating house for the men employed on the work, charged half a crown for every meal.

Other explanations for the name mentioned by Molly Akers in her history of Opiki, *From Fibre to Food* [1] are:

1. That the land in the vicinity of the present junction of Alve and Opiki Roads was believed to have been sold for half a crown an acre (before the Alves arrived) - a low value because of continual flooding.
2. Half a crown was the return fare charged charabanc (bus) travelers from here to Palmerston North.

Rupert Adolph Alve, the last of Carl and Theresia's children, was born on 29 September 1902 at Rangitāne, in the room that later became the office in the homestead. Henry, Eddie, Clara and Dolph all spent time attending the Oroua Bridge (later Rangiotū) school, as the seventy fifth jubilee (1957) picture below indicates. The name change seems to have happened around the turn of the century. The term Oroua related to various settlements along the Oroua River, so it was changed to Rangiotū in honour of the local Rangitāne chief, Hoani Meihana Te Rangiotū. Other relatives, notably Bill Busch and Alex Wallace, also spent time at Rangiotū School during their stays with the Alves during the first decades of the twentieth century.

At the end of 1902, with their move to the Manawatū complete, Carl and Theresia had been in Aotearoa New Zealand for over 26 years. Their family had grown from the one child, Mary, with whom they had arrived in Aotearoa New Zealand, to thirteen children, two of whom were deceased.

In financial terms they had made modest headway, enough to pay a deposit on another area of virgin, bush-clad land adjacent the western side of the Tararua Range. Life had been very difficult, especially during the sixteen years in Alfredton Road near Eketāhuna. If the burden of debt and meagre income pervaded their years in the Wairarapa; the problem of flooding in the Manawatū would now come to dominate their lives.

The Manawatū Standard 9 July 1902 reported,

One of the largest ever recorded floods on the Manawatū R. happened mid-1902.

The newly acquired Alve land would have been affected by this flood, although little or no stock had been acquired at this time. Farming efforts will have been directed to clearing the land of bush and trees. Perhaps cut timber will have been swept away in the floodwaters. The problem of slash is not a new thing!

The scene was now set for the first herd of cows to start grazing the newly cleared farmland, and for the family to begin engaging with the Rangiotū and Manawatū communities amongst which they lived. Connection to the Opiki community was not common until the construction of the suspension bridge two decades later, although there was a wire rope across the nearby Manawatū River which allowed some connection.

In 1904, Mr Louis Seifert built the *Rangitāne* flax mill on the Palmerston side of the river. This mill was adjacent to the Alve boundary near the first cowshed. The mill was connected with the *River* mill on the other side of the river by a wire rope *Flying Fox* arrangement long before the *Swing Bridge* was completed around 1920. Henry and Eddie Alve graphically described how in 1905 one of the mill workers was swept to his death while trying to rescue a stranded Mr Seifert from the marooned cage suspended from the wire rope during a fresh in the river. One of Mr Seifert's would-be rescuers, Mr J.A. Campbell, was swept away when their boat capsized. His body was found near Foxton two months later.

About the same time that Ernie Nash built the cowshed (about 1906), he built four more rooms and a passage and a veranda on to the original lean-to. Prior to this an outbuilding was erected by two Māori builders. This building comprised a storeroom and a bedroom, later used for a wash house. An out-building was put up by Carl Alve and used for a honey house, workshop and temporary bedroom.

Just a short while before Tom Purdom and Lena Alve married, Anna Alve died (10th March) at home of goitre. She is buried in the Catholic section of the Palmerston North cemetery in the same plot as her parents, brother Charles and his wife "Dolly".

Lena Alve was the first cook at the Rangitāne mill and Carl supplied milk to the cookhouse. For some years there was no road from the mill to the Palmerston-Foxton highway, and Mr Tom Purdom carted the bales of fibre to the Rangiotū Railway Station through Māori land adjoining the Alve's farm. The same Tom and Lena were married in St Patrick's Catholic Church, Palmerston North on the 5 April 1906. Lena and Tom began married life living in the house at the top of the farm occupied later by Charlie and Dolly. It was probably built earlier for staff at the flax mill on Nevilles Point. Their first daughter, Gwen Davie, reports that her parents were living there when she was born in 1907. They later moved to a farm near the junction of the Oroua and Manawatū rivers.

On 18 July in the same year (1906) another huge flood (100,000 cusecs) inundated the farm. The Manawatū River was reported to be higher than ever before! No dry land could be seen from Glen Oroua to Jackeytown. The effects on the family are not known, but it can be assumed they were worse than in 1902 because the land was clearer and the farming operation more developed. It is interesting that there are no anecdotal reports of this flood given by early family members.

In August 1908 Theresia married Herbert Simmons in All Saints, Anglican Church, Palmerston North. Theresia and Bert went to live at Mangawhata on land his father (a butcher) had bought in 1902 for the two brothers - Bert and Charlie. One of Bert's claims to fame was that he was responsible for issuing a challenge from the *Huia Rugby Club* (based at Rangiotū) to the newly formed Manawatū representative team. The Huia team was captained by Billy Larkins and had some notable players at the time. The game, played in Palmerston North, was won by Huia 8-6!

Another visitor to the Alve household before 1910 was Bill Busch - eldest child of Mary Busch (née Alve). After her marriage, Mary continued to live in the Wairarapa after the family moved to Rangitāne. Bill did some of his schooling at Rangiotū, while staying with his grandparents. He finished standard six there in 1914 and returned home. Bill writes that he,

> *...was there when Anna (1906) and Carl (1910) died .... My mother, always known as Mary, never told us much of their early life .... I well remember the old people Carl and Theresia Alve. Carl was a typical German and had very little respect for women and bossed all the family but did nothing himself!*

It might be noted that Carl had chronic myocarditis (heart trouble) from about 1905 onwards and would have been physically very limited. This may have accounted for his grumpy temperament observed by his grandchildren. Colin Alve reported that his father observed Carl was a short, stocky man with a very quick temper. Colin retells the story of him fencing with Henry one day. When he told Henry to do something, Henry was heard muttering under his breath before he was hit in the backside with Carl's thrown hammer. On the contrary, Theresia was very placid. She would often have to lie awake at night listening to her husband's *ravings*. Lena is said to have preserved her mother's temperament. Carl mentioned little about his relations or Germany.

Carl died in Palmerston North hospital on 21 September 1910. He died because of a ruptured aneurism of the left ventricle i.e. heart attack. His funeral was held in the Palmerston North Catholic Church, and he was buried in the Catholic section of the Palmerston North cemetery, adjacent Anna, on 24 September. He was survived by his wife Maria Theresia; five daughters - Mary, Theresia, Lena, Beth and Clara; and five sons - Charlie, Alfred, Henry, Eddie and Dolph. At the time of his death, as noted his daughters Mary, Theresia and Lena had married.

Carl's passing marked the end of an era. He, with his wife Theresia, had emigrated newlywed from northern Europe to the antipodes in most trying circumstances. His life was a testimony of courage, adventure, determination and, as the above story relates, exceedingly hard work. All who are their descendants can look back and with proud gratitude recall that they have as forbears people who contributed significantly to the early development of their young nation - Aotearoa New Zealand.

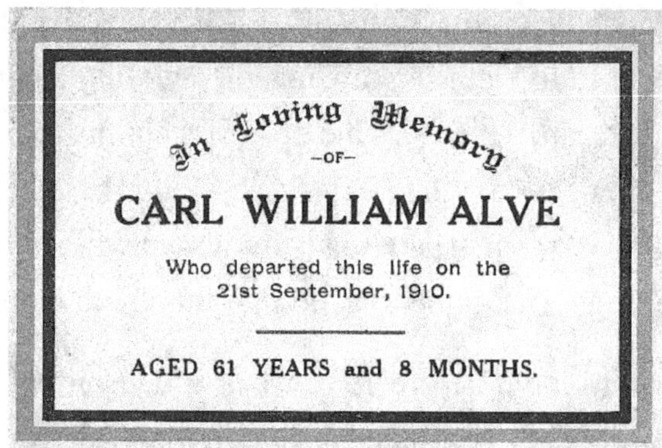

Figure 41 - Carl's Funeral Acknowledgement.

The *Manawatū Evening Standard* printed the following obituary to Carl Alve in its edition of 23 September 1910, [li]

> *The late Mr Carl William Alve whose death at Rangitane was announced in yesterday's issue of the Standard, was born in the Rhine province of Germany in 1849 and came to N.Z. in the ship Gutenburg in 1875. After residing in the Featherston district for four or five years he took up land at Eketāhuna and endured the hardships incidental to the early period of settling that district. After 16 yrs. farming, principally dairying in the Forty Mile Bush, he went back to Featherston, but did not stay there long as he acquired the land at Rangitane, near Palmerston North, where he has resided ever since. Mr Alve made friends wherever he settled and was highly respected by all who knew him. Deceased leaves a wife and family of ten children, most of whom are grown up, three of the daughters being married and there are a number of grandchildren. The funeral takes place tomorrow.*

Carl's will and probate records indicated Theresa (sic) Alve was appointed sole Executrix, Trustee and Beneficiary of his will. [lii] On 1 December 1910 the Manawatū Herald reported that in the Wellington region during November the estates of 252 deceased persons were certified by the Commissioner of Stamps. The principal estates were listed as:

Robert Hunter	£27,438
Mary Ann Doorley	£12,827
Elizabeth Hogg	£ 8,085
Charles Stantiall	£ 5,791
Margaret Fergusson	£ 3,028
Carl Alve	£ 2,852

…and 27 others, with the lowest value of these estates being £332. [liii]

£2,852 in late 1910, adjusted for inflation, would be worth just under $600,000 today. Quite an improvement on the poverty Carl and Theresia knew when they left Germany at the end of 1875!

We conclude with this picture from 1957, where the youngest surviving four of the family pose as past pupils of the Rangiotū School attending in the first decade of the twentieth century. On Dolph's left shoulder is Wiremu Te Awe Awe, a *Rangatira* of the Rangitāne Māori people of Rangiotū, with whom he played much music during the 1920s.

Figure 42 - Rangiotū School 75th Jubilee 1957. Four Alves attended between 1900-1909;
1. Dolph, 2. Eddie, 3. Henry, and 4. Clara.

As I end this story that canvases most of what I know of my great-grand-parents Carl and Theresia Alve to 1910, which began with the marriages of their parents in 1846 Hückeswagen and 1848 Beckum respectively, I reflect on their Gelsenkirchen romance and the life that flowed from it. I have met many people along the way, family, friends and neighbours who help to paint the picture. I have noted our forbears' fortitude and endurance as a couple who knew significant hardship in a rapidly changing Prussia and, who exchanged that for an equally challenging pionéering life in early Aotearoa New Zealand. "For better, or for worse – *auf Gedeih und Verderb"* Theresia and Carl had said to one another in that group wedding service in St Augustine's in Gelsenkirchen on Valentine's Day 1874. Thirty-six years later as Carl's death parted them, they had cause to reflect positively on the many nuances that their wedding promise had delivered them. Their romance in Gelsenkirchen was the prelude to a life of significant achievements and laid the foundation for their emerging families to endure hardship, celebrate success, contribute to their community and lovingly care for their whānau and communities.

Of course, their story does not end here at the end of 1910. The family would continue to develop their Manawatū dairy farm to become a very viable unit supporting five families. And their children will find partners and have more *mokopuna* (grandchildren) for Theresia – thirty-six in total. In the process, life's trials will continue to challenge them as it had done; and their resilience as a whānau will continue and develop.

Mary, Lena and Theresia had begun families of their own by 1910 when Carl died. There were eight *mokopuna* (grandchildren): Bill, Fred, John, Theresa and Rosa Busch; Harold Simmons; and Gwendoline and Daphne Purdom. These and others of the children would bear many more, except for Charlie who married but was childless. Four of the Alve brothers: Charlie, Henry, Eddie and Dolph would farm and develop the Alve land; offering support for their fifth brother Alfred, to farm nearby.

Epilogue

Eighty-five years were to pass after Carl died before one hundred and fifty of the family gathered for the Highden, Awahuri Alve Descendant Reunion in 1995. Between 1994 when I wrote *Alve Road* and the present – 2024 – the development of the world wide web has promoted an explosion of accessible genealogical and historical knowledge. This work builds on my earlier Alve family research recorded in *Alve Road*. I have pondered long and hard about the evidence to hand: genealogical, historical, biographical, religious and familial as I have attempted to dig deeper into the times and circumstances of my Germanic *tupuna* (ancestors) who emigrated to New Zealand during the (southern) summer and autumn of 1875/76.

Theresia's and Carl's were an incredibly challenging existence in the regions of Nordrhein-Westfalen, Germany where they grew up, fell in love and married. Infant mortality was high. Poverty and war were ever present realities that severely impacted them. Religious persecution was present. Industrial pollution was bad. Fatal diseases were around. Yet through all of this they eked out a living and set their sights, as many Germans and Europeans did during this period, on a new and better life for their *tamariki* (children) in new lands full of hope and promise. For the Alves that land was Aotearoa New Zealand.

This work goes some way to filling gaps in my family's early story. In another thirty years new resources and insights will be available to fill more gaps. It will be the task of someone else to produce the next edition of the Alve descendants' story.

May *Valentine's Day 1874,* as I have called this work, be a helpful backdrop for the research and the writing to be done in the future. The beginning of the ongoing story of the Alve family is indicated in the first Aotearoa New Zealand generation biographies in Appendix One. These stories of the thirteen children of Theresia and Carl remind us that while farming was still in the blood of the family for the best part of another century, the family firmly embraced the emerging amalgam which is Aotearoa New Zealand society. And one thing we notice: immigrants still come to this fair land from all around the world looking for a new start in an Island nation that is a great place to call home. Some things never change. And far be it from any of us Alve descendants to be xenophobic towards those who continue to emigrate from places far away, to Aotearoa New Zealand. That would be hypocritical for members of a family who have greatly benefitted from becoming Kiwis. Let us share the *aroh*ā*!*

And in the end, may the descendants of Theresia and Carl Alve be the richer because they know who they are through knowledge of their *whakapapa* and are therefore better able to make meaning of the life, they are called to live here in the twenty first century and beyond.

In closing this saga, may I refer you to the PDF files of *Alve Road,* [liv] the Family website [lv] and Family Facebook page [lvi] as other resources for those interested in things Alve.

And finally, I offer *Pepeha* – a song by the Group *Six60* from Dunedin – recorded and released in 2021. The band wrote on its Instagram page,

> *Proud to share this one, been over a year in the making. 'Pepeha' for the People! A pepeha shows our connection to the physical and spiritual place we call home. This anthemic waiata links significant things – prestige, love, and family – with our environment and to our ancestors.*

Figure 43 - Maunga – Tararua; Awa – Manawatu; Waka – Gutenburg.
Opiki Suspension bridge (centre) with te Manawatu awa in flood

Pepeha a song by Six60

Ko Mana tōku maunga
Ko Aroha te moana
Ko Whānau tōku waka
Ko au e tū atu nei

Mana is my mountain
And Aroha is my sea
Whānau is my waka
And all of that is me

Ahakoa pāmamao
Kei konei koe
Though you are far away
I hold you near

I'll keep the home fires burning
So you can see clear
Kia maumahara mai rā
Nō konei koe

APPENDICES

Appendix One: First Generation Biographies (Revised 2023)

These biographies of the first generation of Aotearoa New Zealand Alves have been amended; they were included in *Alve Road.* They reflect additional information about the early years of the Alve family in Aotearoa New Zealand provided by current descendants. For instance, the bush fire in February 1893 along Alfredton Road that affected the Alve property is mentioned in an extract from the *Wairarapa Daily Times* in the main narrative, and again here in Mary's biography where its personal impact on her is described. More information about the three girls who died young is included. Elizabeth's biography benefits from detailed biographical notes made by Russell Pedersen, her son. New and improved imagery is added to the record.

Anna Maria Catharina Busch - née Alve (1874-1966)

Figure 44 - Mary Busch née Alve.

Born 1 December 1874 in Gelsenkirchen, Germany; Mary had just turned one when she emigrated to Aotearoa New Zealand with her parents during December 1875. The Alves were accompanied during that journey by the Schormann family who they knew in Germany. Mary Gertrud Schormann - later Schwarnwebei – was almost the same age as Mary Alve and the two were to become lifelong friends, living in the Wairarapa. Mary maintained an accent throughout her life, a reminder that her first language was German which was spoken in the home long after her arrival in Aotearoa New Zealand.

Mary often recalled memories of the journey during 1876 from Wellington over the Remutakas to Featherston in a bullock drawn wagon – obviously quite an experience for a toddler of less than two. Mary, the eldest of Carl and Theresia's thirteen children, had a brother – Charles – followed by sisters – Theresia and Anna - by the time she began school at Eketāhuna where the family settled about 1881. During the family's fifteen years there on a small farm they cleared from the surrounding bush, Mary knew the privations and hardships of being the daughter of early Aotearoa New Zealand pioneers. School ended for her when she was in standard four, however she was well able to read and write. In later years she would keep her husband George's financial records and read the newspaper to him at night. George never went to school. During her Eketāhuna years she took violin lessons from neighbour and family friend Heinrich Schormann – her friend Mary's father. In later years before deafness overtook her, she in turn gave lessons using her violin to son Bill and a neighbour's boy. She is reported also as having been a good shot, born of the necessity to save the chickens from hawks and wild cats, and to keep the larder full of pigeons.

During the time they lived in the Eketāhuna district, the Alve property (possibly also the house) was badly affected by a bush fire. For ever after, Mary had a fear of inadvertent fire. She could smell wood smoke almost before it happened.

Shortly after the family moved back to the Featherston region in 1896, Mary met George Busch, also of German descent, whose family had settled first in the Nelson area in 1844 and later in North Canterbury. George was born at Kaiapoi in 1874 and worked in his father's contracting business carting shingle for the local roads board when it was forming many of the roads in the district. After his father's death in 1893 George, with most of his family, moved to Southern Wairarapa. For three years he was a shepherd on the Whatarangi sheep and cattle station at Palliser Bay.

Mary and George were married on 27 December 1898, at her parents' residence in South Featherston. During 1899 they moved to Oporua where George was shepherd manager. Their first son Bill was born in July the following year. Fred and Jack were to follow before, in 1905, George began a most successful contract ploughing and shingle carting business with a team of draught horses that he had assembled. Tis joined the family before George and Mary won by ballot a fifty-acre block of land in the subdivision of the Bidwell estate at Kaiwaiwai near Featherston. There they built a house, and a cowshed and Mary managed a dairy herd while George continued his contracting business which by then was employing labour. The breeding of Clydesdale horses was another enterprise that George began during this period.

Rose and Charlie had arrived at Kaiwaiwai when, in 1912, the Featherston farm was sold to George's brother-in-law. A replacement property - Ngawapurua - after the old settlement on the site of the house was purchased up the Turanganui River on Whakatomotomo Road near Pirinoa. There they built another house which they occupied just after Bess was born in 1914. At this stage George had several teams of horses and was engaged in the building of many roads in the Wairarapa and miles of stop banks around Lake Wairarapa.

Son Bill joined the contracting business upon leaving school in 1914. It was in 1917, around the time that the youngest child Frank was born, that the Busch family acquired their first car - a Model T Ford. George took some time to come to grips with the fact that it was not a horse. Bill reports that on his first drive the wind blew a gate partially shut. His dad pulled on the steering wheel yelling whoa! whoa! whoa! There was many a hair-raising ride after that, including the first over the Remutaka Ranges on the way to the Trentham horse races which ended with the Ford over a bank as the car ran off the road! Mary was injured and this is what possibly led to her developing a prominent humped upper back which got worse as she got older.

In 1919 further property nearby was acquired from the Hume family along Pirinoa Road as the Tauanui estate was divided. This land was dairy farmed by the family until its sale in 1929. Mary was a competent horse rider in her younger days and often rode side saddle. Her old side saddle was still at home when her grandson Nelson Rangi left home in 1945.

With an enterprising husband and a family of seven children, Mary was more than fully occupied during these years. Her family consistently comments on her good nature, her hard work, her kindness and her fondness for saying, "My! My! My!" As well as raising the children, keeping house and doing the gardening she loved, Mary regularly worked on the farm as George promoted and worked his contracting business. Daughter Rose reports that Mary was a marvelous maker of bread and scones. Son Bill knew her as a wonderfully kind and loving mother and remembers how well she knitted and crocheted. She had little social life as she laboured to support George and the family.

Mary's husband George died aged 61 in January 1936. He willed the farm to his youngest son Frank who was nineteen at the time. Mary was to have a life interest in the farm which meant that the farm would provide for her. Unfortunately, the great slump of 1929-33 hit George badly. The Tauanui farm had to be sold as well as another property at Whangaimoana and the Whakatomotomo farm was heavily mortgaged. It would be nearly two decades before all debts were cleared. It was impossible to provide for Mary; the farm barely survived being subject to a mortgagee sale. A family conference agreed that Mary would spend several months at a time with various of the older children including Bill and Mabel, Charlie and Vera, Bess and Bob and (at least twice) with Tis and Charlie Emmens. Charlie was a lighthouse keeper and they lived mostly at Island postings. Mary was with them at Cuvier Island near Great Barrier, and at Dog Island, a desolate Island in Foveaux Strait between South and Stewart Islands. It seems Mary thrived on the remote lifestyle. Some of her grandchildren fondly recall her staying with them. Mary spent some time with her mother who was descending into a form of dementia in the latter part of 1941 and remained there till after her mother's death in April 1942.

Mary's youngest son Frank took over the management of the farm in 1938, about Easter time. Rosa (Rose) who was not living with her husband Frank Rangi, returned to keep house and help Frank who was unmarried. Between sojourns among the family, Mary enjoyed returning to the farm. As she got older, she preferred not to travel and spent increasing time at home. After Frank married in 1944 and daughter Pamela was born in 1945, Rose and her later husband Hune (June) Te Maari moved out. From then on Mary spent most of her time with Rose and later lived with them permanently until her death in 1966.

For many years, Mary's favourite pastime was crocheting. All her work was done with a fine hook and thread, making some extremely intricate pieces. She made complete dining tablecloths with various patterns such as birds, butterflies and flowers, for each of her children and some of her older grandchildren. As she got older, Mary made several dining tablecloths of linen with large, crocheted corners. She made stacks of dressing table crocheted mats, but sadly she had to give it all up with her failing eyesight and loss of dexterity in her hands. Some of her tablecloths and mats to this day remain with, and are loved possessions of, her grand and great grandchildren. She was, of course, very adept at many of the pioneer household crafts such as soap and cheese making, food sourcing and so forth.

Mary's granddaughters Judi & Lynn recall they were in a whare out the back of Rose's house dancing & singing to music. Granny was quite deaf, and her sight was also failing by then and she didn't leave the house anymore. She made it out of the house, down the steps and across the shingle drive to the whare and was cackling in joy at the music. Obviously, she still loved the music. When visiting, she would always give her great grandchildren a silver coin and whisper don't tell your father, because she knew they would get into trouble if they told him. In later years she used to have a cup of tea and a biscuit. She loved using some special China cups she had where the saucer was a plate as well as a saucer. Easier to manage.

Figure 45 - The Busch Family c.1918. Standing: Jack, Bill, Fred, Charlie. Seated: Mary, Theresa, George, Frank. Front: Bessie and Rose.

Charles Henry William Alve (1876-1937)

Charlie was the first Alve to be born in New Zealand. Carl & Theresia with Mary had arrived at Wellington during March 1976. After time in Wellington, they crossed the Remutakas to Featherston where Charlie was born soon after. The birth of Charles William was reported to the registrar by James Cox, Settler of Featherston. The birth date is somewhat in doubt. A birth certificate issued in 1918 has it as 11 November. A certificate issued by a registrar in the Wairarapa has it as 11 December, and his mother's entry in the "Family Bible" has it as 10th December - the date we accept!

Charlie went to school at Eketāhuna after the family moved there about 1881. It was at Eketāhuna that Charlie met Catherine Wallace (1881 - 1967). Catherine was known to the Alves as "Dolly" because of her slight stature. Her father John Henry was a Blacksmith, having earlier served in the New Zealand Wars where he won the N.Z. War Medal. Dolly was born at the Head of the Bay (Duvauchelles), Akaroa on 15th January 1881. John Henry and his wife Ellen (née Pawson) moved to Eketāhuna in 1887 where John worked part-time as a Sawmill Engineer and part-time as a Blacksmith. Catherine had three brothers and three sisters.

Figure 46 - Catherine Wallace and Charles Alve.

Little is known of Catherine's movements from the time Charlie and the Alves left Eketāhuna in 1896 until he and Catherine were married on 13 July 1911 at her parents' home in Eketāhuna. She was then aged thirty years and it is understood that she had lived at Rangitāne sometime before their marriage, although her residence is given as Eketāhuna on the marriage certificate. Witnesses to the marriage were Catherine's father John and her brother George, described as a labourer of Eketāhuna. Charlie and Dolly were married by a Methodist minister - John Pendrey.

Charlie's father, Carl, died the year before their marriage leaving Charlie, his oldest son, very much the senior partner in what was to become the "Alve Brothers" farm. He was responsible, for instance, for acquiring land at Bainesse for Alfred after he married in 1913. With his mother, he also contributed to keeping the family together as the relatively close-knit unit continued into the 1940's.

Dolly's younger brother Alex was a regular visitor to the Alve Rangitāne farm from about 1908. Born in 1899, Alex died in Christchurch during 1994, aged 95. He would travel to visit Dolly and Charlie who lived in the cottage at the top of the Alve farm by the river. He recalls that each of the Alve boys had his job. Charlie was the slaughterman, and he remembers how on the days pigs were killed, the Māoris would gather around and collect the parts that were not wanted. During his visits, Alex was paid by Charlie to cut thistles with a slasher. It was in this way that he was able to earn enough money to buy a stand for his cornet music.

Another visitor to their home in the early days of their marriage was Charlie's nephew Bill Busch. He too would stay with them and other members of the family, until he finished his schooling at Rangiotū School in 1914. Bill's younger brother Charlie Busch was treated like a son by his uncle Charlie who was born two months after he and Dolly married in 1911.

Until they got their share of the land, Charlie and Dolly milked the cows with all the other family members. Access to their land was via a track along the boundary with Gibbons and past the red shed, which had served the flax mill at Neville's Point across the river. A feature of the 50 acres of land they farmed was a two acre stand of native bush preserved during the earlier clearing of the land. Charlie (an early conservationist) was particularly fond of this bush and probably turned in his grave when it was mercilessly cleared in the 1960's during the building of stop banks. Charlie's land bordered his brother Henry's share of the original holding. The two brothers got on well, they had placid natures, and shared in the farming of their land. Charlie and Dolly milked about 35 Jersey cows by hand. They had a boy working for them in the '30s, and Charlie's nephews would also pitch in to help. Evening milking would often not finish until 9pm. Charlie and Dolly also kept 300-400 laying hens and the day was not done until the eggs were ready for sale.

Charlie was blind in one eye, which affected his judgement when driving. Up until 1934 he and Henry shared a Ford Truck. In 1934 a new V8 truck was purchased by Charlie but was always driven by Henry. Charlie was a director of the Manawatū Reliance Dairy Factory at Rangiotū where he supplied milk.

Charlie and Dolly in many ways lived in another world, content not to keep up with technology. While others invested in radios, telephones and milking machines they were happy to live as their parents had. For instance, a trip to Palmerston North was an important occasion if for no other reason than to set their clocks by the town clock.

Dolly's parents, John and Ellen Wallace retired from Eketāhuna to live near Dolly on the Rangiotū Line in the 1920's. They both died while living there - Ellen in 1928 and John in 1932 - and they are both amongst the first who were buried at the new Kelvin Grove cemetery in Palmerston North.

The 1936/37 milking season saw Charlie with a hernia. Despite this he continued his round of farming duties, having lost the assistance of his young farm worker John Muirson, a Flockhouse boy. One morning Henry found him in distress wheelbarrowing his milk. Doctor Barnett was called to assist, and he relieved the hernia. However, that night the problem surfaced again. Charlie was operated on in hospital but early next morning, as Henry and his son Val were having breakfast before milking, they were rung by the hospital to say he was found dead because of a wondering clot, caused by bad bruising of the bowel. Henry had to break the news to Dolly as there was no phone at the house at that time. Charlie died in June 1937 at the age of 60 years. He was buried in the family plot in the Palmerston North cemetery alongside his father Carl and sister Anna. Charlie died intestate. Dolly received two thirds of his estate and his mother Theresia one third, which she subsequently bequeathed back to Dolly upon her death in 1942 - five years later. Henry bought their cows and Dolly gifted him the truck for assistance given. Henry agreed to lease Dolly's land with the right to purchase, which he exercised in the late 1940's. Dolly continued to live in the house taking her share in nursing her mother-in-law, Theresia. The oldest of the family - Mary Busch - also spent quite a lot of time there with Dolly and her mother.

In the early 1950's Dolly lived in the Hamilton area for some time, looking after her aunty Harriet Pawson, wife of her uncle John. During this time her house on the farm was occupied firstly by Henry's son Val Alve and his new wife Joyce, and then by Henry's younger son Ivan Alve and new wife Maree. Dolly returned to the house in 1954 and lived there until the early 1960's. Val's children, who lived nearby, knew her as Aunty Dolly. Their most vivid memory of her is being given cold, boiled potatoes which she had used the juices from to make her bread. A feature of her home was a large collection of shells.

Dolly moved to the Lonsdale Nursing Home at Foxton when her health declined around 1960. Shortly after this, the building of the new Manawatū River stop banks resulted in the demolition of her house. She died in the rest home during 1967 at the age of 86 years. Her brother Alex had contact with her and the Alves during these later years, but it was Val's wife Joyce Alve who took major responsibility for her care and affairs. Alex speaks of problems arranging for her burial in the Catholic section of the Palmerston North cemetery alongside Charlie, presumably because she was not a Catholic.

Charlie & Dolly died without children but are fondly loved and remembered by many nieces and nephews and their descendants.

Myra Jennings, a niece, wrote this of a stay with Aunty Dolly,

> *One time I remember well. She took us to town. We cut across paddocks to get to the Rangitāne railway station. I don't know how she managed in her long dresses, so out of date, but she did. The most vivid memory of our town visit was afternoon tea at Dustin's tearooms in Main Street before getting the train home again. There were still some scrumptious cakes left and much to our delight she told us to, "eat up as they were all paid for." We loved the orchard at Uncle Charlie's and Aunt's place. There was an apple called "Irish Peach" - absolutely beautiful flavour.*

A tribute to Dolly in this era is recorded in the Opiki History [lvii]

> *Many Opiki residents will remember seeing Mrs Charlie Alve walking out to the Main Road to catch the bus to town and will have given her rides. She used to come back laden with her stores. A slightly built woman, she was a marvel for her age and must have lived in that lonely house on her own for nearly forty years.*

Postscripts
1. Dolly's first cousin Adele Farrow married Frank Henry Schormann, Hermann Heinrich and Dorothea's son or grandson. It seems they farmed sheep for some time from the 1920's onwards in Putara Road which is adjacent to the foothills of the Tararua Range, just west of Eketāhuna. It is likely they, or perhaps their children, were honoured by having a Tararua ranges track named after them – the gruelling S-K (Schormann to Kaitoke) tramp has been a legend in the Tararuas. Frank and Adele are buried in the Eketāhuna Lawn Cemetery near the northern gate.

2. Two of Dolly Alve's siblings, like Emma Ida Alve, were buried in the old (now cleared) Eketāhuna First Settlers' cemetery on Alfredton Road and are mentioned on the cairn adjacent.

- Ellen Wallace d.1896
- John (Jack) Wallace d.1909

Theresia Veronika Simmons - née Alve (1878-1960)

Theresia was the third child of Carl and (Maria) Theresia and the second born in New Zealand. She was born at Featherston during October 1878. Her father was working at that time on the construction of the railway line into the Wairarapa, just after the line had been completed over the Remutakas to Featherston. She moved with her family to the Alfredton Road farm when she was about three. She would reflect on those days in later years as the "olden days" when her father was woodcutting in the Forty Mile Bush all week with Scandanavians, coming home at the weekends. She described their home there as mud-thatched with the interior walls covered with newspaper!

She began school when she was seven, her first task being to learn English, having been brought up speaking German. She recalled being laughed at by the storekeeper when sent to get some "Fuller's Earth" (baby powder) by her mother. Her broken English was obviously amusing to him. It was while she was taking lessons in preparation for her first Holy Communion, that the family got offside with the Catholic Church. The priest had come for the baptism of one of the younger children, but was unhappy with the half-crown donated saying, *Is that all you're going to give me? Carl* and Maria from that time kept their distance from the Church, which meant that Theresia was not admitted to Holy Communion. They lamented the fact that the New Zealand priests were so different from those in Germany.

Theresia commented little about her school days, although it seems she progressed well. After her schooling she went to "service" working for the Cotter family as a house servant for some years. During this time, she became engaged, before becoming very ill with hydatids when she was eighteen. She had tumours on her liver and lungs which required surgery, including the removal of a lung at Wellington hospital during 1896. The doctors later expressed their surprise that she recovered so well although, after several months in hospital, she had later to be re-admitted draining the wound that had become infected. It wasn't until about 1920, after the birth of all her children, that she stopped dressing the wound. The hydatids was, it seems, contracted because of picking and eating watercress from alongside the drains which dogs had contaminated. After this debilitating disease and treatment, Theresia's engagement ended; weakened by it, she was deemed to be not a good prospect for a wife it seems. How wrong this judgement was considering the course of her life!

Theresia returned to work with the Cotter's for a short while after her treatment, before rejoining her family at South Featherston where she pitched in to assist with milking at Donald's Dairy. In fact, she continued there with the older children after her parents moved to Manawatū in 1900, joining them at Rangitāne during 1902. She assisted her mother in the home there. She was a good cook and very able with needle and thread. Just after her arrival there the youngest of the family - Dolph - was born.

Theresia met her husband-to-be, Bert Simmons, at a ball she attended at Rangiotū. He was a community-minded man. He organised an early match between the local "Huia" rugby team captained by Billy Larkins, and the newly formed Manawatū team in Palmerston North. For the record, Huia won the match 8-6! Bert a butcher from Ohingaiti, with his brothers Charlie and Jim, had taken up land in Mangawhata Road with help from their father. Before she married Bert in All Saints' Anglican Church, Palmerston North in 1908, Theresia had lost her close sister Anna, and seen Lena her younger sister marry, both in 1906.

Figure 47 - L-R: Charlie Alve, William Simmons, Letty Simmons - later Goss (seated), Bert & Theresia, Elizabeth Alve and Carl Alve (seated).

Theresia and Bert took up residence on the Mangawhata farm that they jointly worked with Charlie Simmons, who would remain a life-long bachelor. During the next ten years, Bert and Theresia had six children, beginning with Harold (1909). Billy (1911) followed. He died of pneumonia two years later. Marjorie (1912) was born prematurely at seven months. This birth repeated Theresia's mother's experience of bearing Alfred alone without any adult assistance. There was no telephone and Bert and Charlie were away at a Rongotea cattle sale. It was lunchtime and the boys Harold and Billy were at the table when Theresia realised the baby was coming. She dashed across the farm and asked the neighbour's son to send his mother over, before giving birth to Marjorie on her own. The neighbour arrived in time to cut the umbilical cord and clean up. The premature baby weighed only about four pounds and was reportedly quite unattractive, but grew to be a strong, robust person. Myra (1916) followed before Alice (1917) was born prematurely the following year, living less than a day. Elza (1918) - known as Micky - completed the family, arriving as the Great War ended.

At the conclusion of the War, Charlie Simmons returned to the Mangawhata farm and resumed his partnership with Bert. In the latter part of the 1920's the decision was made to divide the farm - Theresia and Bert retaining the front and homestead, and Charlie the back half on Pyke Road with the addition of a corrugated cottage relocated from Mangawhata Road. Despite that separation, Theresia's daughter Myra recalled that her mother continued to provide Charlie with a cooked midday meal, cups of tea throughout the day and some food for his evening meal! The whole family shared the responsibility of hand milking the herd of cows. Myra described her mother as a crackerjack in the role, taking on the tough, the touchy and the heavy milking cows. Theresia also had good nursing skills, caring not only for herself after her hydatid surgery, but each of the children's serious illnesses and injuries. A skilled seamstress, there are many photos of clothing and costumes made for her children and their friends when they performed at community events. The wedding dress she made for Myra in 1937 is still in the care of her family (1994). Theresia planted and maintained a flower garden, described in a poem by her daughter, Marjorie, as her *pride and joy*.

Theresia became more reliant on her children and Charlie Simmons to manage the farm as Bert's health deteriorated prior to his death in 1936. The support she had from the extended Alve family, especially her sister Elizabeth, was also significant. After each daughter married and moved away from the district, Theresia, Harold and Charlie continued living and working on the farm until the decision was taken in the 1940s to put share milkers in charge. Theresia and Harold moved to a rented house in Tiakitahuna for a few years and then together to a home at 223 Ferguson Street, Palmerston North, purchased by Harold after the sale of the Mangawhata farm. Theresia always claimed she "owned" one floorboard because Harold was a little "short" of cash on the day of settlement.

Back in Palmerston North, Theresia became a devoted parishioner of All Saints Church where she and Bert had been married. There were regular visits with members of the extended Alve family and occasionally Bert's brothers Charlie and Bill Simmons. Harold also drove his Mother on longer trips visiting Myra and her family who had relocated to a farm in Pihama, Taranaki in 1954. Myra would usually visit her mother, with her two younger children Elaine and Bill, each May school holidays. Marjorie and Micky had a longer distance to travel to see their mother, however in January 1959 all of Theresia's adult children came together in Palmerston North for the marriage of her granddaughter, Barbara Jennings, in All Saints Church. An occasion that allowed Theresia to host many of the older members of her Alve family, and from all accounts, one she very much enjoyed.

Theresia's health declined over the following year. In the winter of 1960, she was admitted to hospital for surgery and discharged to her home in the care of Myra and Mickey, who were with her when she died in the early hours of 27 July 1960.

All Saint's Church was filled with family and friends for Theresia's funeral on 28 July, before her interment in the same plot as Bert in the Terrace End Cemetery. The family arranged for a plaque in memory of their mother to be placed at the end of the pew where Theresia preferred to sit in All Saints Church. She was described as a "well known and respected resident" of the city and of "retiring disposition" in an obituary published in the local newspaper. Her children loved her deeply and would have said she was a hardworking, tolerant woman who overcame many hardships during her 81 years, always maintaining her strong posture and appearance.

Mother

Our darling Mother is very dear to us,
She never complained or made a fuss.
Our Memory of her will always be,
From the day she passed, to Eternity.
We see her lovely face from day to day,
And of all the things she used to say.
She had many friends far and wide.
Who will be thinking of her day by day.
Now she is with Dear God at peace and rest.
Dear soul, she wanted it that way.

A poem written by Marjorie after her mother, Theresia Simmon's, death.

Anna Alve 1880 -1906

Figure 48 - Anna Alve.

Anna, the fourth of Carl & Theresia's thirteen children, was born on 25 August 1880 in Featherston. Soon after her birth her mother and siblings moved to the pioneer farmhouse Carl prepared near Eketāhuna for their arrival. This was her home for her first sixteen years. She attended Eketāhuna School. In 1891 she passed her school exams when she was in standard two. [lviii]

With the older children she worked on the family farm at South Featherston before moving with them to Rangitāne in the Manawatū around 1901.

She had a goiter which grew progressively worse at Rangitāne. This caused her to choke to death in 1906, at the age of 26. Her nephew, Bill Busch was a child staying with his grandparents at the time. He reports that it happened during the night. Anna was sleeping in with Elizabeth and someone came out and woke the boys in the sleepout appealing for them to get a doctor for Anna.

Anna was the first buried in the Alve family plot in the Catholic section of the Palmerston North old cemetery. She is buried there with her parents, brother Charlie and his wife Dolly. Her death came less than a month before Lena Alve's wedding. The tribute on the following page is offered by the author in memory of Anna – his great aunty.

Anna

Anna of old was a prayerful prophetess
Who lived wise and long as she prayed,
Praising God when the Christ child came.
Optimistic Anna was Arendelle's Queen
Striving for the people she loved in Frozen
As she sang, "Love is an Open Door".
But Anna of Rangitāne, forgotten by most,
Invites us to remember the fragile and the frail.
People who speak to us of another way;
The pathway of deep anguish and limitation
Yet, whose meaningful lives remind us
That the short-lived are most to be honoured
For they bravely, like Christ, died youthful,
And speak to us of another life, more eternal.

Terry Alve - 2023

Carolena Purdom - née Alve (1882-1934)

Figure 49 - Carolena Purdom née Alve.

Lena was born in August 1882, not long after the family settled at Alfredton Road, Eketāhuna. She did her schooling there before moving with the family to South Featherston in 1896, where she helped with the milking at Alves' Donald Dairy farm.

After she moved with her family to Rangitāne at the turn of the century, Lena found work at Louis Seifert's "River" flax mill in 1904 as the mill's first cook. It was through working there that she met her husband Tom Purdom who was employed to transport the flax from the mills to the Oroua Bridge railway station for shipment to the Port of Foxton. His route passed through the Alve land and the adjacent Māori land, which ensured regular contact with the Alves.

Tom's family hailed from Christchurch, where Tom was born in 1879, and later Timaru where he grew up and trained as a stone mason. He was the third born in a family of five boys and four girls. His father, William Purdom had emigrated from Cumberland, England and married Selina Taylor in Christchurch during 1875. It is unknown why Tom, with his brothers Lionel (who married Clara Alve) and Fred found their ways to the Manawatū. It is possible that there was a connection with the Busch family in southern Wairarapa. It is known that Lionel later worked at Pirinoa as a shepherd before coming to Manawatū. There is also a suggestion that Tom at least had work with the railways and that he transferred to Manawatū.

Lena and Tom's wedding in 1906 was somewhat overshadowed by the death of Lena's next older sister Anna Alve, just a month before. Lena and Tom were married in St Patrick's Catholic Church, Palmerston North at the "bottom of the altar" because they, or at least Tom, were not Catholics. They settled into the house at the top of the Alve farm which was later to be Charlie and Dolly's home. It had previously been used by flax millers who worked at Neville's Point across the river. Within a few months of their moving there, the huge 1906 Manawatū River flood surrounded them.

It was while living in this house that Gwen (1907) was born a year after their marriage, and a year later Daphne (1908). From 1911 until 1915 Tom and Lena farmed a dairy unit with a herd of about 20 cows near the junction of the Manawatū and Oroua Rivers, near Rangiotū. Between milkings Tom spent his days clearing the still standing bush across the road - it was very rough country in those days just before the First World War. Daughter Gwen remembers getting lost after delivering food to her dad. She had to climb a great tree trunk which typically had been sawn well above ground level. From this she shouted until she was found.

The family spent a short time at the beginning of the First World War minding a home in Palmerston North while the owners were away. It was while living there that Lena bore Olga (1915). Later, during the war, they moved to Bert and Theresia Simmons' farm near the Main Drain to help while Charlie Simmons was away in the war. When Charlie came back from war service, Tom moved to work cleaning drains and driving horses for Isaac Cooksley, living near Bainesse for two years.

In 1920 the family moved to live in Palmerston North where Tom drove for Banbury contractors before working a drag line excavating shingle from the Manawatū River. Marion (1921) was born shortly after the move to Palmerston North, completing the family of four girls. By this time Gwen was away from home working for different of Lena's brothers and sisters. Gradually Tom became incapacitated with arthritis which began to cripple him. This derived, at least in part, from the laborious, damp work he had undertaken.

Lena, after moving to town, became involved with the Brethren Church. It was women of this church who provided her with housework which meant income when Tom could not work. For a period in the 1920's it was a family occasion to go to church on Sunday evenings. Lena with her mother, children, brother Dolph and sister Theresia attended, gathering at the Purdom's afterwards for supper. Eventually Tom also joined the family at church. Her children remembered Lena as a wonderful mother whom they did not fully appreciate when they were younger. She rarely hit them, and when she did it was for good reasons. Neighbours regularly brought their troubles to her.

Tom's illness reduced the family income in the depression years and the pressure on Lena eventually told when she was admitted to hospital. During this time, she suffered severe memory loss, even forgetting her involvement with the church which had earlier been so important to her. Lena's illness culminated in her wandering from home in July 1934. Members of the family undertook an extensive search for her which included dragging parts of the Manawatū River. However, Lena was never seen alive again, her remains being discovered by a hunter in the Tararua Ranges near Tiritea in 1947. These were interred in the newly opened Kelvin Grove cemetery after a Coroner's inquest ruled her death was due to unknown causes.

After Lena's disappearance, daughter Daphne largely took responsibility for the family, with Gwen away married in South Canterbury by this time. Olga, Jack and their family lived with Tom for a period before Daphne took him to be with her and Charlie Reckin at Eastbourne near Wellington, sometime after their marriage in 1939. There he lived in a caravan reasonably able to fend for himself, despite contracting diabetes and losing a leg to it in his latter days. He maintained his sense of humour through all this as indicated by his quipping in a letter to grandson Terry Davie in Timaru who wanted him to visit, "I'll come down when the other leg grows!" Tom died at the good old age of 76, just before Christmas 1955.

Elizabeth Pedersen - née Alve (1884-1966)

Figure 50 - Elizabeth Alve.

The fifth daughter of Carl & Theresia, Elizabeth was by many accounts her father's favourite. Like him she was very musical, learning the violin from a German teacher in Palmerston North, with whom she lived for a while and did housework for recompense. Earlier, when younger, she was introduced to music, possibly by Heinrich Schormann while living at Eketahuna. At the age of sixteen she gave a concert and later taught the violin herself - a Mr Inkpen was one she taught. She also took oil painting lessons later. She regularly gave family members paintings she had done.

Elizabeth, or Beth as she was known to the family, was born in 1884 in the early days of the settlement near Eketāhuna. She attended school there and at Kaiwaiwai, having completed her schooling by the time the family began to move to Rangitāne in 1900. She would regularly drive a gig to Palmerston North where she taught music. On one occasion the horse shied and spilt her into the roadside ditch!

The Pedersens, a Danish family of ten children, lived nearby dairy farming at Jackeytown. Peter the third and oldest boy in the family, had been away for some years in Australia and bush-felling. On his return to Manawatū about 1908, he and Beth met and were married in 1911. They went to live and milk their own cows on a leased farm near Ohakea on Tangimoana Road.

Thelma (1914) and Hazel (1915) were born while they lived there and Thelma recalls that she was four when they moved to Palmerston North, living in Princess Street. Towards the end of the First World War Peter was called up by the army and passed A1 fit, but the war ended shortly after. Russell (1918) was born in Palmerston North.

From Palmerston North, Peter worked on some of the Alve farms at Rangitāne and Rangiotū. They worked and lived on Henry's farm while he and Theresa and baby Phil visited Theresa's relatives in Tasmania about 1919-20. They subsequently bought and briefly worked a farm at Oroua Downs about 1920. They built a house at Foxton Beach about 1921 where they lived for four years. There Peter had a commercial fishing launch and a taxi service plying mainly between Foxton and the Beach, over the rough metalled road. Foxton was then still a port. They returned to farming at Himitangi in 1925, with the girls pitching in with milking after they left school. Later, about 1936, they moved to a sheep farm at Glen Oroua owned by Paddy Quinn, a prominent Manawatū-Horowhenua landowner. They moved to Mangawhata in 1938 near to Bert and Theresia Simmons, from where Hazel and Russell were married two years later in 1940, and Thelma in 1941.

During these days Beth was involved with others of the Alve family in the Brethren Church and regularly attended with the children. This had begun at Himitangi. The families were encouraged to make their own amusement and to visit among themselves. Typical entertainment included musical evenings, with Beth playing violin, and ping pong and tennis. Eddie's wife Laura would come and sing, and Dolph would bring his piano accordion.

Beth and Peter, with the children all away married, moved from Mangawhata to farm work with Malcolm Guy at Koputaroa in 1941. Their son Russell left for WW2 service on his twenty fourth birthday in December 1942. He was not to return home until January 1946, having served in North Africa and Europe and attaining the rank of Captain in the Army. By this time his and his wife Thelma's daughter Valentine Pedersen was five nearing six years old. [lix]

In 1944 Beth and Peter bought a house and a small piece of land from Eddie Alve at Rangitāne. On this land Peter grew big, juicy raspberries which were in high demand around Christmastime when he sold them at the gate. They lived there, adjacent to the river until Peter's death from a heart attack in April 1953, just after the massive '53 Manawatu River flood. Dianne and June Avery, grandchildren, were having part of their summer holiday with Beth and Peter at the time when the flood came. June, who was five, remembers waking in the middle of the night and hearing the great noise of the flood as water broke through the banks nearby. They could see massive tree trunks and animal carcasses floating in the rushing, muddy water which was contained by the bank just behind the house. Peter had raised this with sandbags. He had put aside some water and prepared a way to get onto the roof quickly if need be. It was not long afterwards that Peter died, and the family thought that the stress of this flood contributed.

After Peter's death, Thelma and Bert with their girls moved from Wellington to live with Beth at Rangitāne for nine months. In 1954 they bought a house in Palmerston North where Beth joined them, living there until she died in 1966, aged 81, after a brief stay in the Lonsdale Nursing Home at Foxton. During these years she regularly moved around the family staying with Hazel and Darcy in Christchurch, and Russell and Thelma in Auckland, a couple of months at a time.

Beth kept reasonably good health in her latter years, although she was hospitalised with bronchitis for a time towards the end. She also had a goitre removed when she was 78. In Palmerston North Beth attended the Presbyterian Church, before embracing the faith of the Church of Jesus Christ and Latter-Day Saints. She was baptised into this Church, and her funeral service was held there before she was buried at the Kelvin Grove cemetery in Palmerston North.

Alfred Ernest Alve (1887-1953)

Figure 51 - Alfred Alve.

Born on 28 January 1887, Alf was the second of Carl and Theresia's five sons. He was born when no one was around, the family returning home to find him, and his mum cleaned up and in bed! He began school at Eketāhuna and finished at Kaiwaiwai, Featherston. When he was thirteen, he was part of the advance party, sent in 1900 to help prepare the Rangitane land for the coming of the family. They cleared some land and built the first shelter which, it is understood, had a canvas cover over a wooden frame and an earth floor.

After working with the family to clear the land and establish the Rangitāne farm, Alf left early to work for Harry Simpson ploughing, before moving to his Bainesse land and marrying Florrie Alsop in 1913 whose family lived and farmed at "Westmere", about a mile down the river from the Alve's near Rangiotū. During the first war Florrie's parents and family moved to another farm near to them at Bainesse. They were still living on this land when Mr Alsop died in 1930.

Alf and Florrie had three children while living at Bainesse - Meryl (1916), Noeline (1920) and Colin (1921). Their fourth - Dick (1923) died within a short time of birth just after they left. The family were farewelled by the Bainesse community in 1923 as recorded in this newspaper report in *The Manawatū Evening Standard* dated Wednesday 20 June 1923.

> *On Friday last a farewell social was tendered to Mr & Mrs A. Alve who are leaving the district shortly. During the evening items were contributed by Miss Townsend (encored), Miss Thompson and Master W. Pollard. Mr Alve was presented with an aneroid barometer and Mrs Alve with an electro-plated entree dish, both suitably inscribed. Mr Metcalfe in a neat speech, spoke of the good qualities of the recipients, Mr Alve responding. The company then sang, "For they are jolly good fellows." Dancing followed. The music being supplied by Mr Palliser (piano) and Mr D. Alve (clarinet). The singing of the National Anthem and "Auld Lang Syne" brought the evening to a close.*

The aneroid barometer (Colin) and the entree dish (Merle) were still in the possession of the family in 1994. A black, mantel piece chiming clock, possibly given at their wedding was gifted by the family to the Mellemskov - Eketāhuna museum where it is on display.

Alf moved to work in the Rangiotū Dairy factory for a year living with his family in a house they purchased near Rangiotū School. This house was later occupied by Mrs Alsop until her death in 1936. The following year saw Alf sharemilking on a farm in Riverbank Road before moving to Raupo Road, Mangawhata in 1925 to share milk for Tom Saunders. He continued there for seven years, moving to Tokomaru briefly in 1932. During the following five years they farmed at Norm Gibbons' station *Opiki* until 1938. A short move to brother Eddie Alve's farm at Rangitane led to a further five years' share milking there until 1943. During the latter part of this time son Colin was in the army, and in 1939 Meryl left home when she married.

In 1943 Alf and Florrie, with Noeline and Colin, moved back to the Riverbank Road property where they had earlier been sharemilking. They purchased this thirty-six-acre farm and milked about thirty cows on it until 1962. Like the Rangitāne land, this farm adjacent to the Manawatū River flooded badly.

Like his father Carl, brother Dolph and sister Elizabeth, Alf was very musical. He had earlier played the accordion in Bainesse dances, and in later years could get a tune out of anything: a mouth organ, even a comb and a piece of grass!

Alf died of cancer on 2 January 1953 shortly before the massive 1953 flood inundated the farmland!

Colin and his mother Florrie farmed on at Riverbank Road after Noeline married in 1955. In 1962 they moved together to their home in Summerhill Drive, Aokautere. Florrie died while staying with Noeline in 1969, after suffering a diabetic coma.

Henry Wilhelm Alve (1989-1968)

Figure 52 - Henry Alve & Theresa Wagner.

Born on 19 October 1889 at Eketāhuna, Henry was six when the family moved to South Featherston. He continued his schooling there as the family moved to Rangitāne at the turn of the century, joining them in 1902. After a brief time at Rangiotū School, he joined the family working at the Rangitāne farm.

Henry began farming his fifteen seven acres, which included the Rangitāne homestead and original cowshed, in 1916. He married Theresa Christina Wagner the following year in March.

Theresa Wagner was a Tasmanian of German descent. Her parents were Philip Wagner and Caroline Hauke of Woodsdale in the Midlands, whose families had emigrated via different ships from the Hesse region of southern Germany in 1855. She was the second youngest in a family of thirteen. She was stranded while holidaying in New Zealand by the outbreak of the first world war. She was classified as a German 'alien' as the war intensified and she was unable to travel back to Tasmania as planned. Her brother Phillip, who was a carpenter working for the Westport mines, and his wife Coralie had their first child there. Theresa spent some time assisting with child minding for them. An association with the Parkers, who were Tasmanian relatives living at Rangitāne, may have brought her into contact with the Alves. A family anecdote tells that Theresa determined to win Henry for herself from his then current girlfriend. She continued beyond her marriage, a woman of some determination. Family members would comment on her striking appearance, and particularly her dark brown eyes.

Henry and Theresa's wedding took place in March 1917 in All Saints' Anglican Church, Palmerston North. Witnesses to the signing of certificates were Henry's siblings Clara and Alfred. The newlyweds moved into the homestead at Rangitāne living with Henry's mother Theresia and his sister Clara, and possibly Dolph for some of the time.

Their first child Phillip was born in December 1918. When he was about eighteen months old in 1920, Henry and Theresa found their way with him to visit family in Tasmania - possibly arriving just before (or shortly after) Theresa's father, Philip Wagner's, death in September 1920. While they were away Henry's sister Elizabeth and husband Peter Pedersen with their family came and lived in the homestead, managing the farm. A postcard sent by Henry to his mother detailed their travels and notes that they were staying with Theresa's older sister, Janey Hyland. They were planning to spend Christmas 1920 with Theresa's recently widowed mother Caroline.

Dolph Alve share-milked with Henry for some time. Around the time he turned twenty-one (the day before Henry's son Valentine was born in 1923) Dolph occupied the land acquired over Whiskey Creek west of the early farm.

Phillip began school at Rangiotū in 1924, transferring as an opening day pupil to Opiki School on 28 June 1928. Henry's and Eddie's children attending school at that time were invited by the Akers family to transfer to the nearer Opiki School in order to ensure that adequate numbers of pupils were offering, to justify the establishment of the school. The school opened in a marquee and Val began school there later in 1928 when he reached five. By the time Harry began at Opiki School in 1931 there were two rooms.

During the boys' younger years, Hilda Hersey was employed to assist Theresa with domestic duties. When Theresa took a second journey to Tasmania in 1930 to be with her ailing mother, she sailed out of the Port of Bluff near Invercargill. Henry's niece Rose Busch helped keep house while she was away. Rose was particularly fond of her uncle Henry, often staying in the home during her visits across the Tararuas. She tells graphically of Henry's sense of humour. One incident involved a visit from zealous Christians seeking for his conversion and assuring him thereby of a place in heaven. Naively he countered that if Theresa his wife was not going there, he would sooner be where she was! Rose suggested to Henry, having noted his tendency to act dumb, that people would think he was silly. He agreed but assured her that he did that deliberately to string people along and get more out of them!

Theresa returned from Tasmania to Wellington by ship with her niece Nellie Bender later in 1930. Nellie stayed for several weeks, and the boys remember her particularly for her needlework. Shortly after Theresa's return from Tasmania, Ivan was born to complete the family. Contact with Tasmanian relatives declined after this. Theresa was not a good correspondent, although she did receive regular copies of the *Tasmanian Courier* from relatives in subsequent years. Theresa's sons have in later years revived contact with their Tasmanian cousins, particularly through Reita Dolan and Nina Banks. Another link with Tasmania was through Peter Palmer who farmed at Colyton. Peter's two sisters Mary and Kate had married two of Theresa's brothers, Robert and Len Wagner in Tasmania. Each Christmas Day for some years Peter and wife Jessie and girls would visit the Alve home, with the Alve's reciprocating on Boxing Day.

Other friends of the family included the Parkers mentioned above, and another flax milling family who had lived next door - the Evans. Mrs Evans had been one of the Burgess family who had also lived next door. The Evans later moved to Rongotea where Harry Alve worked in the butter factory. Don Nagle and his family at Opiki were Jewish Germans with whom the Alve's also had a friendship over the years.

Henry was an easy-going man, proud of his German heritage and often given to singing, sometimes in German, and reciting poetry. He was destined to be a farmer in those pioneering days when it was all hands to the plough but in some ways, he had a sense of missed vocation, a sense that had earlier been encouraged by his schoolteacher who had remarked that he would make a good teacher. That vocation was to be left for his son Phillip and granddaughter Margaret who were to enter the ranks of schoolteachers later.

Technological change was rapid during this time. In 1929/30 milking season a Moffat-Virtue milking machine arrived from the Wairarapa. The cows still needed stripping after the cups were removed, but the milking process was significantly quickened. In 1932 the first AC (mains) radio was acquired - it was a good quality "Courier", still in the hands of the family at Longburn. During the 1930's trucks were used to transport milk to the factory, although the last of the draught horses survived until the mid-1950's. The family also obtained a car in the 1930's and eventually a 1938 Ford V8 which had been a taxi in the early 1940's. The first tractor arrived in 1947 - a Massey Harris.

Val helped with milking during his school years, replacing the boy employed for this in the early 1930's. He worked on the farm full-time at the end of his primary schooling in mid-1938, just before he turned fifteen. A year before, Charlie had died leaving Henry with increased responsibility with a larger dairy herd and twice the acreage to farm. Val worked for "pocket money" until 1948 when he was taken on by his father as a sharemilker.

During the late 30's Henry & Theresa established the Westfalia Friesian Stud with cows and bulls purchased from various places, including some from "Ruaview" near Raetihi. The name "Westfalia" was given to this stud, recognising the origins of the family in the German province of the same name, where Henry's mother Theresia had grown up and married Carl Alve. It is possible that Theresa, Henry's wife, received an inheritance upon the death of her mother in 1931, although there are no records of the same. The establishment of the Stud may have been facilitated by this inheritance, as may have the acquisition of Dolly's farm after Charlie's death and the early mechanisation of the farming operation.

Val continued sharemilking through his marriage, living in Dolly's house at the top of the farm 1951-53, before moving away and allowing Ivan to share milk for a season. Harry filled the breach during 1954-1956, before Joyce and Val returned to live in the homestead and resume sharemilking in mid-1956.

Henry and Theresa, with Harry, lived in Bainesse Road next to the Caskes from 1957-59. Henry commuted back to the farm regularly, which in those days also included a run-off on Kellows Line, near Himitangi. The next three years 1959-62 had them back in Eddie's house at Rangitāne before they retired to Ngaire Street, Longburn later in 1962. This was shortly before the Manawatū River Control Scheme went through, cutting 30 acres from the size of the farm.

The farm was sold to his son Val in 1963, at the time a new farmhouse was built because of the demolition and removal of the old homestead which found itself behind the new stop banks.

Henry and Theresa lived in retirement at Longburn celebrating their Golden Wedding anniversary in March 1967. Henry was the only child of Carl and Theresia to reach this milestone. A few months later Henry succumbed to prostate cancer, dying on 3 January 1968. Henry took great pride in the Alve settlement and development of the land at Rangitāne. His death signaled the last chapter in that occupation, the last of the Alve farmland at Rangitāne being sold by Val two years later. Theresa survived Henry for three years, dying of a stroke in February 1971. Their Longburn home continued as son Harry's residence until his death in 2004 when Phil used it as his home away from Wellington. The house was sold in 2014 after Phil's death, having been cleared and put on the market by Ivan's son Paul who lives in Longburn.

Edward Otto Alve (1891-1965)

Figure 53 - Edward Alve and Laura Spink.

Eddie, as he was known in the family, was born at Eketāhuna in January 1891. He shared a birthday (29 January) with his father Carl and his daughter Elvene. Being younger than the rest of the family he, and Clara his sister, moved to Rangitāne with their parents in 1900 ahead of the rest of the family. Later he would recall what they found there upon arrival,

> *... there was a slab whare just cut out of the trees. The mosquitoes were terrible, he asserted. It was just one constant buzz all night long and you had a terrible job to get any sleep at all.... When I first arrived here, I saw the remains of an old jetty just at the back of the house and I made a few enquiries. Both the Māoris and their Pakeha neighbours told me that it was where the food used to come up by punt for Palmerston in the early days, and from there in bullock wagons it was transported through to Palmerston North.*
> lx

Eddie attended Rangiotū, then known as Oroua Bridge, school along with Henry and Clara. Eddie related very well to the Māori iwi who lived in the Ngāwhakarau village adjacent to the farm. He was later to lease/purchase the meeting house, orchard and land from the Rangitāne people in 1923. Hilton recalls going with his father to negotiate with various Māoris to lease/purchase further land during the 1930's. This was a long, tortuous process that involved contacting many people and having to pay for their co-operation. He had also purchased a Māori canoe from the Māori in the early years which he kept until it was swept away in the 1953 flood. This is possibly the canoe preserved in a museum at Santoff near Bulls.

Eddie was a keen hunter and shooter, roaming the uncleared, swampy Taonui basin northwest of the farm where there were untold amounts of wildlife - ducks, pukekos, weka, etc. amongst the large stands of cabbage trees. He also spent time with his Busch cousins shooting on the Whatarangi station in the southern Wairarapa where there were deer, pigs and goats. He kept several game trophies in his home before it burned. He also hunted Zamba deer at Himitangi near the lakes. In earlier years he hunted rabbits with ferrets which he kept in his pockets! He also kept bees in his orchard, fearlessly tending them and suffering no ill effects from stings.

Eddie married a Welsh lady, Laura Spink, in 1915. Laura had immigrated to New Zealand with her mother in 1913 after her father William had settled at Rangitāne the previous year. William worked at the flax mills as a carpenter after building wharves in Auckland. They lived in a house adjacent to the Red Shed at the top of the farm, upstream by the Manawatū River.

Initially, Eddie farmed the Rangitāne Alve land in partnership with his brothers, before being allotted his share about 1923. By this time Lisle (1917) and Elvene (1920) were born. Hilton was born in 1926. During 1929 his wife Laura returned to the U.K. for eight months while Eddie employed a housekeeper. Lisle left school in 1931 and worked on the farm for a year before leaving and returning briefly in 1933. It was during the spring of 1935 that Eddie's and Laura's house was burned down. This, and other tensions, had Laura move to live in Palmerston North with Hilton where she managed a delicatessen shop for three years before purchasing a rooming house at 50 Queen Street, where she charged fifteen shillings a week per room to board professionals and businessmen.

In 1939, after a clearing sale, Eddie leased the farm to his brother Alfred. He then moved to Hawkes Bay where he worked for the Government Public Works for about two years, clearing roads in the Esk Valley and out towards Tongoia. He returned to the Manawatū as a night watchman at the Longburn Freezing Works, before taking up farming again once Alf's lease expired about 1944. This was shortly after his brief marriage to Mona Simpson who died a month after their wedding in January 1944. Eddie and Mona met in Palmerston North where Eddie lived in a bach behind the Johansen home, in Slacks Road. Mrs Ethel Johansen was friendly with Mona's sister Beryl Simpson (later Seifert), and it was Ethel who introduced them.

In 1951 Eddie married Ina Donnell (née Rasmussen), the daughter of a Danish settler family. Eddie shared with her the care of her three young daughters - Rachael, Margaret and Jenny Donnell - until they left home. After the birth of his son William (1955), Eddie sold his farm to nephew Charlie Busch before moving to live at Foxton Beach. At the Beach, Eddie was employed by the Manawatū County Council to keep the beach front tidy. Around 1961 Eddy, with Ina and Billy, returned to Rangitāne living in the house located adjacent to the river in one corner of the farm he had sold to Charlie Busch. This house was moved further from the river by the catchment board in 1962 when the high banks were constructed.

In his later years Eddie grew raspberries and gooseberries and kept bees on his small plot of land. He died on 30 October 1965 at the age of 74. His wife Ina lived on with son Billy in the Rangitāne house until her death in 1993. Billy, the last of the Rangitāne Alves, remained living in the house there until it was burned when a truck crashed into it in the early 2000's.

While Eddie was a quick-tempered man it seems, like his father Carl, he is remembered by many for his kindness and care of others. During the depression years he was always ready to invite a swagger home for a meal, even if his family had to go without. He was also generous, especially to his Māori neighbours in earlier years, loaning possessions like his guns to them. His open-hearted kindness was not always reciprocated.

Rosa Ellen (1893-1896)

Rosa was born on New Year's Day 1893. She was the tenth born of the children of Theresia and Carl. She was three when she died from diphtheria on 21 August 1896, very soon after the family moved to Kaiwaiwai, Featherston South during the winter of 1896 to work for Donald's Dairies. She had been ill with diphtheria for six days before her death. It is reported that there was a diphtheria epidemic locally, around the time of Rosa's death, and that a few children who died from this are buried in the Featherston cemetery near Rosa. She is buried in the Catholic section. Hers is the first identifiable Alve grave in Aotearoa New Zealand, and the second Kiwi death in the family (following Emma's) after they immigrated.

It is possible (even likely) that Rosa was named after her father Carl's elder sister, variously named in the genealogical records as Rosette, Rosa or Rosalia who married Mathias Hausmann in Gelsenkirchen, Germany in the early 1870's.

Figure 54 - Rosa is buried in the Featherston Cemetery where her grave remains as pictured in 2023.

A project associated with the February 2024 Alve Descendant Reunion raised funds to restore Anna's grave headstone in Featherston. The local Council were approached and offered guidelines. Donations were collected around the time of the Reunion.

The restoration allowed a plaque to be added on this grave acknowledging Emma Ida Alve's birth and death in May 1896. It was completed at the end of May 2024 and an unveiling is planned for around the time of Anne's birth date of 20 August. The mahi was undertaken by Black Axe Contractors, Featherston and William E. Jones, Monumental Masons, Palmerston North under the supervision of Julianne Alve.

Figure 55 – Terry's wife Margaret Alve and Isaiah Perris their grandson visited the newly restored memorial to Anna and Emma Alve at Featherston 2 June 2024.

Emma Ida (1896)

Emma was the next child born after Rosa. She was born prematurely, living only eight hours before dying on 10 March 1896. I understand Emma was buried in the Eketāhuna First Settlers' cemetery near the family farm in Alfredton Road. There is no record available of her burial, nor sign of the grave. The cemetery was cleared in the 1970s with a cairn placed nearby on Alfredton Road just east of Eketāhuna. Around the time of writing, a memorial to Emma was added to her sister Rosa's grave in Featherston. Funding for this project was associated with the February 2024 Alve Descendant Reunion in Pahiatua.

Emma was the first Alve to die in Aotearoa New Zealand. The two early Alve infant deaths (Emma and Rosa) are indicators of the hardship the family faced as the New Zealand economic depression took hold. In a few months during 1896 Theresia and Carl lost their two young daughters. One either side of their move off the Eketāhuna farm to Kaiwaiwai, Featherston. These losses added to the grief that was associated with leaving land they had cleared and farmed since 1880. Their sense of loss must have been devastating for them and the older children. And ten years later in 1906, when Anna died at Rangitane, these earlier experiences of deep sadness will have been very much in mind. Carl died of heart failure in 1910, was this an element of his broken heart? We can hardly imagine what it was like for Theresia to lose all four of them during this period.

Figure 56 - Emma Alve is thought to have been buried here in the cleared First Settler Cemetery, Alfredton Road, Eketāhuna.

Recently Emma Ida's namesake, Carl Alve's brother Ewald's daughter Emma, was found to have lived and died in Gelsenkirchen, Germany 10 September 1887. In naming their daughter

Emma, Carl and Theresia may have been aware through correspondence of the first Emma's short life which preceded that of their prematurely born, and short-lived daughter, in 1896.

Clara Else Purdom - née Alve (1897-1975)

Figure 57 - Clara Alve.

Clara was the youngest girl and second last of her family, born on 25 July 1897, a year after the family moved to South Featherston. She was born a year after the deaths of her sisters Rosa and Emma.

She moved with her parents to Rangitāne three years later in 1900. A very fair-haired child, Clara was a favourite among the Māori living nearby who loved to have her at the pa. She attended the Rangiotū/Oroua Bridge School. As the youngest girl in a large family, she was somewhat spoilt as a child.

After she finished school, Clara did housework around the district with her family and others before marrying Lionel Purdom in 1920 at All Saints' Anglican Church in Palmerston North. Lionel was the younger brother of her sister Lena's husband Tom - two Alve sisters married two Purdom brothers. Lionel had come north from Timaru where he was born. He worked as a shepherd firstly at Nightcaps, Southland before and then at Pirinoa, South Wairarapa (Busch territory) after the Great War. During this war he served with the NZ army overseas, rising to the rank of sergeant.

After marrying, Clara and Lionel lived for a while at Pirinoa before moving to a small dairy farm on Pyke Road, Bainesse that had belonged to Hedley Wilton. They were able to purchase this with assistance from a rehabilitation loan that Lionel received after his war service. They had a redundant flax mill house transported there from Rangitāne. The farm was near the Simmons'. Clara's sister Theresia and nieces Myra and Micky Simmons would often come over and stay.

They were particularly fond of Aunty Clara's marvelous cooking. It was quite an isolated area, which meant no electricity right up to the time they left this farm. They were dependent on kerosene for lighting and to run the stove. There was also a coal range. Milking machines arrived about 1929. These were driven by an Anderson petrol engine. Eventually a radio was obtained that required batteries which were bulky.

Her only child, Lionel Alve Purdom, who was known as *Alve*, arrived in 1925. He remembers his mum as always being there for him when he got home from school. Clara was active helping Lionel on the farm. Community involvement included membership of the Country Women's Institute which met at Rangiotū.

Alve was about twelve in 1937 when they left the farm which had proved unprofitable, despite their having 'slogged their hearts out' in very poor conditions. After a short stay with Lionel's sister Jeannie Wright and her husband Bob in Roy Street, Palmerston North the family moved into their own home at 67 Stanley Avenue. Lionel took work selling Electrolux vacuum cleaners. Later work during the war had him selling lubricators and oil filters for cars from which he derived a reasonable income. Towards war's end Lionel was relief driving buses for Madge Motors on the Palmerston North - Foxton route. This also involved moving troops to Wellington and Trentham, and Sunday tours around the district.

An interesting anecdote from Lionel's bus driving years tells of him transporting, for payment in kind, mason jars full of whitebait from Foxton to Palmerston. In those days whitebait was plentiful, so much so that son Alve remembers Māoris digging whitebait into their gardens because they could not sell them!

Clara, along with other members of the family, took her turn caring for her aging mother during these years. It was while she was staying with Clara in Palmerston North, her mother Theresia died in 1942.

Without warning, apart from complaining of indigestion, Lionel died of a heart attack in 1952 while still employed as a bus driver. Perhaps the shock of his death led to Clara suffering poor health afterwards. For a time, she lived with her sister Theresia before returning home. Son, Alve left home in 1957, the year Clara sold her home at Stanley Street and moved to Wellsbourne Street.

Niece, Myra Simmons tended her in Clara's latter years, and she notes at the time Clara loved to talk about the Alves and her younger years at Rangitāne. She was saddened the Alves had all moved from Rangitāne. She moved into Willard Home shortly before she died of cancer in 1975 - the last of the thirteen children of Carl and Theresia to pass away. Her death on the 19

September came three months short of the centenary of Carl, Theresia and Mary Alve boarding the Gutenburg at Bremerhaven, Germany for New Zealand on 18 December 1875.

Rupert Adolph Alve (1902-1967)

Figure 58 - Rupert Adolph Alve and Nita Shailer.

Adolph was born soon after his family moved to the Rangitāne farm. He had been promised a nice present for his eighth birthday, but his father died a week before that. He attended Rangiotū School helping his brothers at the same time with milking. He later reported that this was very tiring. Dolph spent some time working with Alf at his Bainesse farm before he returned to farm at Rangitāne, on the block that was to become his on his 21st birthday in 1923. At this time his mother Theresia was living with him and housekeeping - his siblings all married by 1920. Dolph and his mother lived initially in rooms transported from the Rangitāne flax mill by Mr Cawley. These became part of the cowshed that was built on the farm - the house being built later.

During the 1920's Dolph played saxaphone for *Billy Larkin's Elite Orchestra*. This orchestra consisted of two saxaphonists, two violinists, a drummer and Billy Larkins on piano. Between 1923-1925 this involved him several nights per week, which eventually became too much with farm work required during the day! Dolph, like his father and others of the family, was gifted musically. He also played the accordion and claviola.

Dolph met Nita Shailer through her sister Gladys who cared for old Mrs Jane Fawcett next door to the farm. Nita lived at Oroua Downs, and they were married in Palmerston North at the end of 1931.

Dolph was involved with his mother and other family members in the Open Brethren Church, regularly attending meetings in Palmerston North. Later Dolph and Nita joined the Presbyterian Church at Rangiotū. He eventually became a Sunday School teacher there. He later became an elder in St John's Presbyterian Church and the first session clerk at St Marks in Palmerston North. He also served on the School Committee at Rangiotū, serving as chairman for a period.

Dolph and Nita's two sons, Jack (1932) and Dennis (1940), joined them at Rangitāne. Theresia Alve lived with them, and other members of the family, during the 1930's. Her 80th birthday was celebrated at their place in 1936 with Jack, as the youngest grandchild, helping to blow out the candles on her cake. Dairy farming continued through the 1930's as a challenging life, especially with flooding a constant threat. Shortly after Dennis' birth, and life-threatening surgery, the 1941 flood poured water through their farm and home. They were rescued by boat, with Dolph's mother Theresia, and taken to safety at Rangiotū after escaping through the roof. This flood drowned ten cows and, the following year twelve more were condemned with T.B. These out of a herd of forty were a great loss.

In the late 1940's Dolph's health failed, and Eric Jensen was employed to help on the farm, and then Mace Joosten. Charlie Busch, a nephew, began sharemilking on the farm in 1950 and the family moved to their College Street home in Palmerston North. After Charlie moved to Eddie Alve's farm, Dolph's farm was leased: first to Neil Harvey and then to George Little between 1952 and 1962.

In Palmerston North, Dolph became a Rawleighs dealer. His health improved until in 1961, following the death of his brother-in-law Peter Fawcett, he was diagnosed with cancer.

Dolph and Nita returned to the Rangitāne farm with Jack, who began farming it in 1962. Dolph lived until 22 February 1967 having helped Jack on the farm after their return to it. He died of cancer and is buried at the Kelvin Grove cemetery. Nita lived on with Jack (and Mary) after they married, until in 1970 she moved to Palmerston North to care for her brother-in-law Stan Shailer who died in 1975. Thereafter she lived in his house, with a boarder, until her death in 1986.

Appendix Two: First Two Generations in Aotearoa New Zealand

In 1994, when I wrote *Alve Road,* I included a genealogical list of descendants and their marriages to the fourth generation in New Zealand. At that time sensitivity about privacy, legally and socially, was a little more relaxed than it is today. Nowadays the convention (and the law) is that we do not publish details of those living, at least not without their permission. In the lists of the first two generations that follow there are two living Alve descendants and one Alve marriage partner, viz: Ivan, William and Jean Alve. I have permission from them to publish their information.

THERESIA MÖLLERS AND CARL ALVE

Maria Theresia, daughter of Bernard Wilhelm Möllers and Catharina Elisabeth Spahr, was born on Jul. 3, 1856 in Beckum, Münster, North Rhine-Westphalia, Germany and died on Apr. 30, 1942 in Palmerston North, NZ.
Carl Wilhelm (Jnr) Alve was born on Jan. 29, 1849 in Hückeswagen, Germany and died on Sep. 21, 1910 in Palmerston North, NZ. They married on Feb. 14, 1874 in St Augustine's Catholic Church, Gelsenkirchen, Germany.

1ST GENERATION (13 CHILDREN)

Children of Maria Theresia Möllers and Carl Wilhelm (Jnr) Alve

1. Anna Maria Catherina Alve was born on Dec. 1, 1874 in Gelsenkirchen, Germany and died on Aug. 19, 1966 in Wairarapa, NZ.

2. Charles William Alve was born on Dec. 10, 1876 in Featherston, NZ and died on Jun. 22, 1937 in Palmerston North, NZ.

3. Theresia Veronika Alve was born on Oct. 23, 1878 in Featherston, NZ and died on Jul. 27, 1960 in Palmerston North, NZ.

4. Anna Alve was born on Aug. 25, 1880 in Featherston, NZ and died on Mar. 10, 1906 in Rangitāne, Manawatū, NZ.

5. Carolena (Lena) Alve was born on Aug. 28, 1882 in Eketāhuna, NZ and died on Jul. 18, 1934 in Manawatū, NZ.

6. Elizabeth Alve was born on Dec. 14, 1884 in Eketāhuna, NZ and died on Sep. 25, 1966 in Palmerston North, New Zealand.

7. Alfred Ernest Alve was born on Jan. 28, 1887 in Eketāhuna, NZ and died on Jan. 2, 1953 in Palmerston North, NZ.

8. Henry Wilhelm Alve was born on Oct. 19, 1889 in Eketāhuna, NZ and died on Jan. 3, 1968 in Palmerston North, NZ.

9. Edward Otto (Eddie) Alve was born on Jan. 29, 1891 in Eketāhuna, NZ and died on Oct. 30, 1965 in Palmerston North, NZ.

10. Rosa Ellen Alve was born on Jan. 1, 1893 in Eketāhuna, NZ and died on Aug. 21, 1896 in Featherston, NZ.
11. Emma Ida Alve was born on May 9, 1896 in Eketāhuna, NZ and died on May 10, 1896 in Eketāhuna, NZ.

12. Clara Else Alve was born on Jul. 25, 1897 in Featherston, NZ and died on Sep. 19, 1975 in Palmerston North, NZ.

13. Rupert Adolph Alve was born on Sep. 29, 1902 in Rangitāne, Manawatū, NZ and died on Feb. 22, 1967 in Palmerston North, NZ.

IN SUMMARY

Ten of Carl & Theresia's thirteen children married, and nine of these had children. Charlie and Dolly remained childless. The three who did not marry were the girls Anna, Rosa and Emma who died young, between 1896 and 1906, as above. This generation was born from 1874 (Mary) through to 1902 (Rupert Adolph), over twenty-eight years.

1ST GENERATION (WITH PARTNERS & THEIR 36 CHILDREN)

1. Anna Maria Catherina Alve was born on Dec. 1, 1874 in Gelsenkirchen, Germany and died on Aug. 19, 1966 in Wairarapa, NZ. She married George William Henry Busch on Dec. 27, 1898 in Featherston, NZ. George William Henry, son of Hans Heinrich Theodor Busch and Sarah Mercy Streeter, was born on Jun. 11, 1874 in Kaiapoi, Canterbury, NZ. and died on Jan. 5, 1936 in Wairarapa, NZ.

Children of Anna Maria Catherina Alve and George William Henry Busch

1.1. William John Busch

1.2. Frederick George Busch

1.3. John Clifford Stanley Busch

1.4. Theresa Annie Busch

1.5. Rosa Selina Busch

1.6. Charles Henry Alve Busch

1.7. Elizabeth Caroline Busch

1.8. Frank Edward Busch

2. Charles William Alve was born on Dec. 10, 1876 in Featherston NZ and died on Jun. 22, 1937 in Palmerston North NZ. He married Catherine 'Dolly' Wallace on Jul. 13, 1911 in Wallace Res. Eketāhuna, NZ. Catherine 'Dolly', daughter of John Henry 'Jack' Wallace and Ellen Pawson, was born on Jan. 15, 1881 in Head of the Bay, Akaroa, NZ and died on Feb. 18, 1967 in Foxton, Manawatū, NZ.

3. Theresia Veronika Alve was born on Oct. 23, 1878 in Featherston, NZ and died on Jul. 27, 1960 in Palmerston North, NZ. She married Herbert (Bert) Hamilton Couls Simmons on Aug. 27, 1908 in All Saints, Palmerston North, NZ. Bert was born on May 26, 1881 in NZ died on Dec. 20, 1936 in Palmerston North, NZ.

Children of Theresia Veronika Alve and Herbert Hamilton Couls Simmons

3.1. Harold Herbert Simmons

3.2. William Alve Simmons

3.3. Marjorie Veronica Simmons

3.4. Myra Rosa Simmons

3.5. Alice Simmons

3.6. Elza Theresa Simmons

4. Anna Alve was born on Aug. 25, 1880 in Featherston, NZ and died on Mar. 10, 1906 in Rangitāne, Manawatū, NZ.

5. Carolena (Lena) Alve was born on Aug. 28, 1882 in Eketāhuna, NZ and died on Jul. 18, 1934 in Manawatū, NZ. She married Thomas (Tom) Purdom on Apr. 5, 1906 in St Patrick's P.N. Tom, son of William Robert Purdom and Selina Amelia Taylor, was born on Jun. 25, 1879 in Christchurch, NZ - NZBDM 1879/6582 - Tom died on Dec. 5, 1955 in Petone, Wellington, NZ.

Children of Carolena (Lena) Alve and Thomas (Tom) Purdom

5.1. Gwendoline Theresia Purdom

5.2. Daphne Selina Purdom

5.3. Olga Carolena Purdom

5.4. Marion Elizabeth Purdom

6. Elizabeth Alve was born on Dec. 14, 1884 in Eketāhuna, Manawatū-Wanganui, NZ and died on Sep. 25, 1966 in Palmerston North, NZ. She married Peter Pedersen on Jun. 15, 1911 in Oroua, Manawatū-Wanganui, NZ. Peter, son of Celius Pedersen and Catharine Anne Winter, was born on Nov. 9, 1880 in Mauriceville, NZ. and died on Apr. 25, 1953 in Oroua, NZ.

Children of Elizabeth Alve and Peter Pedersen

6.1. Thelma Catherine Elizabeth Pedersen

6.2. Hazel Teresa Nelle Pedersen

6.3. Russell Pedersen

7. Alfred Ernest Alve was born on Jan. 28, 1887 in Eketāhuna, NZ and died on Jan. 2, 1953 in Palmerston North, NZ. He married Florence May Alsop on Dec. 3, 1913. Florence, daughter of Arthur Amos Alsop and Mary Harker, was born on May 23, 1890 in Hanmer Springs, NZ and died on Nov. 16, 1969 in Palmerston North, NZ.

Children of Alfred Ernest Alve and Florence May Alsop

7.1. Freda Meryl Alve

7.2. Noeline May Alve

7.3. Alfred Colin Alve

7.4. Richard Harker Alve

8. Henry Wilhelm Alve was born on Oct. 19, 1889 in Eketāhuna, NZ and died on Jan. 3, 1968 in Palmerston North, NZ. He married Theresa Christina Wagner on Mar. 7, 1917 in All Saints, Palmerston North, NZ. Theresa Christina, daughter of Philip Conrad Wagner and Caroline Maria Hauke, was born on Sep. 18, 1888 in Spring Bay, Tasmania, Australia and died on Feb. 8, 1971 in Palmerston North, NZ.

Children of Henry Wilhelm Alve and Theresa Christina Wagner

8.1. Phillip Carl Alve

8.2. Valentine Wagner Alve

8.3. Henry Adolph Alve

8.4. Ivan Charles Alve

9. Edward Otto (Eddie) Alve was born on Jan. 29, 1891 in Eketāhuna, NZ and died on Oct. 30, 1965 in Palmerston North, NZ.

He married 1st Laura Spink on Jul. 22, 1915 in Palmerston North, NZ. Laura, daughter of Ezra Williamson Spink and Elvira Thomas, was born on Aug. 28, 1891 in Cardiff, Wales and died on Nov. 21, 1962 in Hastings, NZ.

He married 2nd Mona Comforth Simpson on Dec. 16, 1943 in Palmerston North, NZ. Mona Comforth, daughter of George Gerard Augustus Lovelock Simpson and Sarah Ann Westwood, was born on Jan. 25, 1899 in Foxton, NZ and died on Jan. 30, 1944 in Palmerston North, NZ.

He married 3rd Ina Daphne Rasmussen on Jun. 12, 1951 in Otaki, NZ. Ina Daphne, daughter of Frederick William Rasmussen and Annie Robinson, was born on Jun. 26, 1920 in Palmerston North, NZ and died on Sep. 3, 1993 in Palmerston North, NZ.

Children of Edward Otto (Eddie) Alve and Laura Spink

9.1. Lisle Edward Ezra Alve

9.2. Elvene Laura Alve

9.3. Hilton Alve

Children of Edward Otto (Eddie) Alve and Ina Daphne Rasmussen

9.4. William Edward Alve

10. Rosa Ellen Alve was born on Jan. 1, 1893 in Eketāhuna, NZ and died on Aug. 21, 1896 in Featherston NZ.

11. Emma Ida Alve was born on May 9, 1896 in Eketāhuna, NZ and died on May 10, 1896 in Eketāhuna, NZ.

12. Clara Else Alve was born on Jul. 25, 1897 in Featherston, NZ and died on Sep. 19, 1975 in Palmerston North, NZ. She married Lionel Saunders Purdom on Mar. 24, 1920 in Palmerston North, NZ. Lionel Saunders, son of William Robert Purdom and Selina Amelia Taylor, was born on Jan. 25, 1890 in Timaru, NZ (Poss. b. 4 Jan 1890 - NZBDM 1890/8104) and died on Jun. 6, 1952 in Palmerston North, NZ - NZBDM 1952/30934.

Children of Clara Else Alve and Lionel Saunders Purdom

12.1. Lionel Alve Purdom

13. Rupert Adolph Alve was born on Sep. 29, 1902 in Rangitāne, Manawatū, NZ and died on Feb. 22, 1967 in Palmerston North, NZ. He married Nita Maud Shailer on Dec. 9, 1931 in Palmerston North, NZ. Nita Maud, daughter of Charles Henry Shailer and Elizabeth Ann Collis, was born on Sep. 4, 1909 in Carnarvon, NZ and died on Oct. 22, 1986 in Palmerston North, NZ.

Children of Rupert Adolph Alve and Nita Maud Shailer

13.1. Jack Reginald Alve

13.2. Dennis Charles William Alve

2ND GENERATION (37 GRANDCHILDREN & PARTNERS)

1.1. William John Busch was born on Jul. 23, 1900 in Pirinoa NZ and died on Dec. 24, 1996 in Masterton, NZ. He married Mabel Brown on Oct. 12, 1922 in Pirinoa, NZ. Mabel, daughter of Norman (Twin) Brown and Robina Liddle, was born on Mar. 22, 1902 in Leicester, UK and died on Jul. 11, 1957 in Masterton, NZ.

1.2. Frederick George Busch was born on Jul. 21, 1902 in Wairarapa, NZ and died on Jan. 14, 1984. He married Aura Wilmer Rhoda Simmons. Aura Wilmer Rhoda was born on May 18, 1900 and died on Jun. 26, 1982.

1.3. John Clifford Stanley Busch was born on Jul. 22, 1904 in Wairarapa, NZ and died on Mar. 6, 1985. He married 1st Hazel Lilian Russell in 1929 in New Zealand. Hazel Lilian was born in 1909 in Waimate, Canterbury, NZ and died on an unknown date.
He married 2nd Nola Margaret Dryden. Nola Margaret, daughter of Albert Edward Dryden and Eleanor Margaret Morris, was born on Dec. 11, 1915 in Napier, Hawke's Bay, NZ and died on Nov. 7, 1979 in Wellington, NZ.

1.4. Theresa Annie Busch was born on Dec. 6, 1905 in South Featherston, NZ and died on Sep. 13, 2001 in Carterton, NZ. She married Charles Cecil Emmens on Jun. 1, 1927 in NZ. Charles Cecil, son of (Unknown) and Marion May Emmens, was born on Jun. 8, 1905 in South Bend, St. Joseph, Indiana, USA and died on Jul. 24, 1980 in 27 Bethune Street, Featherston, Wairarapa, NZ.

1.5. Rosa Selina Busch was born on Jan. 15, 1908 in South Featherston, Wairarapa, NZ and died on Apr. 18, 1996 in Lakeland Health Hospital, Rotorua, NZ.
She married 1st Francis Harold Rangi on Sep. 18, 1929 in New Zealand. Francis Harold was born on Dec. 6, 1905 in NZ and died in 1973 in Putaruru, Waikato, NZ.
She married 2nd Hune Tokoarangi Te Maari on Oct. 3, 1947 in Masterton, NZ. Hune, son of Tokoarangi Te Maari and Meremionga Hiroti, was born on Dec. 13, 1920 in Pirinoa, NZ and died on Mar. 25, 1974 in Masterton, NZ.

1.6. Charles Henry Alve Busch was born on Sep. 19, 1911 in Wairarapa, NZ and died on Dec. 11, 1987 in Palmerston North, NZ. He married Vera Gwendoline Thomas in Feb. 1939 in Pirinoa, NZ. Vera Gwendoline was born on Apr. 6, 1912 and died on Dec. 5, 1987 in Palmerston North, NZ.

1.7. Elizabeth Caroline Busch was born on Feb. 17, 1914 in Pirinoa, NZ and died on Sep. 6, 2004 in Hutt Hospital, Lower Hutt, NZ. She married Charles Owen Evans in Martinborough, NZ. Charles Owen, son of Frederick Owen Evans and Alice Maud Garrett, was born on Jun. 18, 1901 in Mangaweka, Rangitikei, NZ and died in 1987 in Wellington, NZ.

1.8. Frank Edward Busch was born on Jun. 14, 1916 in NZ and died on Mar. 30, 1983 in Masterton Hospital, NZ. He married Wilma Ellen Herrick on Aug. 26, 1944. Wilma Ellen was born on Sep. 21, 1925 in Martinborough, Wairarapa, NZ and died on Dec. 24, 2004.

3.1. Harold Herbert Simmons was born on Sep. 23, 1909 in Palmerston North, NZ and died on Apr. 23, 1991 in Palmerston North, NZ.

3.2. William Alve Simmons was born on May 26, 1911 in Mangawhata, Manawatū, NZ and died on Jun. 16, 1913.

3.3. Marjorie Veronica Simmons was born on May 7, 1912 in Mangawhata, Manawatū, NZ and died on Oct. 3, 1976 in Katikati, NZ. She married Edmund Stanbra on May 10, 1933 in All Saints Palmerston North, NZ. Edmund was born on Jun. 28, 1902 in Wiggington, Oxfordshire, UK and died on Jul. 5, 1965 in Katikati, NZ.

3.4. Myra Rosa Simmons was born on Sep. 9, 1916 in Mangawhata, Manawatū, NZ and died on Feb. 4, 2001 in Palmerston North, NZ.
She married 1st Arthur Alexander Jennings on Dec. 23, 1937 in Palmerston North, NZ. Arthur Alexander, son of Thomas Percy Jennings and Susan Ada Thompson, was born on Dec. 7, 1909 in Portsmouth, Hampshire, UK and died on Mar. 25, 1988 in Palmerston North, NZ.
She married 2nd Cecil Percy Jennings on Aug. 6, 1948 in Palmerston North, NZ. Cecil Percy, son of Thomas Percy Jennings and Susan Ada Thompson, was born on Dec. 7, 1909 in Portsmouth, Hampshire, UK and died on Jul. 16, 2000 in Palmerston North, NZ.

3.5. Alice Simmons was born on Jul. 26, 1917 in Mangawhata, Manawatū, NZ and died on Jul. 27, 1917 in Mangawhata, NZ.

3.6. Elza Theresa Simmons was born on Oct. 2, 1918 in Palmerston North, NZ and died on Dec. 8, 1978 in Auckland, NZ. She married William Henry Rhol Ellis in Feb. 1942 in Auckland, NZ. William Henry Rhol, son of Henry William Ellis and Margaret Mary Hall, was born on Sep. 8, 1906 in Auckland, NZ and died on Jun. 20, 1975 in Auckland, NZ.

5.1. Gwendoline Theresia Purdom was born on Jun. 28, 1907 in Rangitāne, Manawatū, NZ and died on May 17, 1999 in Timaru, New Zealand. She married Robert Frederick Davie on Feb. 25, 1932 in the Registry Office, Timaru, NZ. Robert Frederick was born on Feb. 10, 1909 in South Canterbury, NZ and died on Aug. 27, 1994 in Timaru, NZ.

5.2. Daphne Selina Purdom was born on Oct. 7, 1908 in Rangitāne, Manawatū NZ (NZBDM 1908/23917 with spelling errors) and died on May 31, 1991 in Napier, NZ. She married Charles

Reckin on Jul. 14, 1939 in Wellington, NZ. Charles, son of Herman Richard Paul Reckin and Babetta Kuhn, was born on May 7, 1899 in London, UK and died on May 26, 1980 in Napier, NZ.

5.3. Olga Carolena Purdom was born on Dec. 4, 1915 in Palmerston North, NZ and died on Jul. 28, 1999 in Greytown, NZ.
She married 1st (Unknown).
She married 2nd Archibald (Jack) Palenski on Aug. 6, 1938 in Palmerston North, NZ. Archibald (Jack), son of Axubold Karl Herman (Arnold or Paddy) Palenski and Andria Gloria (Elori) Madsen, was born on Nov. 14, 1912 in Halcombe, Manawatū District, NZ and died on Apr. 30, 1961 in Palmerston North, NZ.

5.4. Marion Elizabeth Purdom was born on Jun. 7, 1921 in Palmerston North, NZ and died on Oct. 12, 2012 in New Zealand. She married Arthur Miritene Karipa. Arthur Miritene, son of Herepete Ihaka Karipa and Alice Cole, was born on Jan. 25, 1920 in Awahuri, Manawatū, NZ and died on Jan. 3, 1986 in Hamilton, NZ.

6.1. Thelma Catherine Elizabeth Pedersen was born on Jan. 20, 1914 in Palmerston North, NZ and died on Sep. 4, 2013 in Palmerston North, NZ. She married Thomas Handley Vernon Avery on Jun. 5, 1941 in All Saints Anglican Church, Palmerston North, NZ. Thomas Handley Vernon, son of Henry Avery and Florence Hunt, was born on Feb. 24, 1917 in Pahiatua, NZ and died on May 2, 1991 in Kelvin Grove, Palmerston North, NZ.

6.2. Hazel Teresa Nelle Pedersen was born on Jul. 6, 1915 in Ohakea, Manawatū, NZ and died on Jul. 9, 2004 in Palmerston North, NZ. She married Leonard McCarthy D'Arcy Bailey on Aug. 14, 1940 in Palmerston North, NZ. Leonard McCarthy D'Arcy, son of Leonard McCarthy Bailey and Florence Kathleen Mora, was born on Aug. 4, 1918 in Christchurch, NZ and died on Oct. 4, 1983 in Levin, NZ.

6.3. Russell Pedersen was born on Dec. 12, 1918 in Palmerston North, NZ and died on Oct. 14, 2006 in Nanaimo, British Columbia, Canada. He married Thelma Gwendoline Louisa Cooksley on Mar. 28, 1940 in Palmerston North, NZ. Thelma Gwendoline Louisa, daughter of Isaac Daniel Sage Cooksley and Maude Violet Aldridge, was born on Jun. 25, 1923 in Mangawhata, Manawatū, NZ and died on Sep. 3, 2014 in Nanaimo, British Columbia, Canada.

7.1. Freda Meryl Alve was born on Oct. 28, 1916 in Palmerston North, NZ and died on Nov. 24, 2009 in Hawkes Bay, NZ. She married Allan Evan McPherson on Sep. 6, 1939 in Palmerston

North, NZ. Allan Evan, son of Alfred Campbell McPherson and Ann Lillian Tillyard, was born on Feb. 2, 1910 in Eketāhuna, NZ and died on Jun. 8, 1981 in Pahiatua, NZ.

7.2. Noeline May Alve was born on Mar. 24, 1920 in Palmerston North, NZ and died on Jul. 4, 2012 in Arohanui Hospice, Palmerston North, NZ. She married Alfred Harold King on Apr. 30, 1955 in St Paul's Church, Palmerston North, NZ. Alfred Harold was born on Jun. 28, 1920 in Feilding, NZ and died on Oct. 29, 2004 in Palmerston North, NZ.

7.3. Alfred Colin Alve was born on Aug. 31, 1921 in Palmerston North, NZ and died on Feb. 5, 2006 in Palmerston North, NZ. He married Margaret Rose Gillanders on May 9, 1970 in Palmerston North, NZ. Margaret Rose, daughter of Edward Charles (Sandy) Gillanders and Ivy Mildred Haycock, was born on Nov. 30, 1923 in Palmerston North, NZ and died on Mar. 18, 1987 in Palmerston North, NZ.

7.4. Richard Harker Alve was born on Aug. 21, 1923 in Palmerston North, NZ and died on Aug. 22, 1923.

8.1. Phillip Carl Alve was born on Dec. 8, 1918 in Palmerston North, NZ and died on Jul. 20, 2012 in Palmerston North, NZ.

8.2. Valentine Wagner Alve was born on Sep. 30, 1923 in Palmerston North, NZ and died on Oct. 4, 1999 in Palmerston North Hospital, NZ. He married Joyce Mildred Elcox on Feb. 3, 1951 in Palmerston North, NZ. Joyce Mildred, daughter of Thomas Richard Elcox and Annie Mabel Farmer, was born on Nov. 19, 1929 in Palmerston North, NZ and died on Aug. 12, 2015 in Palmerston North, NZ.

8.3. Henry Adolph Alve was born on May 25, 1926 in Palmerston North, NZ and died on Jun. 15, 2004 in Longburn, Manawatū, NZ.

8.4. Ivan Charles Alve was born on Jun. 17, 1931 in Palmerston North, NZ. He married Maree Olive Marston on Feb. 7, 1953 in Palmerston North, NZ. Maree Olive, daughter of Ernest Stanley Marston and Daphne Madge Burton, was born on Dec. 31, 1932 in Palmerston North, NZ and died on Sep. 2, 1996 in Palmerston North Hospital, NZ.

9.1. Lisle Edward Ezra Alve was born on Mar. 18, 1917 in Palmerston North, NZ and died on Jan. 6, 2006 in Hastings, NZ. He married Elizabeth Matekino (Liz) Walker on Aug. 26, 1948. Elizabeth Matekino (Liz), daughter of Walker and Merekahia Savage, was born on Mar. 18, 1922 in Te Kaha, NZ and died on Jun. 30, 2003 in Hastings, Hawke's Bay, NZ.

9.2. Elvene Laura Alve was born on Jan. 29, 1920 in Palmerston North, NZ and died on Oct. 19, 1996 in Taurima Rest Home, New Plymouth, NZ. She married Edwin James Peter Meech on Jun. 9, 1951 in St Andrews Church, Palmerston North, NZ. Edwin James Peter, son of Ernest Augustus Meech and Jeannie Forsythe, was born on May 6, 1916 in Masterton, NZ and died on Sep. 19, 1994 in Taurima Rest Home, New Plymouth, NZ.

9.4. Hilton Alve was born on Mar. 15, 1926 in Palmerston North, NZ and died on Sep. 24, 2015 in Taupo, NZ. He married Margaret Jean Parker on Dec. 16, 1950 in Woodville, NZ. Margaret Jean, daughter of Percy George Parker and Alice Lusk, was born on Jan. 18, 1931 in Waitara, NZ.

9.5. William Edward Alve was born on Apr. 6, 1955 in Palmerston North, NZ.

12.1. Lionel Alve Purdom was born on May 27, 1925 in Palmerston North, NZ and died on Mar. 29, 2015 in Palmerston North, NZ. He married Lila May Grundy on Jun. 7, 1958 in Whanganui, NZ. Lila May was born on Apr. 21, 1931 in Palmerston North, NZ and died on Sep. 13, 2013 in Wanganui, NZ.

13.1. Jack Reginald Alve was born on Jun. 5, 1932 in Palmerston North, NZ and died on Oct. 5, 2005 in Palmerston North, NZ. He married Mary Elizabeth Fawcett on Jun. 28, 1969 in Methodist Trinity Church, Palmerston North, N.Z. Mary Elizabeth, daughter of William James Fawcett and Florence Ethel Mary Shailer, was born on Oct. 30, 1931 in Palmerston North, NZ and died on Aug. 14, 2011 in Whanganui, NZ.

13.2. Dennis Charles William Alve was born on Jun. 4, 1940 in Palmerston North, NZ and died on Aug. 14, 2010 in Palmerston North, NZ.
He married 1st Heather Mildred Stirling on Jul. 2, 1966. Heather Mildred, daughter of William David Stirling and Ida Meryl Wilton, was born on Mar. 12, 1947 in Palmerston North, NZ.
He married 2nd Marelyn Irene Gage on Mar. 5, 1983 in Hamilton, NZ. Marelyn Irene, daughter of David John Gage, was born on Dec. 21,1946 in Whakatane, NZ and died on Nov. 18, 2005 in Queensland, Australia.
He married 3rd Gayle Roth Harris on Apr. 18, 2009 in Palmerston North, NZ. Gayle was born on Apr. 9, 1937 and died on Nov. 26, 2018 in Palmerston North, NZ.

SURVIVING SECOND GENERATION DESCENDANTS

Figure 59 - Ivan Alve (1931-)
Henry's Son.

Figure 60 - Jean Alve (1931-)
Hilton's Wife.

Figure 61 - William Alve (1955-)
Eddie's Son.

THIRD GENERATION DESCENDANTS

Figure 62 - Nelson Rangi (1929-)
Eldest surviving 3rd Generation Descendant (2024).

Figure 63 - Julianne Alve (1973-)
Youngest 3rd Generation Descendant.

IN SUMMARY

These first-generation descendants bore 37 children in the second generation – mokopuna for Theresia and Carl. These second-generation children arrived 1900 (Bill Busch) to 1940 (Dennis Alve), over forty years.

The second-generation descendants bore 95 children – more mokopuna for Theresia and Carl. These third-generation descendants arrived from 1923 (Ray Busch) to 1973 (Julianne Alve), over fifty years.

While we do not have an exact count, I expect that there are about two fifty descendants born in the fourth generation. 197 of these are recorded in *Alve Road* published at the end of 1994 and currently 210 of the fourth generation are in *My Heritage* family tree (2024). I have assumed 250 fourth generation descendants for the sake of the graph below. This fourth generation began with the birth of Warwick Leslie Busch to Ken and Rosalie Busch on 29 October 1947 and ended with Liam John Gordon Alve's birth to John and Ellen late in 2001, according to my records. A time span of fifty-four years.

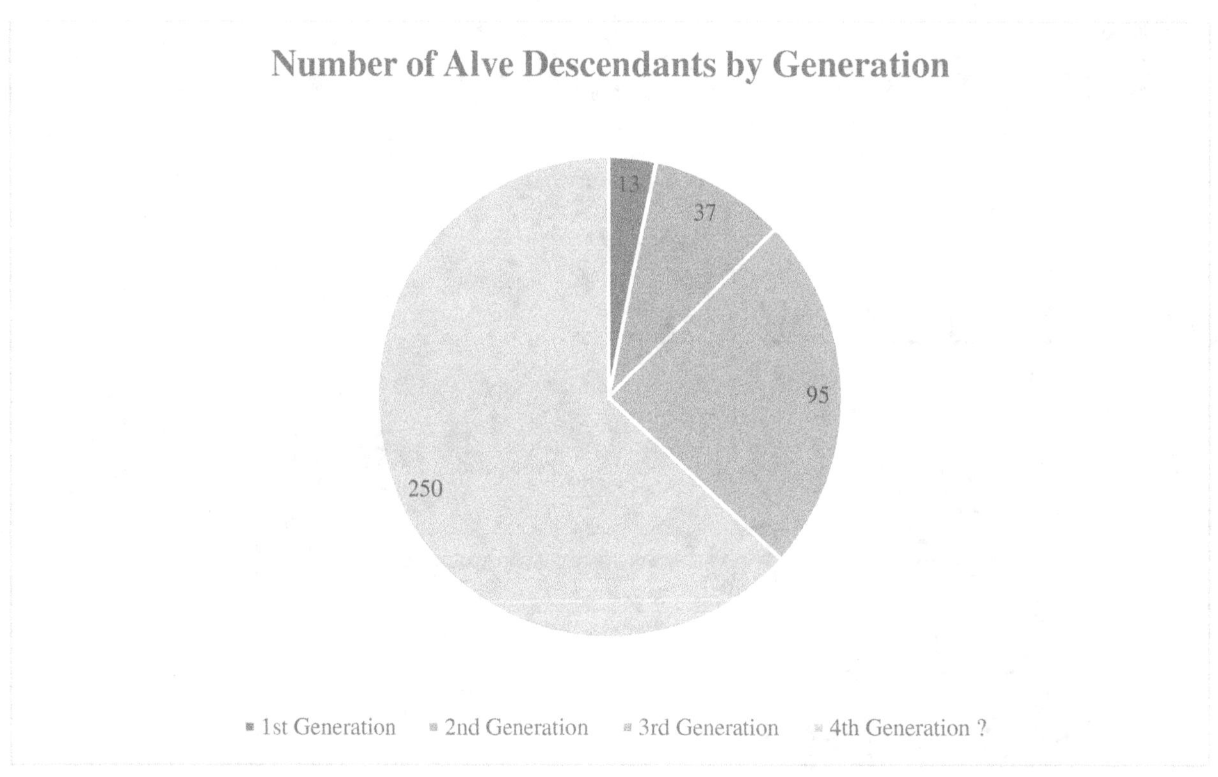

Figure 64 - Number of Alve Descendants over Four Generations.

Appendix Three: The Gutenburg Passenger List

HAMBURG/BREMERHAVEN TO WELLINGTON

File IM 15/258 - National Archives, Wellington, N.Z.
Left: Bremerhaven, Germany on 18 December 1875
Arrived: Wellington, New Zealand on 23 March 1876

1 RASMUSSEN Rasmus SM 26 Denmark Labourer

2 DINESEN Johan Fr. SM 27 Denmark Labourer

3 LYNGBY Jacob W SM 25 Denmark Labourer

4 JENSEN Chr. Hansz SM 23 Denmark Labourer

5 JOHANSEN Jens Chr. SM 22 Denmark Labourer

6 GARAZZA Lucia SW 32 Italy Servant

7 ANTICO Carlo MM 32 Italy Labourer Nicolina MW 34

8 CALAMAI Egisto MM 34 Italy Labourer Alsunta MW 26

9 SMIDT Tulma SW 22 Denmark Servant

10 HANSEN Simon SM 20 Denmark Labourer

11 SCHULZE Heinrich SM 29 Prussia Labourer

12 HAASE Wilhelm MM 38 Prussia Labourer Franzisca MW 32

13 JANSSAN Johan SM 21 Sweden Labourer

14 RUSTERHOLZ Ferdinand SM 26 Italy Labourer

15 BAY Harold SM 19 Norway Labourer

16 HANSEN Christen E. SM 31 Norway Labourer

17 STENBERG Johan E. SM 19 Norway Labourer

18 SMITH Harold SM 30 Norway Labourer

19 STENBERG Axel SM 16 Norway Labourer

20 TORKILDSEN Laurtz MM 44 Norway Labourer Anna MW 33 Rudolf B 8 Torkild B 6
Helene G 3 Hans I 6mo.

21 HANSEN Oline SW 35 Norway Servant

22 JACOBSEN Jacob L MM 26 Norway Labourer Theoline MW 25

23 STENBERG Amalie SW 23 Norway Servant Mathildr G 11½

24 PETERSEN Christina C. SW 19 Norway Servant

25 HENDRICKSEN Johannz SW 22 Norway Servant

26 HAUSEN Camilla SW 18 Denmark Servant

27 MEYER Johann D. SW 24 Denmark Servant

28 SURVY Victor SM 27 Prussia Labourer

29 BRIESEMANN Neins SM 25 Prussia Farmer

30 JENSEN Ane Margt. SW 25 Denmark Servant

31 PEDERSEN Niels SM 29 Denmark Labourer

32 RUDOLPHI Paoli SM 20 Italy Labourer

33 GILASIO Landi SM 23 Italy Labourer

34 MORADEI Auguste SM 23 Italy Labourer

35 MEYER August SM 34 Saxony Labourer

36 POLIT Julius SM 28 Prussia Labourer

37 SCHIPPER August SM 16 Austria Labourer

38 NIELSEN Ane Margt. SW 45 Denmark Marie G 9½ Niels B 3

39 PAASKE Jorgen SM 17 Scheswig Labourer

40 NIELSEN Anders SM 23 Denmark Labourer

41 RENNER Julius SM 36 Hanover Machinist

42 GEORG Christensen SM 45 Prussia Farm Lab.

43 BARDASINI Salvatore MM 26 Italy Farm Lab. Maria MW 22

44 (no entry)

45 ERMER Franz MM 40 Prussia Farm Lab. Pauline MW 38

46 PRENNS Gottfried SM 40 Prussia Farm Lab.

47 LIEBGUT August SM 32 Prussia Farm Lab.

48 WIDMAIN Georg SM 41 Prussia Farm Lab.

49 WALLAT Friedrick MM 26 Prussia Farm Lab. Caroline MW 25 Otto B 1½

50 BARCHERT Gustav SM 24 Prussia Farm Lab.

51 GHEZZANE Pilade SM 21 Italy Farm Lab.

52 FRANDI Aristodome MM 34 Italy Farm Lab. Anarchiate MW 35 Franzisca B 9 Asco B1½ Italia G 6

53 TURCHI Carlo MM 45 Italy Labourer Zantina MW 35 Maria SW 17 Carola SW 13 Erico B 9 Louisa G 8 Emma G 5 Catharina G 3 Franzcisco I 6mo.

54 BIANCHINI Antonia MM 36 Italy Labourer Louisa MW 26 Odovardo B 4

55 SIMIAN Essila SW 16 Italy

56 VOLTI Cesare SM 20 Italy Labourer

57 CORRADO Pietro SM 22 Italy Labourer

58 GAMANASI Dante SM 25 Italy Labourer

59 GERMANO Giuseppe SM 31 Italy Labourer

60 KLEEMAN Wilhelm MM 43 Prussia Farm Lab. Auguste MW 43 Emilie G 7

61 FIEINUS Carl MM 28 Prussia Farm Lab. Bertha MW 28

62 BERTHOLD Wilhelm MM 49 Prussia Farm Lab. Wilhelmine MW 49 Emil SM 14

63 MUDRACK Robert MM 24 Prussia Farm Lab. Auguste MW 23 Martha I 9mo.

64 BIEDOW Rudolph MM 38 Prussia Farm Lab. Marie MW 44 Reinhold SM 15 Anna SW 13

65 MAUL Friedrich MM 34 Prussia Farm Lab. Wilhelmine MW 35 Friedrich B 9½ Wilhelmine G 7

66 MALLGRAFF Johann MM 40 Prussia Farm Lab. Johanna MW 49 Clara SW 15 Auguste G 11? WEISS Pauline SW 45 Prussia

67 WEISSE Paul Julius SM 23 Prussia Labourer

68 SCHIRNACK Carl MM 42 Prussia Labourer Wilhelmine MW 38 Franzisca SW Emil SM 17

69 NISSEN Georg SM 28 Prussia Farm Lab.

70 KOHLER Ewald MM 38 Prussia Farm Lab. Auguste MW 35 Waldemar B 11 Hedwig G 7

71 HOFFMANN Heinr. SM 35 Prussia Farm Lab.

72 LENZ Wilhelm MM 22 Prussia Farm Lab Alma MW 27

73 MANZ Friedrich MM 47 Prussia Farm Lab. Pauline MW 45 Bertha SW 18 Otto SM 15 Auguste G 11 Emma G 9 Minna G 3

74 SOMMER Heinrich SM 34 Prussia Farm Lab.

75 ALVES Carl MM 27 Prussia Farm Lab. Marie MW 20 Anna G 1½

76 SCHORMANN Heinrich MM 33 Prussia Farm Lab. Dorothea MW 27 Friedrich B 6 Marie G 1½

77 FOSELLO Marco MM 30 Italy Labourer Otavia MW 20

78 TOFAUOIE Benoenuto MM 26 Italy Labourer Albiva MW 30 Feresiua G 2

79 MASCHINI Alfonso SM 30 Italy Labourer

80 PIRLEONI Rafaello MM 36 Italy Labourer Julia MW 22 Ida G 3

81 BINI Guiseppe MM 36 Italy Labourer Marianne MW 36

82 BERGER Hermann SM 29 Saxony Labourer

83 FRIKKER Clemens SM 48 Switzerland Labourer

84 FREI Melchior SM 21 Switzerland Labourer

85 FREI Carl SM 23 Switzerland Labourer

86 HABER Gottleib MM 27 Switzerland Labourer Elise MW 26 Rosiuis I 6mo.

87 MULLER Johannes SM 23 Switzerland Labourer

88 SCHMIED Johann SM 30 Switzerland Labourer

89 SCOPLER Emerensia SW 20 Switzerland Servant

90 FEDERLI Giovanni SM 35 Italy Labourer

91 BIERL Alexandra SM 22 Italy Labourer

92 M SM 28 Italy Labourer

KEY: SM – Single man; MM – Married man; SW – Single woman; MW – Married woman; G – Girl; B – Boy; I – Infant (under 1).

Appendix Four: Closing the Historical Gap

Know Your History; Know Yourself!

The following abbreviated summary [lxi] of the history of Germany and German-speaking peoples is offered to fill the gap between our pre-historic forbears and the immediate aftermath of the Franco-Prussian war of 1871. This summary is taken from a *New World Encyclopedia* online article about *Germany*. The online version contains liberal imagery and other enhancements that may invite you to consider reading this information there. I found this summary of German history to be the best I have discovered to date.

-o-OO-o-

"People from the eastern Mediterranean began working copper and tin deposits in central Germany, Bohemia, and Austria about 2500 B.C.E. Around 2300 B.C.E., battleaxe-wielding Indo-Europeans, probably from southern Russia, settled in northern and central Germany, while Slavic peoples settled in the east, and Celts in the south and west. The Bell-Beaker people, who were skilled metalworkers, moved east from Spain and Portugal about the year 2000 B.C.E., and developed a thriving Bronze Age culture in Germany. From 1800 to 400 B.C.E., Celtic people in southern Germany and Austria developed the Urnfield, Hallstatt, and La Tène metalworking cultures, introduced the use of iron for tools and weapons, and used ox-drawn ploughs and wheeled vehicles.

Under Augustus (63 B.C.E. to 14 C.E.), the Roman General Publius Quinctilius Varus began to invade Germania (a term used by the Romans for territory from the Rhine to the Urals), and it was in this period that the Germanic tribes became familiar with Roman tactics of warfare.

The Christian Era (C.E.)

In 9 C.E., three Roman legions led by Varus were defeated by the Cheruscan leader Arminius in the Battle of the Teutoburg Forest. Modern Germany, as far as the Rhine and the Danube, thus remained outside the Roman Empire. By 100 C.E., the time of Tacitus' Germania, Germanic tribes settled along the Rhine and the Danube (the Limes Germanicus), occupying most of the area of modern Germany. The third century saw the emergence of a number of large West Germanic tribes: Alamanni, Franks, Chatti, Saxons, Frisians, Sicambri, and Thuringii.

In 376, the emperor Valens admitted Visigoths as allies to farm and defend the frontier. In the fourth and fifth centuries, nomadic Huns, sweeping in from Asia, set off waves of migration, during which the Ostrogoths, Visigoths, Vandals, Franks, Lombards, and other Germanic peoples overran the Roman Empire.

The Roman provinces north of the Alps had been Christianized since the fourth century and dioceses such as that of Augsburg were maintained after the end of the Roman Empire. However, from around 600, Irish-Scottish monks founded monasteries at Würzburg, Regensburg, Reichenau, and other places. The missionary activity in the Merovingian kingdom was continued by the Anglo-Saxon monk Boniface (672–754), who established the first monastery east of the Rhine Fritzlar, about 200km east of Hückeswagen. Bishoprics under papal authority were established.

Clovis I (c. 466 – 511) conquered neighboring Frankish tribes and established himself as sole king. He succeeded his father Childeric I in 481 as King of the Salian Franks, who occupied the area west of the lower Rhine, with their center around Tournai and Cambrai along the modern frontier between France and Belgium. Clovis converted to Roman Catholicism, as opposed to the Arianism common among Germanic peoples, at the instigation of his wife, the Burgundian Clotilda, a Catholic. He was baptized in the Cathedral of Rheims. This act was of immense importance in the subsequent history of France and Western Europe in general, for Clovis expanded his dominion over almost all of the old Roman province of Gaul (roughly modern France). He is considered the founder both of France (which his state closely resembled geographically at his death) and the Merovingian dynasty which ruled the Franks from the mid-fifth to the mid-eighth century. Merovingian rule was ended by a palace coup in 751 when Pippin the Short formally deposed Childeric III, beginning the Carolingian monarchy.

The Carolingian Dynasty (751-c.900)

The Carolingian dynasty (known variously as the Carlovingians or Karlings) was a Frankish noble family with its origins in the Arnulfing and Pippinid clans of the seventh century. The name Carolingian itself comes from Charles Martel, who lived from 686 to 741 (from the Latin Carolus Martellus), who defeated the Moors at the Battle of Tours in 732. The greatest Carolingian monarch was Charlemagne (742 or 747 to 814), a champion of Christianity and supporter of the papacy. Charlemagne fought the Slavs south of the Danube, annexed southern Germany, and subdued and converted pagan Saxons in the northwest. Charlemagne had himself crowned Emperor by Pope Leo III at Rome in 800, an event which revived the Roman imperial tradition in the west and set a precedent for the dependence of the emperors on papal approval. He is often seen as the Father of Europe and is an iconic figure, instrumental in defining European identity. His was the first truly imperial power in the West since the fall of Rome.

Latin was the official language of the court and the Church, although the West Franks in Gaul adopted the Latinate vernacular that became French. East Franks and other Germanic people spoke various languages that became German. Carolingian rulers encouraged missionary work among the Germans. Non-Frankish Germans, however, retained much pagan belief beneath their newly acquired faith.

The Carolingians had the practice of making their sons (sub-)kings in the various regions (regna) of the Empire, which they would inherit on the death of their father. They also followed the traditional Frankish (and Merovingian) practice of dividing inheritances among heirs, instead of passing everything to the eldest son (primogeniture). The Carolingians disallowed inheritance to illegitimate offspring.

Charlemagne's third son Louis the Pious (778–840) was Emperor and King of the Franks from 814 to his death in 840. The surviving adult Carolingians fought a three-year civil war ending in the Treaty of Verdun (843), which divided the empire among Charlemagne's three grandsons. One received West Francia (modern France), another acquired the imperial title and a territory extending from the North Sea to Italy, while the third, Louis the German (804–876), received East Francia (modern Germany). The Treaty of Mersen (870) divided the middle kingdom, with Lotharingia going to East Francia and the rest to West Francia. In 881, Charles the Fat (839–888) of East Francia, heir of Louis the German, received the imperial title. Six years later he was deposed by Arnulf of Carinthia (850–899), a bastard child of a legitimate Carolingian king, the last Carolingian emperor.

By the tenth century, pagan Danes, Magyars, and Moravians invaded East Francia from the north and east, while rival Frankish tribes fought. The Carolingians had granted lands as temporary fiefs to dukes (tribal military leaders), counts (appointed officials), and clergy for their services to the state. As central royal authority declined, feudal lords provided local government and defense, and the fiefs became hereditary. The five main duchies were Franconia, Swabia, Bavaria, Saxony, and Lorraine. Lesser warriors served dukes out of tribal loyalty and in exchange for grants of land. Common people lost the right to bear arms and worked the fields in return for protection and a share of the crops. By ancient German tradition, the kings were elected, a system that delayed the emergence of a strong German state.

Germanic Peoples United

The last Carolingian died without an heir, so the Franks and Saxons elected Conrad, Duke of Franconia (890–918), as their king, who proved incompetent. Next elected was the Saxon Duke Henry I (876–936), the Fowler, a sober, practical soldier, who made peace with a rival king, defeated Magyars and Slavs, and regained Lorraine. He united the Germanic peoples (Franks, Saxons, Swabians, and Bavarians) and for the first time, the term Kingdom (Empire) of the Germans (Regnum Teutonicorum) was applied to a Frankish kingdom, even though teutonicorum meant something closer to 'Realm of the Germanic peoples.'

In 936, Otto I the Great (912–973) was crowned at Aachen. He strengthened the royal authority by appointing bishops and abbots as princes of the Empire (Reichsfürsten), thereby establishing a national church (Reichskirche). Outside threats to the kingdom were contained with the decisive defeat of the Magyars of Hungary near Augsburg at the Battle of Lechfeld in 955 and the subjugation of Slavs between the Elbe and the Oder rivers. In 962, Otto I was crowned emperor in Rome, taking the succession of Charlemagne and establishing a strong Frankish influence over the papacy.

Otto became entangled in Italy, a rich land, and a scene of feudal disorder and Saracen invasions. When Adelheid, widowed queen of the Lombards, asked Otto for help against her captor, Berengar, King of Italy, Otto invaded Italy in 951, and married the widowed Queen, thereby winning the Lombard crown. Pope John XII appealed to Otto for aid against Berengar, so Otto invaded Italy a second time, defeated Berengar, and was crowned Emperor by the pope in 962. A treaty called the Ottonian Privilege guaranteed the pope's claim to papal lands, while future papal candidates had to swear fealty to the emperor.

Otto II (955–983) established the Eastern March (Austria) as a military outpost, but he was defeated by the Saracens in his efforts to secure southern Italy. The pious Otto III (980–1002) attempted to revive the glory and power of ancient Rome with himself at the head of a theocratic state. He engineered the election of his cousin Bruno of Carinthia as Pope Gregory V, the first German pope.

From 1000 C.E.
The childless Henry II (972–1022), gentle and devout, encouraged the Cluniac movement and sent out missionaries from his court in the new bishopric of Bamberg. He was crowned King of Germany in 1002, and King of Italy in 1004. He was the only German king to be canonized.

The Salian dynasty was a dynasty in the High Middle Ages of four German Kings (1024–1125), also known as the Frankish dynasty after the family's origin and role as dukes of Franconia. All of these kings were also crowned Holy Roman Emperor (1027–1125). Under the reign of the Salian emperors, the Holy Roman Empire absorbed northern Italy and Burgundy.

Conrad II (990–1039), was a clever and ruthless ruler, who proved that the monarchy no longer depended on contracts between sovereign and territorial nobles—he made the fiefs of lesser nobles hereditary and appointed lower-class men responsible directly to him as officials and soldiers. He had Burgundy bequeathed to him, strengthened his hold on northern Italy, and had Poland return lands previously taken in conquest.

During the reign of Conrad's eldest son Henry III, the Black (1017–1056), the Holy Roman Empire supported the Cluniac reform of the Church, a series of changes within medieval monasticism focused on restoring the traditional monastic life, encouraging art, and caring for the poor, as well as the prohibition of simony (the purchase of clerical offices). Imperial authority over the Pope reached its peak. An imperial stronghold (Pfalz) was built at Goslar, as the Empire continued its expansion to the East.

A controversy began between Henry IV (1050–1106) and Pope Gregory VII (1025–1085) over appointments to ecclesiastical offices. Henry crushed a Saxon rebellion in 1075 and confiscated land, thus intensifying their hatred of him. When Gregory forbade lay investiture of churchmen, Henry had the Synod of Worms in 1076 depose him. The pope excommunicated Henry and freed his subjects from their oath of loyalty. The emperor was compelled to submit to the Pope at Canossa in 1077.

The princes elected a rival king, Rudolf of Swabia (1025–1080). In 1080, Gregory excommunicated Henry again and recognized Rudolf. Henry marched on Rome, deposed Gregory, installed the Antipope Clement III, and was crowned emperor in 1084. Henry returned to Germany to continue the civil war against a new rival king, since Rudolf had died in 1080. Finally, betrayed and imprisoned by his son Henry, the emperor was forced to abdicate.

In 1122, a temporary reconciliation was reached between Henry V (1086–1125) and the pope with the Concordat of Worms, which stipulated German clerical elections would take place in the imperial presence without simony. The emperor was to invest the candidate with the symbols of his temporal office before a bishop invested him with the spiritual symbols. The consequences of the investiture dispute were a weakening of the Ottonian National Church, Reichskirche, and a strengthening of the Imperial secular princes.

New Towns Founded from 1100

From 1100, new towns were founded around imperial strongholds, castles, bishops' palaces, and monasteries. The towns began to establish municipal rights and liberties, while the rural population remained in a state of serfdom. In particular, several cities became Imperial Free Cities, which did not depend on princes or bishops, but were directly subject to the emperor. The towns were ruled by patricians (merchants carrying on long-distance trade). Craftsmen formed guilds, governed by strict rules, which sought to obtain control of the towns. Trade with the east and north intensified. Germans colonized and chartered new towns and villages in largely Slav-inhabited territories east of the Oder, such as Bohemia, Silesia, Pomerania, Poland, and Livonia.

Henry V died childless in 1125. His nephews Frederick and Conrad Hohenstaufen were passed over in favor of Lothair III of Supplinburg (1075–1137), Duke of Saxony. During his reign, a succession dispute broke out between the houses of Welf and Staufen; the latter was led by Frederick II and his brother Duke Conrad of Franconia. The Hohenstaufen, or Waiblingen, of Swabia, who were known as Ghibellines in Italy, held the German and imperial crowns, while the Welfs of Bavaria and Saxony, known as Guelphs in Italy, sided with the papacy. In Germany, Lothair fought a civil war with the Hohenstaufen princes, who refused to accept him as emperor. At Lothair's death, the princes chose Conrad of Hohenstaufen (who reigned 1138–1152), and civil war erupted.

Frederick I Barbarossa (1122–1190) was elected and crowned King of Germany in 1152, crowned King of Italy in 1154, Holy Roman Emperor in 1155, and King of Burgundy in 1178. Handsome and intelligent, warlike, just, and charming, Frederick Barbarossa was the ideal of the medieval Christian king. Regarding himself as the successor of Augustus, Charlemagne, and Otto the Great, he spent most of his reign shuttling between Germany and Italy trying to restore imperial glory in both.

An accommodation was reached with the rival Guelph party by the grant of the duchy of Bavaria to Henry the Lion (1129–1195), duke of Saxony. Austria became a separate duchy in 1156. Barbarossa tried to reassert his control over Italy, and in 1177 a final reconciliation was reached between the emperor and the Pope. In 1180, Henry the Lion was outlawed, and Bavaria was given to Otto of Wittelsbach (founder of the Wittelsbach dynasty which was to rule Bavaria until 1918), while Saxony was divided.

From 1184 to 1186, the Hohenstaufen empire under Barbarossa reached its peak during the Reichsfest (imperial celebrations) held at Mainz and with the marriage of his son Henry in Milan to the Norman princess Constance of Sicily. The power of the feudal lords was undermined by the appointment of *ministerials* (unfree servants of the emperor) as officials. Chivalry and the court life flowered, leading to a development of German culture and literature.

Frederick died leading the Third Crusade. His son Henry VI (1165–1197) put down a rebellion by the returned exile Henry the Lion and then restored him to power, forced the northern Italian cities to submit to him, seized Sicily from a usurping Norman king, but died suddenly in 1197 while planning a crusade to the Holy Land. The empire fell apart.

Kings Frederick I and II

Frederick II (1194–1250) was raised and lived most of his life in Sicily, his mother, Constance, being the daughter of Roger II of Sicily. He was known in his own time as Stupor mundi ('wonder of the world') and was said to speak nine languages and be literate in seven. Frederick was a ruler very much ahead of his time, being an avid patron of science and the arts. Frederick II was a religious skeptic, which was unusual for the era in which he lived, and to his contemporaries, highly shocking and scandalous. Of his relations with the Saracens of Sicily, rather than exterminate them, he allowed them to settle on the mainland and build mosques. Not least, he enlisted them in his—Christian—army and even into his personal bodyguards. His empire was frequently at war with the Papal States, so it is unsurprising that he was excommunicated twice and often vilified in chronicles of the time. Pope Gregory IX went so far as to call him the Antichrist. After his death the idea of his second coming where he would rule a 1000-year reich took hold, possibly in part because of this.

Between 1212 and 1250, he established a modern, professionally administered state in Sicily. He resumed the conquest of Italy, leading to further conflict with the papacy. In the Empire, extensive sovereign powers were granted to ecclesiastical and secular princes, leading to the rise of independent territorial states. The popes regarded Frederick as dangerous. When Frederick led a crusade to Jerusalem in 1228, Pope Gregory IX invaded Sicily. Frederick returned home and made peace, but by 1237 he battled the second Lombard League of cities that was allied with the pope. Frederick seized the Papal States, and the new pope, Innocent IV, fled to Lyon.

Frederick died peacefully, wearing the habit of a Cistercian monk, on December 13, 1250, in Castel Fiorentino near Lucera, in Puglia, after an attack of dysentery. His legitimate son Conrad IV inherited the Imperial and Sicilian crowns, but Conrad died four years later, and the Hohenstaufen dynasty fell. There followed the Great Interregnum (1254–1273) between the end of Hohenstaufen rule and the beginning of Habsburg rule, during which there was no emperor.

Beginning in 1226 under the auspices of Emperor Frederick II, the Teutonic Knights began their conquest of Prussia after being invited to Chełmno Land by the Polish Duke Konrad I of Masovia. The native Baltic Prussians were conquered and Christianized by the Knights with much warfare, and numerous German towns were established along the eastern shore of the Baltic Sea. From 1300, however, the Empire started to lose territory on all its frontiers.

The empire had lost Poland and Hungary by the late thirteenth century and had lost control of Burgundy and Italy. Seven princes, whose principalities were virtually autonomous, chose weak kings. The Church was a dominant force in society. Towns paid taxes to the emperors in exchange for freedom from feudal obligations. Trade greatly increased. Towns began to form trade associations, the most powerful of which was the Hanseatic League. Rich burghers built city walls, cathedrals, and elaborate town halls and guildhalls. Lofty, richly decorated Gothic cathedrals were built in Bamberg, Strasbourg, Naumburg, and Cologne.

The Habsburgs Rise

By the late Middle Ages, the Habsburgs, Wittelsbachs, and Luxembourgs struggled for the imperial crown. The Great Interregnum ended in 1273, with the selection of Rudolf of Habsburg

(1218–1291), a minor Swabian prince who made the Habsburgs one of the great powers in the empire. On Rudolf's death the electors chose Adolf of Nassau (1255–1298), followed by Albert of Austria, then by Henry, Count of Luxembourg (1275–1313), who crossed the Alps in 1310 and temporarily subdued Lombardy. The Roman people crowned him, because the popes had left Rome and were living in Avignon, France, in the Avignon Papacy, the period from 1309 to 1377, during which seven French popes resided in Avignon.

Civil war raged until the Wittelsbach candidate, Louis IV the Bavarian (1282–1347), defeated his Habsburg rival at the Battle of Mühldorf in 1322. The failure of negotiations between Emperor Louis IV and the papacy led in 1338 to the declaration at Rhense by six electors to the effect that election by all, or the majority of, the electors automatically conferred the royal title and rule over the empire, without papal confirmation. Between 1346 and 1378 Emperor Charles IV of Luxembourg, king of Bohemia, sought to restore the imperial authority. Around 1350, the Black Death ravaged Germany and most of Europe, killing about one-third of the population.

Pope Clement VI (1291–1351) opened negotiations with Charles IV, King of Bohemia (1316-1378), who was chosen in 1347. Charles IV, of the House of Luxembourg, ignored the question of papal assent. In the edict of the Golden Bull in 1356, which provided the basic constitution of the empire up to its dissolution, he specified the seven electors, made their lands indivisible, granted them monopolies on mining and tolls, and secured them "gifts" from candidates, making them the strongest princes. Charles entrenched his own dynasty in Bohemia, bought Brandenburg and took Silesia from Poland, and to obtain cash, he encouraged the silver, glass, and paper industries of Bohemia.

Emperor Sigismund (1368–1437), who was King of Bohemia, made Antipope John XXIII call the Council of Constance (1414–1418), to end the Papal schism which had resulted from the Avignon Papacy. (John XXIII, born Baldassarre Cossa [1370 – 1419], was antipope during the Western Schism.) The council was attended by roughly 29 cardinals, 100 'learned doctors of law and divinity,' 134 abbots, 183 bishops and archbishops, and 1000 prostitutes! Bohemia was convulsed by the Hussite movement, which combined Czech nationalism with a desire for Church reform. Sigismund invited the Czech religious reformer Jan Hus (1369–1415) to state his views, under imperial protection, at the Council of Constance. But the council subsequently had him burned as a heretic, prompting the inconclusive Hussite Wars (1420–1434) against and among the followers of Hus in Bohemia.

Around the middle of the fourteenth century, the Black Death ravaged Germany and Europe. From 1438, the Habsburgs, who controlled most of the southeast of the empire (more or less modern-day Austria, Slovenia, Bohemia, and Moravia after the death of King Louis II in 1526), maintained a constant grip on the position of the Holy Roman Emperor until 1806.

Emperors included Albert II (1397–1439), who engaged in defending Hungary against the attacks of the Turks, died on October 27, 1439 at Neszmély and was buried at Székesfehérvár; and Frederick III (1415–1493). During his reign from 1493 to 1519, Maximilian I tried to reform the Empire: An Imperial Supreme Court (Reichskammergericht) was established, imperial taxes were levied, the power of the Imperial Diet (Reichstag) was increased. The reforms were frustrated by the continued territorial fragmentation of the empire, which gave rise to increased disunity among the empire's territorial rulers and prevented the formation of nations in the manner of France and England.

Early-modern European society gradually came into being as a result of economic, religious, and political changes. Gradually, a proto-capitalistic system evolved out of feudalism. The Fugger family gained prominence through commercial and financial activities and became financiers to both ecclesiastical and secular rulers. The knightly classes found their monopoly on arms and military skill undermined by the introduction of mercenary armies and foot soldiers. Predatory activity by "robber knights" became common.

Martin Luther and the Protestant Reformation

Figure 65 - A statue of Martin Luther the great religious reformer depicted with the 95 theses he nailed to a church door in Wittenberg during 1517.

Martin Luther (1483–1546), a German monk, theologian, and church reformer, was particularly aroused by an unscrupulous campaign by the Church to sell indulgences, or remissions of punishment for sin. In 1517, Luther published a list of 95 theses attacking indulgences, and in 1520, he published his beliefs, which affirmed the liberty of the Christian conscience informed only by the Bible, a priesthood of all believers, and a State-supported Church. Pope Leo X (1475–1521) condemned Luther's works, and when Luther burned the papal condemnation, he was excommunicated. Charles V (1500–1558), who became Holy Roman Emperor in 1519, summoned Luther to defend himself at the Diet of Worms (1521). The free city of Worms is south from Mainz and north of Mannheim on the Rhine River. Luther refused to recant, so he was outlawed. Hiding in the Wartburg Castle near Eisenach, Luther translated the Bible, and in so doing established the basis of the modern German language.

Luther's ideas spread rapidly. The fanatical theologian Andreas Karlstadt (1486–1541) urged iconoclastic attacks on church painting, statuary, and stained glass. The Peasants' War (1524–1526) broke out in Swabia, Franconia, and Thuringia against ruling princes and lords, following the preachings of Reformist priests. But the revolts, which were assisted by war-experienced noblemen like Götz von Berlichingen and Florian Geyer (in Franconia), and by the theologian Thomas Münzer (in Thuringia), were soon repressed by territorial princes. The peasants lost all rights and sense of initiative, and princes set up state churches in which the service was in German, and the clergy were allowed to marry.

Besides followers of Luther, Protestants were divided between Reformed Christians following Swiss theologian Ulrich Zwingli (1484–1531), who wanted to set up Bible-based theocratic states, and radical Anabaptists, poor people who wanted churches independent of the state. Without peaceful compromise, Charles V routed the Protestant princes and cities at the Battle of Mühlberg in 1547. But many nobles, who had acquired Catholic lands and were staunch Protestants, forced on Charles V the Peace of Augsburg in 1555, which recognized the Lutheran faith, and stipulated that the religion of a state was to be that of its ruler.

The Council of Trent (1545–1563), an ecumenical council of the Catholic Church, abolished the sale of indulgences and reformulated doctrine and worship to preclude reconciliation with Protestantism. The Jesuit order, founded by the Spaniard Ignatius of Loyola (1491–1556), set up centers in German cities, and the rulers of Bavaria, Austria, Salzburg, Bamberg, and Würzburg restored Catholicism by force, creating a Catholic bloc in southern Germany. Protestant princes under Frederick IV (1574–1610) formed the Protestant Union in 1608, while in 1609, Maximilian I, Duke of Bavaria, led the Catholic princes into the Catholic League.

The Thirty Years War
The Thirty Years' War, fought between 1618 and 1648, was ostensibly a religious conflict between Protestants and Catholics, although the rivalry between the Habsburg dynasty and other powers was a more central motive. Catholic France under the de facto rule of Cardinal Richelieu supported the Protestant side in order to weaken the Habsburgs, thereby furthering France's

position as the pre-eminent European power. This increased the France-Habsburg rivalry which led later to direct war between France and Spain. The war was fought principally on the territory of today's Germany and involved most of the major European continental powers. Mercenary armies were extensively used, devastated entire regions scavenged bare by the foraging armies. Episodes of widespread famine and disease devastated the population of the German states and, to a lesser extent, the Low Countries and Italy, while bankrupting many of the powers involved.

The war ended with the Treaty of Munster, a part of the wider Peace of Westphalia in 1648. The treaty recognized the independence of each Holy Roman Empire state, making the Holy Roman Emperor powerless. The prince of each German state would determine its religion, meaning that Habsburg lands and those to the south and west were Catholic. The treaty recognized the Reformed faith and agreed that Protestants could retain acquired lands. But Germany had lost about one-third of its population to war, famine, and plague, as well as much of its livestock, capital, and trade. Refugees and mercenaries roamed, seizing what they could.

The Peace of Westphalia

From 1640, Brandenburg-Prussia had started to rise under the Great Elector of the House of Hohenzollern, Frederick William (1620–1688). The Peace of Westphalia in 1648 strengthened it even further, through the acquisition of East Pomerania. A system of rule based on absolutism was established. In 1701, Elector Frederick of Brandenburg was crowned "King in Prussia." From 1713 to 1740, King Frederick William I, also known as the "Soldier King," established a highly centralized state, with an efficient bureaucracy, which filled the treasury and paid for a large standing army. Meanwhile, the Wettins of Saxony became kings of Poland. The Welfs of Brunswick-Lüneburg gained great influence when Elector George inherited the throne of England as George I in 1714. The Wittelsbachs of Bavaria sought a crown in the Spanish Netherlands, and the Habsburgs of Austria held Bohemia and Hungary.

The German princes became involved in four wars with France—the War of the Devolution (1667–1668), the Dutch War (1672–1678), the War of the League of Augsburg (1688–1697), which won Great Elector Frederick William of Brandenburg Strasbourg and Alsace, and the War of the Spanish Succession (1701–1714), which ended in the Peace of Utrecht. The German princes came into conflict with Sweden in the Baltic, in the First Northern War (1655-1660), and the Great Northern War (1700–1721).

In 1683, the Turks were defeated outside Vienna by a Polish relief army led by King Jan Sobieski of Poland while the city itself was defended by Imperial and Austrian troops under the command of Charles IV, Duke of Lorraine. Hungary was reconquered, and later became a new destination for German settlers. Austria, under the Habsburgs, developed into a great power.

The Rise of Prussia

After the Peace of Hubertusburg in 1763, Prussia became a European great power. The rivalry between Prussia and Austria for the leadership of Germany began.

The War of Austrian Succession (1740–1748) began under the pretext that Maria Theresa of Austria was not eligible to succeed her father, Charles VI, Holy Roman Emperor, as ruler of the extensive Habsburg domains because Salic law precluded royal inheritance by a woman. The Bavarians, Saxons, and French invaded Austria and Bohemia, while Great Britain, the Netherlands, and Russia came to the aid of Austria. Frederick II's military victories prompted Maria Theresa to make peace with him in 1742, ceding him Silesia. Austria and its allies drove the French from Bohemia and conquering Bavaria. By the Treaty of Aix-la-Chapelle (1748), Maria Theresa's husband, Francis, Duke of Lorraine, was recognized as emperor (although she ruled), and Maria Theresa gave up Bavaria and let Prussia keep Silesia.

But in the three Silesian Wars (1740–1763) and in the Seven Years' War (1756–1763) she had to cede Silesia to Frederick II, the Great, of Prussia. After the Peace of Hubertsburg in 1763 between Austria, Prussia, and Saxony, Prussia became a European great power. This started the rivalry between Prussia and Austria for the leadership of Germany.

"Enlightened absolutism" was established in Prussia and Austria starting in 1763. The ruler was to be "the first servant of the state." Frederick II, the Great (1712–1786), a proponent of the revised absolutism, modernized the Prussian civil service and promoted religious toleration. Frederick patronized the arts and philosophers. Reforms included the abolition of torture, improvement in the status of Jews, emancipation of peasants, while education was promoted. In the eighteenth century, after the religious wars and Turkish threat, German culture flowered. The princes centralized their governments, established mercantile economies, and built palaces, churches, museums, theaters, gardens, and universities. Burghers and peasants were scorned as uncouth, and useful only for paying taxes. Enlightenment theories of representative government, combined with Romantic ideas of freedom and national identity, fostered a desire for national unification.

The French Revolution and Napoleon Bonaparte

The French Revolution (1789–1799) was a period of political and social upheaval in France and Europe, during which the French government structure, previously an absolute monarchy with feudal privileges for the aristocracy and Catholic clergy, underwent radical change to forms based on Enlightenment principles of republic, citizenship, and inalienable rights.

This revolution sparked five wars of defense between the well-trained armies of Napoleonic France and neighbors including Prussia and Austria. Following the first two wars, the Peace of Basel in 1795 ceded the left bank of the Rhine to France. In the third, Napoleon conquered Vienna and Berlin. In 1803, Napoleon I of France (1769–1821) abolished almost all the ecclesiastical and the smaller secular German states and most of the imperial free cities. New medium-sized states were established in southwestern Germany. In turn, Prussia gained territory in northwestern Germany.

The Holy Roman Empire was formally dissolved on August 6, 1806, when the last Holy Roman Emperor, Francis II (1768–1835), resigned. In 1806 the Confederation of the Rhine was established under Napoleon's protection. In 1809, Austria led a fourth war against France, while Napoleon was occupied in Spain, but lost more land. In 1813, the Wars of Liberation began, following the destruction of Napoleon's army in Russia (1812). After the Battle of the Nations at Leipzig, in October 1813, Germany was liberated from French rule, and the Confederation of the Rhine was dissolved.

Political Map Redrawn after Napoleon's Demise

The Congress of Vienna was a conference between ambassadors from the major powers in Europe that was chaired by the Austrian statesman Klemens Wenzel von Metternich and held in Vienna, Austria, from late September 1814 to June 9, 1815. Its purpose was to settle issues and redraw the continent's political map after the defeat of Napoleonic France the previous spring, which would also reflect the change in status caused by the dissolution of the Holy Roman Empire eight years before. The discussions continued despite the ex-Emperor Napoleon I's return from exile and resumption of power in France in March 1815, and the Congress's Final Act was signed nine days before his final defeat at Waterloo on June 18, 1815, by Britain's Duke of Wellington and by Prussia's Gebhard Leberecht von Blücher.

The German Confederation was an association of 39 Central European states created by the Congress of Vienna in 1815 to serve as the successor to the 240-state Holy Roman Empire of the German Nation, which had been abolished in 1806. Its states were represented by a powerless legislature, known as a diet. Disagreement with the restoration politics led to a liberal movement seeking a government on British and French models, with a constitution guaranteeing popular representation, trial by jury, and free speech, along with national unification. However, the rulers of Prussia and Austria, and the kings of Bavaria, Hanover, Württemberg, and Saxony, bitterly opposed liberalism and nationalism. Austria, Prussia, Russia, and Britain formed the Quadruple Alliance to resist any threat to the Vienna settlement.

Social Uprising

On October 18, 1817, students held a gathering to exchange ideas, the high point of which was the burning of works by authors like August von Kotzebue, who were against a united German state. A second such meeting attracted 30,000 people from all social classes and regions to the *Hambacher* celebration. There for the first time, the colors of black, red, and gold were chosen to represent the movement, which later became the national colours. Meanwhile, the growing industrialization in Europe contributed to a wave of poverty, fueling social uprisings.

A July Revolution in Paris in 1830 set off uprisings in numerous German states. The confederation banned public meetings and petitions. In 1848, further revolutions, beginning in Paris, spread through Europe. Nationalist groups revolted in Hungary, Bohemia, Moravia, Galicia, Lombardy, Bavaria, Prussia, and southwest Germany. Metternich resigned and Emperor Ferdinand I (1793–1875) abdicated in favor of his nephew Francis Joseph I. In May, the German National Assembly (the Frankfurt Parliament) met in St. Paul's Church in Frankfurt am Main to draw up a national German constitution. But the 1848 revolution turned out to be unsuccessful. King Frederick William IV of Prussia refused the imperial crown, the Frankfurt parliament was dissolved, the ruling princes repressed the uprisings by military force, and the German Confederation was re-established by 1850.

Otto von Bismarck

In 1862, conflict between the Prussian King Wilhelm I and the increasingly liberal parliament erupted over military reforms. The king appointed Otto von Bismarck (1815–1898) the new Prime Minister of Prussia, who solved the conflict with difficulty and used the desire for national unification to further the interests of the Prussian monarchy. In 1863–64, disputes between Prussia and Denmark grew over Schleswig, which—unlike Holstein—was not part of the German Confederation, and which Danish nationalists wanted to incorporate into the Danish kingdom. The dispute led to the Second War of Schleswig, during which Prussia, joined by Austria, defeated Denmark. Denmark was forced to cede both the duchy of Schleswig and the duchy of Holstein to Austria and Prussia. In the aftermath, the management of the two duchies caused growing tensions between Austria and Prussia, which ultimately led to the Austro-Prussian War (1866). The Prussians were victorious in this war, carrying a decisive victory at the Battle of Königgratz.

In 1867, the North German Federation (German: *Norddeutscher Bund*) under the leadership of Prussia replaced the German Confederation, which was dissolved in 1866. Austria was excluded and would remain outside German affairs for most of the remaining nineteenth and the twentieth centuries. The North German Federation existed from 1867 to 1871, until the founding of the German Empire, led by Otto Von Bismarck who was declared chancellor. With it, Prussia established control over the 22 states of northern Germany and, via the Zollverein, southern Germany.

Franco-Prussian War

Differences between France and Prussia over the possible accession to the Spanish throne of a German candidate—whom France opposed—was the French pretext to declare the Franco-Prussian War (1870–71). Due to their defensive treaties, joint southern-German and Prussian troops repelled French troops which had occupied Saarbrücken and proceeded to invade France in August 1870. After a few weeks, the French army was forced to capitulate in the fortress of Sedan. French Emperor Napoleon III was taken prisoner and the Second French Empire collapsed. Months after the Siege of Paris was lifted, the Peace Treaty of Frankfurt was signed: France was obliged to cede what became known as Alsace-Lorraine to Germany.

During the Siege of Paris, the German princes assembled in the Hall of Mirrors of the Palace of Versailles and proclaimed the Prussian King Wilhelm I as the *German Emperor* on January 18, 1871. The German Empire was thus founded, with 25 states, three of which were Hanseatic free cities, and Bismarck, again, served as Chancellor. It was dubbed the "Little German" solution, since Austria was not included.

National Isolation

Beginning in 1884 Germany established several colonies. The young emperor's foreign policy was opposed to that of Bismarck, who had established a system of alliances in the era called *Gründerzeit*, securing Germany's position as a great nation, isolating France using diplomatic means, and avoiding war for decades. Under Wilhelm II, however, Germany took an imperialistic course, not unlike other powers, but it led to friction with neighboring countries. Most alliances in which Germany had been previously involved were not renewed, and new alliances excluded the country. Specifically, France established new relations by signing the *Entente Cordiale* with the United Kingdom, and established ties with Russia. Austria-Hungary and Germany became increasingly isolated …."

Appendix Five: The Foreword to *Alve Road*

Figure 66 - William John Busch 1900-1996 – eldest of the Second-Generation Descendants.

I lived with the Alves on two or three occasions as a boy between 1906 and 1914. I was more or less brought up with them and I finished my schooling there at Rangiotū. I was the oldest grandchild, and my mother was Mary.

I knew all the family particularly well before they were married. Lena was the first one to marry I think. Anna died of goitre while I was there. There was Theresia and Elizabeth and Charlie who unfortunately passed away very suddenly later. Alfred married an Allsop and Henry married a Tasmanian girl. Eddie married an English woman and Clara was married later to a Purdom. Dolfy, he was the youngest of the family and he had two boys.

My memories of Alve's are very much alive. The old man Alve - Carl Wilhelm - he was a hot-headed old boy who used to fly into a rage very often and go crook at the family. But he had his sense of humour. He was a good singer and he used to love sitting on the chair playing the accordion singing, all in German of course - *sprechen sie Deutsch?* Grannie Theresia, she was a dear old lady; a wonderful woman. She did a great job looking after all the family and I thought a lot of her.

The Alve's were a fine old family.

Bill Busch, Wharekaka Home, Martinborough, New Zealand – 25th October 1994.

Author's Note: Bill Busch is the eldest of the second generation of Alve descendants born in New Zealand. His mother Mary Busch (née Alve), born in Germany a year before the Alve family emigrated to New Zealand, was the eldest of the first generation born in New Zealand.

Appendix Six: A Poem by Ken Busch
[First printed in Alve Road in 1995 where *Theresia* is referred to as *Maria*, her first name.]

Carl & Maria Theresia Alve

Caught in the first flow of freedom.

A man and a woman of their day.

Released from centuries of serfdom.

Looking for a far better way.

Adverts for migrants from Hamburg.

New Zealand a British Colony.

Dare we, Maria, go free?

Mother and father and child preparing.

Awaiting to see where this new land would be.

Refusing to doubt the wisdom of their sailing.

Instinct of faith sustaining their grieving.

All this great daring for you and for me.

At last Pacific skies blow steady and blue.

Long months have passed with the Atlantic at play.

Villagers from Germany give loud praise to their crew.

Even as we give thanks, for their vision, this day.

Figure 67 - Ken Busch, the second son of Bill Busch and second of the third generation Alve descendants – his elder brother Ray was the eldest of the third generation.

Appendix Seven: A Hymn in Honor of Ancestors

Ecclesiasticus or Sirach 44:1-15

New Revised Standard Bible Version – Catholic Edition

1 Let us now sing the praises of famous ones,
our ancestors in their generations.
2 The Lord apportioned to them great glory,
his majesty from the beginning.
3 There were those who ruled in their kingdoms,
and made a name for themselves by their valor;
those who gave counsel because they were intelligent;
those who spoke in prophetic oracles;
4 those who led the people by their counsels
and by their knowledge of the people's lore;
they were wise in their words of instruction;
5 those who composed musical tunes,
or put verses in writing;
6 rich ones endowed with resources,
living peacefully in their homes—
7 all these were honored in their generations,
and were the pride of their times.
8 Some of them have left behind a name,
so that others declare their praise.

9 But of others there is no memory;
they have perished as though they had never existed;
they have become as though they had never been born,
they and their children after them.
10 But these also were godly ones,
whose righteous deeds have not been forgotten;
11 their wealth will remain with their descendants,
and their inheritance with their children's children
12 Their descendants stand by the covenants;
their children also, for their sake.
13 Their offspring will continue forever,
and their glory will never be blotted out.
14 Their bodies are buried in peace,
but their name lives on generation after generation.
15 The assembly declares their wisdom,
and the congregation proclaims their praise.

Appendix Eight: Alve Descendant Reunions

The 2024 Alve Descendant Reunion

Figure 68 - 2024 Reunion Attendees at Masters Hall, Pahiatua Saturday 17 February

Figure 69 - Canadian cousins, Dave Farrant & Gregory Pedersen beneath the gnarled old macrocarpa tree which is adjacent to the original Alve farmhouse, Fauvel's Road near Eketahuna.

Sixty-one people gathered for this Reunion on the weekend of 17-18 February 2024. Prior to gathering for Saturday afternoon tea at Master's Hall, Pahiatua several attendees gathered in Palmerston North for two Saturday events:

Figure 70 - Peter Alve RIP 1970-2023

- The unveiling of Peter Alve's headstone at Kelvin Grove Cemetery was attended by over 100 relatives and friends from both sides of his family. Peter who died on 9 October 2023, had an abiding interest in family matters and an amazing ability to recall family births, deaths and marriages and use it to keep in touch with whānau.

- A vigil at the Terrace End, Palmerston North old cemetery where Theresia (1942) & Carl (1910), Charles (1937) & Dolly (1967) and Anna Alve (1906) are interred in the Catholic section. Family heard about Julianne Alve's recent work upgrading this grave, Nelson Rangi offered boyhood memories about Theresia, and various others shared anecdotes, even a poem about Anna from this book!

Figure 71 - The Old Alve Grave, Terrace End, Palmerston North

Following afternoon tea at Master's Hall formal family group and informal photos were taken by Ingrid & Dave Alve. A lot of catching up and new meetings followed before the Tararua Lions cooked and served a wholesome barbecue dinner.

A Saturday evening function was co-ordinated by Christine Alve from Taupo which included:

- A welcome from the Tararua Mayor Tracey Collis;

- Storytelling factual and apocryphal - Dave Farrant & Nelson Rangi took the prizes;

- Margaret Weir, Julianne Alve & Christine Rose talked to historic family objects they had brought: glassware, crochet, Dolly's paua necklace, accordion, Carl's walking stick, etc;

- Terry Alve talked about the writing of the new book *Valentine's Day 1874: a Ruhr Valley Romance* which focuses on Theresia and Carl's relationship from 1849-1910;

- This was followed by a ten-minute video narrated by Theresia (using AI) who tells of their life in Germany and in New Zealand until 1902;

- Julianne Alve reported on the Rosa Grave, Featherston upgrade that was the subject of a Reunion appeal;

- Senior relatives present - Jean Alve and Nelson Rangi - cut the Reunion cake before we shared supper together.

After Sunday breakfast 30-40 viewed another video, this time narrated by Carl, before they participated in a **half hour worship service** during which Caroline Newson and William Hopgood read a moving passage which is a hymn in honour of ancestors written in Ecclesiasticus 44:1-15 and Greg Pedersen read from 1Corinthians 13 before making brief comments. The service also included hymn singing and a Waiata led by Margaret Alve and Caroline Newson and prayers led by Terry Alve. The service concluded with lacquered Paua shells and other gifts being given to the 8 Canadian family members and others present.

Figure 72 - The star marks the area family walked at the Woodhouse Farm near Eketahuna where Theresia, Carl and Family lived 1880-1896. This area is adjacent to the large macrocarpa tree pictured above and includes the high point where we had a panoramic view of the farm.

Thirty-three descendants then boarded a **bus to Eketahuna** at 10 am where for three hours they:

- Visited the Eketahuna (Mellemskov) Museum viewing an Alf Alve clock and a possible image of Carl, among other things.

- Wandered through the Sacred Heart Catholic Church of the Eketahuna parish Carl, Theresia and family attended.

- Viewed the memorial cairn adjacent the Early Settlers Cemetery on the edge of Eketahuna where Emma Alve was buried – the first family death in A-NZ.

- Walked on and viewed the original Alve land on Fauvels Road (formerly part of Alfredton Road), now farmed by the Woodhouse family.

- Spent time in the Mangaoranga Cemetery where Heinrich and Dorothea Schormann (immigrant friends and joint landowners) were buried along with their 15-year-old Scharnweber grandson and several others, notably Scandanavians including Pedersens whom our Canadian cousins took particular interest in.

Figure 73 - That's Carl (on the right), asserted Trevor Alve at the Eketahuna Museum.
There is confusion over the date of this photo. If it is 1880 (see Te Ara Online Encyclopedia) it may be.
If it is c.1900, as the image donor suggested, then Carl was heading for Rangitane from Featherston and it is likely not him.
This image is held at Te Pūranga Kōrero o Wairarapa / Wairarapa Archive, Masterton

Returning to Masters Hall around 1pm we were surprised at the high quality of the packed lunch that *Thyme 2 Ryes* of Pahiatua provided us hungry travellers. Following lunch, farewells were profuse and extensive for the next hour as family members bade farewell to one another and headed into the world.

Finally, we acknowledge Margaret Alve who oversaw the Reunion shopping and catering. Thank you for yummy food.

Organisers: Elaine Newson & Terry Alve

Figure 74 - Elaine Newson –
Reunion Co-Organiser

The 2015 Alve Descendant Reunion

Figure 75 - Those who attended the 2015 Alve Descendant Reunion in Palmerston North.

Easter 2015 marked 20 years since nearly 150 descendants and partners of Carl and Maria Alve gathered at Highden, Awahuri for a major reunion. To mark the occasion and to continue celebrating our family heritage a day event was held in the Palmerston North Convention Centre on Easter Sunday 5 April 2015.

60 people (pictured) attended this reunion, including some of the last of the 2nd generation family & spouses. Descendants of six of the nine 1st generation Alve families were present: descendants of Theresia, Lena, Henry, Eddie, Clara and Dolph.

Sadly, the weekend before the Reunion two who were planning to attend died, viz. Alve Purdom and Ken McLeod.

Figure 76 - Standing: Ivan Alve and Jean Alve. Seated Joyce Alve and Hilton Alve.
Surviving descendants and partners who attended the 2015 Descendant Reunion.
Both Joyce and Hilton died later that year.

The 1995 Alve Descendant Reunion

Figure 77 - 1995 Reunion Organisers L-R: Julianne, Val, Joyce, Maree, Peter, Ivan & Terry Alve, Theresa Flintoff, Phil Alve, Thelma
Avery, Gordon Alve and Christine Lockett

Two years of planning, the publication of "Alve Road" - a history of the Alve Family - and travel arrangements for nearly 150 family members culminated in a family descendant reunion during Easter Weekend 1995.

From the first gathering on Good Friday evening (14 April) the tone was one of relaxed informality. The organising committee chaired by Gordon Alve did an excellent job. "Highden" at Awahuri, the stately old homestead venue chosen, was the ideal setting with its early 20th century flavour, its extensive lawns and gardens, accommodation, chapel and friendly family staff who catered superbly for the weekend.

Family members arriving found their registration packs filled with helpful information about the region, a list of all attending, creative name badges colour-coded according to family and with details of the events and meals each was registered for. Souvenir teaspoons, letter openers and key rings all with Carl's and Theresia's photo on were there for those who had ordered them and available for purchase for those who hadn't. In addition, framed, coloured photos of Carl & Maria (200m x 150mm). "Alve Rd" - AA miniature road signs - were also for sale.

Another of the weekend's highlights was the marvelous display of photographs grouped by families, and genealogical information that Peter & Julianne Alve had painstakingly mounted. They had done their homework well and many memories were prompted as this display was viewed. Many photos in this display were ordered by family members.

Morning Welcome & Photographs
Saturday morning dawned brilliantly sunny and still highlighting the wonderful facility that Highden is. Soon after 10am Manawatu District Council mayor Caryll Clausen formally opened the Reunion and movingly spoke of the good name of the Alve's in the district. She mentioned their good relations with the Māori tangata whenua of the local Rangitāne tribe and of their community-mindedness. Her husband was one of a Danish pioneer settler family who had farmed near the Alves at Rangitāne.

Her welcome speech was followed by comments from Frau Annett Gunther, 2nd secretary from the German embassy in Wellington who was accompanied by Frauline Cornelia Luck who had a week before arrived from Germany to work at the embassy. Annett and Cornelia stayed until mid-afternoon mixing with family gathered and tangibly reminding them of their heritage.

Brendan, the formal photographer, took over at that point and from his balcony camera position cajoled the family into a kind of ordered chaos as they gathered on the lawn outside for the whole group (140-150) family photograph. With 2nd generation family members seated in front, the crowd responded well to his, "look down-1-2-look up" command. After a 2nd generation photo, each family was formally photographed in order from Mary's to Dolph's descendants.

Some light relief was found as three of Mary's granddaughters (Frank's girls: Pam, Kaye and Judi) insisted they be photographed back on to show off their special tee shirts emblazoned with the words, "I'm Anna Maria Catherina's Grand Daughter."

Afternoon - Lunch to Tea

Lunch was enjoyed inside and outside as people spread out, catching up with those they had not seen for a while, and meeting family who hitherto had only been a name or unknown. The afternoon passed quickly and then it was time to cut the reunion cake which had been made by Joyce Alve and iced by her daughter Christine Lockett. This was cut by the oldest grandchild of Carl and Maria present - Tis Emmens from Featherston and the eldest grandson present - Lisle Alve from Hastings. This cake was served with afternoon tea as the results of the Easter Raffle were announced. Jack Alve of Kimbolton took first prize and Levon Evans of Stokes Valley took the second prize.

The Banquet

The family dispersed to rest before the Reunion Banquet in the evening. Nearly 100 were present for this as Nelson Rangi of Kawerau ably gave the welcome speech with much storytelling and levity. He spoke on behalf of everyone present as he warmly thanked the organisers for their efforts.

After the main course, specially invited guest Mr Rolf Panny of Ashhurst gave the keynote address. Rolf, a first-generation German-New Zealander is a retired lecturer in German studies (1971-1990) at Massey University. He contributed to, "The German Connection" published in 1993, writing of German settlement in the Lower North Island. Rolf movingly highlighted the hard-working role of the family's pioneering women and paid special tribute to them. He also reflected on the difficult conditions that German emigrants left behind to come to New Zealand and other lands.

Terry Alve thanked Rolf for his informative and entertaining remarks and led those assembled in recognising Keryn Rowe's 38th birthday with singing, "For she's a jolly good fellow.". Keryn was the only family member celebrating a birthday during the weekend gathering.

Later in the evening entertainment was provided by Caroline Newson (violin), Maree Newson (piano) and Theresa, Caroline and Maree Newson accompanied by Peter Nicols (dancing). The rest of the evening, into the wee small hours, was taken up with much reminiscing.

Easter Morning in the Chapel

Sunday morning celebrations began with chapel thanksgiving service attended by about forty of the family. Ken Busch read his poem dedicated to Carl and Maria which is recorded inside the front cover of "Alve Road". Margaret Alve and Lila Purdom provided music. Jack Alve read the lesson from Psalm 139 and Russell Pedersen read the gospel story of the resurrection from Luke 24. Terry Alve in a short message noted and reflected on the important role women had in the resurrection story, echoing comments made by Rolf Panny the night before. He went on to develop the thought that each one of us is important and precious in God's sight, regardless of who we are and what we have done.

Down Memory Lanes

After Sunday lunch, a bus tour departed for the Kelvin Grove cemetery on the northern edge of Palmerston North. There 40-50 visited the graves of about twenty-five 1st, 2nd and 3rd generation descendants which had been marked with flags. This was followed by a stop at the Terrace End old cemetery where the restored gravesite of Carl, Maria Theresia, Anna, Charlie and Dolly Alve was visited and thoughtfully admired. The restoration work had been arranged and overseen by Jack Alve and family. Prayers were offered. While at this cemetery the gravesite

Figure 78 - Around 150 people attended the 1995 Alve Descendant Reunion, including several from the second generation seated at the front.

of Theresia, Bert and William Simmons was viewed. They are the only other Alve descendants buried at the Terrace End site.

The bus tour continued through the ring road at Massey University with commentary by Phillip Alve. The tour paused at the Opiki Hall for afternoon tea which had been prepared by Val and Joyce, Ivan and Maree Alve assisted by their daughters Theresa Flintoff and Christine Lockett.

Then it was over the Manawatu River to the former Alve farmland at Rangitāne. Time was spent viewing the remnants of Henry's and Val's cowshed and yards and at the Alve Road signpost where several photographs were taken.

The tour continued through Rangiotū where many of the family attended school. At Pyke Road Alve Purdom indicated the sites where his family and the Simmon's lived. Thence it was over the Oroua river and through the Kairanga district back to Highden at Awahuri after nearly five hours on the road!

It was a poignant moment as darkness fell to see a huge Easter full moon rising languidly over the Tararua Ranges in the east as the bus arrived at Highden. A final meal of barbecued sausages and steak closed a weekend reunion that will be long remembered by those who attended for many things, but especially for its friendliness that reunited us in the bonds of family.

About the Author

Figure 79 - Terence Valentine Alve, Author.

I had an 'aha' moment as a teenager when my great uncle Charlie's brother-in-law, Alex Wallace, told me stories about my great grandparents Theresia and Carl Alve in a way that made their lives come alive. I never knew my *tūpuna,* but the influence of that conversation has driven me to make exploring my family's genealogy and history a life-long quest.

In 1994 I wrote, *Alve Road: How do you spell that?* which chronicled what I knew of the history of the Alve family in Germany and, the better-known history of the family in New Zealand. As part of this work, I wrote over 120 brief biographies of the first four generations of the family, beginning with my forbears Carl Wilhelm and Maria Theresia Alve who emigrated from Germany to New Zealand in 1875-76.

Born in 1952, I attended Rangiotū Primary School and Palmerston North Boys' High School, before completing a *Bachelor of Civil Engineering Honours* degree at Canterbury University. After working for the Christchurch City Council as an engineer, I studied theology at the Bible College of New Zealand and St John's Theological College in Auckland receiving a *Bachelor of Divinity* Degree from the Melbourne College of Divinity. I was ordained for ministry in the Christchurch Anglican Cathedral by Bishop Allan Pyatt in 1980 and served as a Parish priest in several Canterbury (Ashburton, Te Ngawai – Pleasant Point and Spreydon) and Wellington (Tawa, Whitby, Island Bay, Chinese Mission, Northland, Upper Hutt and Porirua) Anglican parishes. I have been Priest in Charge of Porirua Parish since October 2018.

The mainstay of my Christian ministry has been encouraging people to know and tell their faith stories and, in the process, to keep vibrant their God connection. As a tribute to my father in the faith, my father-in-law Don Milne, I published *Don Milne: a most extraordinary man,* in 2023. My writing and presentation skills have been enhanced through my work as a website designer and developer. I am also a self-taught genealogist and family history researcher. I use a variety of internet resources to further this work, including the *MyHeritage* online genealogy platform and the *www.alve.nz* website and Alve Descendant Facebook page.

In 1973 I married Maureen Diver, a devout Catholic from Upper Riccarton who did her schooling at Villa Maria College, Christchurch and who died of cancer the year after we married. Later I married Margaret Milne, from Upper Riccarton and together we have four adult children and nine mokopuna (grandchildren). Margaret and I reside in Tawa, Wellington where we have lived since 1994.

We have travelled extensively overseas in Australia, England, Scotland, Ireland, Germany, Scandinavia, Estonia, Fiji and South Africa, often with family research in mind. I pound the streets and bush tracks of Tawa and Wellington with our miniature Schnauzer dog Pippin who always looks forward with enthusiasm to the next day's walk. Occasionally, I go bush and lodge in a hut in the southern North Island mountains and hills.

List of 80 Illustrations

Bibliography & End Notes

The following texts were consulted during the writing of Alve Road: How do you spell that? Published in 1994.

ADCOCK, Irene, *A Goodly Heritage: Eketāhuna and Districts 100 Years, 1873-1973.* Eketāhuna Borough and County Councils, 1973.

AKERS, Molly, *From Fibre to Food, Opiki - The District and Its Development.* Stylex Print Ltd., Palmerston North, 1978.

AKERS, Molly J., Suspended Access: *Opiki Toll Bridge 1918 - 1969.* Stylex Print, Palmerston North, 2003.

BAGNALL, A.G., *Wairarapa: An Historical Excursion.* Hedley's Bookshop Ltd., for the Masterton Lands Trust, Masterton, 1976.

BRAMSTED, Ernest K., *Germany: The Modern Nations in Historical Perspective.* Prentice Hall Inc., 1974.

BUICK, T. Lindsay, *Old Manawatū or The Wild Days of the West.* Buick & Young, Palmerston North, 1903.

BUICK, T. Lindsay, *Old Manawatū or The Wild Days of the West.* 1903. Reprint - Capper Press, Christchurch, 1975.

BUSCH, Harold, *The Busch Line: from Serfdom to Freedom.* Harold Busch, 1985.

CARLE, C.J., *Forty Mile Bush - A Tribute to the Pionéers.* North Wairarapa News Co. Ltd., 1980.

CAVE, L.M.H., *Writing and Publishing Your Family History.* New Zealand Society of Genealogists Inc., 1986.

CORRICK, Doreen, *The Wallace Family History.* Doreen Corrick, 1988.

DIXON, Maren & WATSON, Ngaire, *A History of Rangiotū.* The Dunmore Press Ltd., 1983.

McLEAN, Gavin., *Local History: A Short Guide to Researching, Writing and Publishing a Local History.* Bridget Williams Books Ltd., 1992.

NATIONAL ARCHIVES, *Family History at National Archives.* Bridget Williams Books Ltd., 1991.

PARKER, V. (Ed.), *The New Zealand Genealogist.* New Zealand Society of Genealogists Inc., 1979-1993.

PETERSEN, G.C., *Palmerston North: A Centennial History.* Reed, 1973.

RAFF, Diether, *A History of Germany from the Medieval Empire to the Present.* Berg, 1988.

STOTT, Bob, *The Remutaka Incline Yesterday and Today.* Southern Press Ltd., 1984.

WOODHOUSE, A.E. (Ed.), *Tales of Pionéer Women.* Whitcombe and Tombs Ltd., 2nd Revised Edition,1940

Subsequently, while much of my research has been online and is referenced in the Endnotes, the following texts have been consulted and/or quoted in this work.

ALVE, Terence V., *Alve Road: How Do You Spell That?* The Alve Family Trust, 1994

BADE, James N. (Editor), *The German Connection.* Oxford University Press Auckland,1993.

BERRY, P.L. *Germans in New Zealand 1840-1870.* M.A. in History Thesis, University of Canterbury, 1964. (PDF file)

DAVIES, Norman, *Europe: A History.* Pimlico, London, 1997.

DUNICK, Mark Edward, *Continental European Assisted Immigrants in 1870s New Zealand.* PhD Thesis, Victoria University of Wellington, 2022

PAAS, MANFRED et al, *1000 Jahre Pfarrei – 100 Jahre Propstei – St Augustinus Gelsenkirchen.* Kunstverlag Josef Fink, 2004.

TENQUIST, J.D. *Rails Over the Ranges.* Featherston Jaycee Inc., 1975

VOSS, Michael E., *140 Years at Karere; The Voss Settler Family History.* Michael E. Voss, February 2022. (I purchased and used the eBook publication)

WATT, Michael, *The Fingal Valley's German Heritage.* Michael Watt, 2022.

End Notes

____

[i] https://en.wikipedia.org/wiki/Neanderthal

[ii] https://www.neanderthal.de/en/home.html

[iii] https://en.wikipedia.org/wiki/Neanderthal_genome_project

[iv] RAFF, Diether. *A History of Germany from the Medieval Empire to the Present*

[v] Marriage Certificate of Anna Lamsfuß and Wilhelm Alfer translated from the High German by Dr Frederick Knowles, Christchurch, NZ c.1993.

[vi] https://commons.wikimedia.org/w/index.php?curid=17594814 Huckeswagen Crest

[vii] CLARK, Christopher, *Revolutionary Spring: Europe Aflame and the Fight for a New World.* Crown Publishing Group, Penguin Random House, 2023

[viii] Ibid

[ix] https://www.landesarchiv-nrw.de/data02/Abt_Rheinland/PA_3103/~023/02371/R_PA_3103_02371_0136.jpg?

[x] DAVIES, Norman, *Europe: A History*. Pimlico, London, 1997, pages 841-2.

[xi] https://en.wikipedia.org/wiki/Franco-Prussian_War

[xii] Sven Jeske (in Quora)

[xiii] https://en.wikipedia.org/wiki/Gelsenkirchen

[xiv] https://www.gelsenkirchener-geschichten.de/wiki/Dernbacher_Schwestern

[xv] https://marienhospital.eu/das-marienhospital/ueber-uns/geschichte-des-mhg

[xvi] *1000 Jahre Pfarrei – 100 Jahre Propstei – St. Augustinus Gelsenkirchen,* 2004. Page 41- I had the German translated into English.

[xvii] Translated from the German text by Larissa Lambrecht from Berlin while living and working as an *au pair* for my son Jonathan's family in Tawa.

[xviii] 1995 Alve Family Reunion - THE ALVE FAMILY

---

xix https://www.germanaustralia.com/d/d-why-emi.htm

xx https://en.wikipedia.org/wiki/Kulturkampf

xxi DUNNICK, Mark Edward, *Continental European Assisted Immigrants in 1870s New Zealand*, Victoria University of Wellington PhD Thesis, 2022

xxii https://en.wikipedia.org/wiki/Donald_Akenson

xxiii https://teara.govt.nz/en/the-voyage-out/page-1#The%20Longest%20Journey

xxiv https://trove.nla.gov.au/newspaper/article/91265396 The South Australian Weekly Chronicle and Mail, Saturday 23 March 1867

xxv Heritage New Zealand Quarterly, Koanga, Spring 2023 and the associated Heritage New Zealand web page https://www.heritage.org.nz/list-details/2895/Listing

xxvi https://www.wrecksite.eu/wreck.aspx?196279 Information about the wreck of the Gutenburg.

xxvii https://tinyurl.com/brookhusen This website is in German. My *Google Translator* gave me a good English rendition.

xxviii WATT, Michael, *The Fingal Valley's German Heritage*. Michael G. Watt, 2022

xxix BERRY, P.L. *Germans in New Zealand 1840-1870*. M.A. in History Thesis, University of Canterbury, 1964. (PDF file)

xxx https://paperspast.natlib.govt.nz/imageserver/parliamentary/P29pZD1BSkhSMTg3Ny1JLjIuMS41LjImZ2V0cGRmPXRydWU=

xxxi DUNNICK, Mark Edward, *Continental European Assisted Immigrants in 1870s New Zealand*, Victoria University of Wellington PhD Thesis, 2022

xxxii https://polishhistorynewzealand.org/fritz-reuter/

xxxiii Causes and Effects of Emigration from Germany (1870s–1880s), published in: German History in Documents and Images, https://germanhistorydocs.org/en/forging-an-empire-bismarckian-germany-1866-1890/ghdi:document-1739 [September 16, 2023].

xxxiv BAGNALL, A.G., *Wairarapa: an Historical Excursion*. Hedley's Bookshop Ltd., for the Masterton Lands Trust, Masterton, 1976.

[xxxv] ADCOCK, Irene, *A Goodly Heritage: Eketāhuna and Districts 100 Years, 1873-1973.* Eketāhuna Borough and County Councils, 1973.

[xxxvi] https://certificateoftitle.nz/wp-content/uploads/wcam/6989/6038_WN7A_163_Title_Historic_View.pdf

[xxxvii] https://www.Eketāhuna.co.nz/?page_id=63

[xxxviii] Ibid.

[xxxix] https://tinyurl.com/EketāhunaschoolC19 Eketāhuna School History PDF

[xl] ADCOCK, Irene, A Goodly Heritage: Eketāhuna and Districts 100 Years, 1873-1973. Eketāhuna Borough and County Councils, 1973.

[xli] https://teara.govt.nz/en/economic-history/page-5

[xlii] PAPERS PAST, Wairarapa Daily Times, Volume XV, Issue 4345, 15 February 1893, Page 2

[xliii] PAPERS PAST, Dominion, Volume 4, Issue 954, 22 October 1910, Page 7

[xliv] A statement by Emeritus Professor Sir Mason DURIE, Hon Sir Edward Taihākurei DURIE and Professor Meihana DURIE of Ngāti Kauwhata and Rangitāne. Extracted from the *The Rangimarie Narrative…* https://cdn-cms.f-static.net/uploads/3114584/normal_5e56dc8846a7e.pdf

[xlv] AKERS, Molly, *Suspended Access - Opiki Toll Bridge 1918-1969* (p.10). Stylex Print, Palmerston North, 2003.

[xlvi] Restoration of Foxton - Longburn railway line into pathway (Stuff - 15 July 2023).

[xlvii] DIXON, Maren & WATSON, Ngaire, *A History of Rangiotū.* The Dunmore Press Ltd., 1983.

[xlviii] BUICK, T. Lindsay, *Old Manawatu or The Wild Days of the West.* Buick & Young, Palmerston North, 1903. [Inserted between pp.112-113]

[xlix] Ibid.

[l] AKERS, Molly, *From Fibre to Food, Opiki - The District and Its Development.* Stylex Print Ltd., Palmerston North, 1978.

[li] Manawatu Standard, Palmerston North, 23 September 1910

[lii] *"New Zealand, Archives New Zealand, Probate Records, 1843-1998," database with images, FamilySearch (https://familysearch.org/ark:/61903/3:1:3QS7-L943-*

KSVN?cc=1865481&wc=4BCL-73D%3A1045248601%2C1045574701:21February2019),
*Palmerston North Court > Probate records 1910 P1/10-P86/10 > image 834 of 1055; Archives
New Zealand, Auckland Regional Office.*

[liii] MANAWATU HERALD, VOLUME XXXII, ISSUE 925, 1 DECEMBER 1910, PAGE 3

[liv] https://www.alve.nz/store/c2/Alve_Road_Digital_Book_Files.html

[lv] https://www.alve.nz

[lvi] https://tinyurl.com/alvefamily

[lvii] AKERS, Molly, *From Fibre to Food, Opiki - The District and Its Development.* Stylex Print
Ltd., Palmerston North, 1978. (p.34)

[lviii] https://tinyurl.com/EketāhunaschoolC19

[lix] RUSSELL PERDERSEN – *My Personal History* transcribed from a Personal Journal given to
Patricia Livingstone (Russell's daughter) by her mother Thelma in 2010.

[lx] Reported in an Interview with Merv Eglinton c.1960 https://milne-
alve.weebly.com/audios.html

[lxi] https://www.newworldencyclopedia.org/entry/Germany